UNDERSTANDING AND DEVELOPING SCIENCE TEACHERS' PEDAGOGICAL CONTENT KNOWLEDGE

UNDERSTANDING AND DEVELOPING SCIENCE TEACHERS' PEDAGOGICAL CONTENT KNOWLEDGE

Professional Learning
Volume 12

Rationale:

This series purposely sets out to illustrate a range of approaches to Professional Learning and to highlight the importance of teachers and teacher educators taking the lead in reframing and responding to their practice, not just to illuminate the field but to foster genuine educational change.

Audience:

The series will be of interest to teachers, teacher educators and others in fields of professional practice as the context and practice of the pedagogue is the prime focus of such work. Professional Learning is closely aligned to much of the ideas associated with reflective practice, action research, practitioner inquiry and teacher as researcher.

Understanding and Developing Science Teachers' Pedagogical Content Knowledge

By

John Loughran
Monash University, Clayton, Australia

Amanda Berry
Monash University, Clayton, Australia

and

Pamela Mulhall
University of Melbourne, Australia

2nd Edition

SENSE PUBLISHERS
ROTTERDAM / BOSTON / TAIPEI

A C.I.P. record for this book is available from the Library of Congress.

ISBN 978-94-6091-788-2 (paperback)
ISBN 978-94-6091-821-6 (e-book)

Published by: Sense Publishers,
P.O. Box 21858, 3001 AW Rotterdam, The Netherlands
https://www.sensepublishers.com/

Printed on acid-free paper

TABLE OF CONTENTS

ACKNOWLEDGEMENTS

Special thanks to all of those science teachers who gave so freely of their time and ideas which were crucial to the research from which this book is based.

Jen Alabaster	Julie Goldsworth	Laura Odgers
Claire Allemand	Belinda Griffiths	Xenia Pappas
Bobby Bailey	Simon Head	Rob Poyntz
Adam Bertram	Stephen Keast	Wayne Reed
Robyn Bowering	Mark Learmonth	Catriona Scott
Angelo Collins	Nicole Lewis	Gary Simpson
Deborah Corrigan	Brian McKittrick	Barbara Sloan
Tony Dennis	Vojtech Markus	Robyn Speedy
Nick Derry	Marion Martin	Vivienne Sullivan
Matthew Dodd	Peter Meehan	Suzanne Vaughan
Patricia Dove	Philippa Milroy	Andrew Walsh
Heather Downing	Ian Mitchell	Lisa Willis
Guy Evans	Terry Mitchelmore	Terry White
Merrin Evergreen	Peter Morgan	Maryanne Young
John Gipps	Wan Ng	

Thanks also to Claude Sironi for setting demonstrations and the accompanying photographs.

Special thanks to Sarah Rutherford for her careful proof reading of this second edition.

The authors are grateful for the research support made possible through funding from the Australian Research Council.

PREFACE TO SECOND EDITION

The first edition of this book was published six years ago. Since then, we have been involved (individually and collectively) in an array of activities derived from the interesting range of possibilities and ideas that CoRes and PaP-eRs have created both for us and for others. We have had the good fortune to be invited to share our ideas with colleagues internationally (e.g. New Zealand, USA, Canada, UK, Taiwan, Hong Kong, Singapore, Sweden and the Netherlands) as teachers and researchers have engaged with CoRes and PaP-eRs as a framework for thinking about practice. Through researching PCK, new and innovative projects have sprung up in many places in ways that have more than demonstrated the allure of the concept to the research community (Hume & Berry, 2010; Nilsson & Loughran, 2010, 2011). Now, as we release this second edition of the book, we take the opportunity to add to our existing Resource Folios, by offering a very different approach to a CoRe with accompanying PaP-eRs on the topic of Genetics (see chapter 9). We have also added some interesting explorations and interpretations of the value and use of CoRes and PaP-eRs from users' and researchers' perspectives.

In this preface to the second edition we now briefly explain how our thinking has developed over time as a consequence of engaging with the construct of PCK, and the understandings that have emerged for us through working with CoRes and PaP-eRs, as both a process and a product.

Initially, we did not realise what we were getting ourselves into when we began to explore what 'pedagogical content knowledge' really means, what it looks like in practice, and how it might be captured and portrayed for others.

In the first instance, the idea of PCK was enticing because it seemed to be such a clever way of imagining what the specialist knowledge of teaching might involve. PCK conjured up an image of cutting-edge knowledge of practice, something special and important, something that could define expertise, something that could illustrate in a meaningful way why teaching needed to be better understood and more highly valued. However, much to our surprise, when we started researching PCK, we found that "seeing" PCK proved to be exceptionally elusive. The teachers with whom we worked struggled to understand what we meant by the term. We found it difficult to ask questions that could "unpack" their specialist knowledge of practice (although we were convinced it existed); and, while we thought we knew what we were doing, we struggled to make progress.

Over time, we slowly developed the CoRe (Content Representation) framework as a consequence of thinking much more deeply about the nature of science content knowledge *for* teaching. Big Science Ideas emerged as an important way of reconsidering what matters most in conceptualizing science topics for teaching. As the prompts took shape (the left hand column in a CoRe), we felt as though we were learning something about science teaching that was new and different – something that had not been put together this way before.

The CoRe framework created a coherent way of conceptualizing science content that reflected (for us) the inherent knowledge of practice that we saw in expert teachers but which they themselves so often struggled to articulate. PaP-eRs (Pedagogical and Professional-experience Repertoires) were developed as a natural consequence of the need to dig deeper into the myriad aspects of the CoRe in order to capture the essence of teachers' pedagogical reasoning and purpose; to make the tacit explicit.

The synergies between CoRes and PaP-eRs were immediately obvious to us as we put them together into a package which we called a Resource Folio. When we assembled our first complete Resource Folio (Particle Theory – see chapter 4), we felt as though we had learnt a great deal about that special amalgam of content and pedagogy that Shulman (1986, 1987) so eloquently described as pedagogical content knowledge, all those years ago.

As we progressed and developed a number of other Resource Folios (see chapters 4–9; chapter 9 being new to this edition) we became increasingly aware of the special and intriguing nature of PCK. Researching PCK had a dramatic impact on our understanding of practice. As we attempted to capture and portray PCK, we were confronted by our own lack of particular science content knowledge on many occasions. As a consequence, we were reminded of how limited understandings of a specific topic inhibit the ability to create the amalgam of content and pedagogy that is PCK. In addition, the essence of PCK is not captured by mere representations of teachers just "knowing what to do" or "how to do it".

Over the course of our long research adventure with PCK, our own views about what PCK is and how it might be described and explained for others have gradually changed as we have become better informed about the idiosyncrasies of the construct. This is not least because of the issues, problems and concerns it created for us in our work.

Just as PCK has captured our attention, it has also done the same for others. The allure of the PCK construct is immediately obvious in the literature where, from time to time as the cycle of interest ebbs and flows, refinements, reconsiderations and adjustments to Shulman's original notion rise and fall. We have found that some of these "additions" have been less than helpful in clarifying the nature of PCK, and in some cases, actually make it more confusing.

We contend that PCK is more conceptual than concrete, and that there is a learning curve about PCK that influences how researchers interpret and use it. For example, it is not unusual to hear of subject-specific PCK – which we would see as tautological. In a similar vein, some describe context specific or context dependent PCK – again, a somewhat redundant use of a signifier. There are also those instances of particular content being injected into the term such as that of TPCK (Technological Pedagogical Content Knowledge), and conversely, even that of generic and specific PCK. On the one hand it seems as though the more that PCK is refined and/or redefined in a bid to make it more concrete, the less valuable it becomes as a descriptor of specialist or expert knowledge of practice. But on the other hand, in its more conceptual form it is almost too abstract to be practical.

In reflecting on our research efforts with PCK (through the development of CoRes and PaP-eRs), we seem to have been caught between the abstract and the concrete, although that is not necessarily a bad thing. The CoRe captures not just an individual's thinking about the teaching and learning of specific content but, also, the collaborative or shared understandings of that content across groups of teachers. On the other hand, PaP-eRs are very specific to a particular aspect of the CoRe and therefore quite distinctive and individual. We came to the view that for a given topic, CoRes and PaP-eRs necessarily combine to illustrate what PCK might involve, but no single aspect of them alone defines PCK. We sought to make PCK concrete through CoRes and PaP-eRs, but also acknowledge the importance of it as an abstract construct; and, we reject our methodology being characterized as a recipe for, or a competency list of, PCK.

It is hard to know now, but perhaps we subconsciously responded to what Shulman described as the generative nature of PCK (Berry, Loughran, & van Driel, 2008a): as we came to understand it better, the need to fully "pin it down" became less important, despite the fact that insights into the nature of PCK were crucially needed. So in many ways, we arrived at a point where being able to illustrate instances that might safely be described as indicative of PCK was more important to us, than categorically stating that something was PCK. Nevertheless, even though CoRes and PaP-eRs, as packaged in a Resource Folio, are very concrete, they also carry strong conceptual underpinnings that allow for a diversity of interpretations and applications. One such variation is through the ways in which teachers have engaged with them.

When we started our research we were very conscious of our own science teaching roots and our desire to do something that would be useful for teachers. We had often bemoaned the difficulties for teachers of finding research outcomes that were applicable in their classroom practice (see for example, Berry & Milroy, 2002) and so pushed ahead with our PCK research in the hope that we might do something to address the issue. However, over time, we found ourselves feeling caught between the needs, expectations and requirements of academia (and research funding) and our concerns for outcomes that would be meaningful for science teachers. From time to time we lamented that our work might appear to be theoretically strong but practically soft. So we were a little surprised, but certainly pleased, when we observed what teachers and teacher educators did with CoRes and PaP-eRs.

Although we did not develop CoRes and PaP-eRs as curriculum documents, many teachers immediately translated them into that form. They used (in particular) CoRes as a way of reconsidering what science content could look like, how it might be arranged and what it meant to organise curriculum conceptually, rather than in a linear fashion. PaP-eRs were a little more challenging. They liked to read them and to interrogate what was being portrayed, but usually found constructing them to be time consuming and not so valuable from a personal perspective (see Adam Bertram's chapter – another addition to this edition). Hence, the value to teachers was in terms of encouraging reflection on practice, creating a shared language for discussing science teaching and learning, and offering insights into practice, all of which became a springboard for their own professional learning.

Some teacher educators, as illustrated in particular by the work of Jim Woolnough, incorporated the teaching of PCK into their science teacher education programs. Jim used CoRes and PaP-eRs to help his student teachers see learning about science teaching in ways that challenged the more typical student teacher need to scramble for "tips and tricks" to build a bank of fun activities (Woolnough, 2009). Jim used CoRes and PaP-eRs as a way of teaching his student teachers about being science teachers, not transmitters of science information. Together, they worked on constructing their own CoRes and PaP-eRs before, during and after their practicum (school experience) in a way that created a vision for what their ongoing professional learning might look like as science teacher specialists. Jim's research into his use of PCK as a development goal in learning to be a science teacher demonstrated how his approach to science teacher education changed along with his student teachers' understanding of, and expectations for, science teaching.

Now, as we complete this edition of the book, we see new possibilities emerging from our work. These new possibilities have come about as a consequence of teachers and teacher educators being attracted to the concept of PCK as an idea, and to CoRes and PaP-eRs as one way of making that idea useable in practice. As is always the case with quality teaching, truly expert teachers (Loughran, 2010) grasp the essence of new approaches to pedagogy and interpret, alter and adjust those ideas and practices to meet their purposes in their classrooms with their students. They create new ways of thinking about the content, their students' learning and their own development as professionals. We believe that CoRes and PaP-eRs create these types of opportunities for teachers and hope that this book continues to be useful in the day to day practice of science teachers, teacher educators and researchers.

CHAPTER ONE

TEACHING

Learning through experience

> I had an awakening ... I had taught science in five different high schools ... believing I was a very good teacher. ... At the time I believed I had 'mastered' teaching, because I knew my science content as well as having accumulated a large repertoire of teaching strategies and hands-on activities. ... Over time, my self-perception as having 'mastered' teaching slowly dissolved. ... I progressively became aware that my teaching of high school science over 14 years was rather mundane ... Upon reflection, I realized that, as a secondary science teacher for 14 years, I knew my science content but very little about how children learn. ... Thus began my awakening about understanding the complex relationships between teaching and learning that is still evolving today. ... In retrospect ... I had such a simplistic conception of teaching during those first 14 years; it is a little embarrassing that I believed I had mastered the job. (Hoban, 2002, pp. xvi - xvii)

Teaching is complex work and like Garry Hoban (above), many teachers come to find that their initial simplistic views of teaching are confronted when the intricacies of their work become clearer over time. Through this process, whereby a growing understanding of teaching begins to emerge largely as a result of learning through experience, a new appreciation of one's skills and abilities compels some to move beyond the simple delivery of information.

This, however, is not as straightforward as it may sound, as a strong and pervasive view of teaching is based on a transmissive model whereby prescribed content or information is delivered to students. Through this transmissive model, the approach of content "delivery" is often misrepresented as that which comprises teaching.

A transmissive view of teaching is in stark contrast to perceiving teaching as a process of enhancing learning through developing a deeper understanding of content, whereby teaching procedures and strategies are selected for particular reasons that are important to shaping learning in ways that are meaningful and valuable to the learner. Clearly then, there are major differences in the implications for teachers, and teaching, when a transmission model is contrasted to the complex model of teaching for understanding, through which expertise in pedagogy is genuinely viewed as skilfully managing (and enhancing) the relationship between teaching and learning.

PROFESSIONAL LEARNING

Just as Garry Hoban experienced an awakening in relation to his views of and subsequent approaches to teaching, for many teachers there are ongoing and subtle reminders of the mismatch between their intentions for teaching and the practice that evolves as a consequence of the dailiness of teaching (Loughran & Northfield, 1996). However, even though the distinction between delivering content and teaching for understanding may be apparent, choosing to do something about it is a completely different matter.

Unfortunately, approaches to professional learning that might encourage teachers to more readily respond to the inherent contradictions between intentions and actions in teaching are not necessarily supported at either a school or systemic level. Therefore, for those who choose to respond, the professional learning journey is often characterised by individual teachers finding themselves questioning their own practice and seeking new ways of constructing teaching and learning experiences without necessarily being supported, encouraged, or rewarded for so doing.

For example, the work of Mandi Berry and Philippa Milroy (2002) demonstrates how difficult it can be to approach teaching science in ways that draw on notions of acknowledging and responding to students' prior views and purposefully addressing alternative conceptions. They set out to 'teach in ways that would better facilitate students' better understanding of science concepts; foster students' responsibility for their own learning; and, work from the position that science is a social process and that science ideas change over time' (Berry & Milroy, 2002, pp. 196 - 197).

Attempting to meet such aims obviously confronts the notion of teaching as the transmission of information. However, in attempting to address these concerns, Mandi and Philippa found it to be demanding work. There was little real support available to them within their school and, perhaps more surprisingly, even less advice and direction in the educational research literature. Therefore, they were left to work through their issues alone and to construct their teaching in new and different ways, whilst simultaneously implementing such changes in their classrooms. They found themselves inventing and implementing, devising and trialling whilst also managing the day to day concerns of teaching the 'prescribed' curriculum.

What Mandi and Philippa then came to recognize was that the changes in their teaching comprised a journey, not an event. They did not teach one way at the start of their adventure and then suddenly transform their teaching overnight to become new and different teachers. They came to develop their teaching as they experimented with their practice and built new understandings of teacher and student learning. Their journey involved many false starts, much frustration, considerably more work and time and the development of new scripts that challenged their previous routines in teaching science. Their professional learning, while being personally rewarding, was not something able to be garnered from a book on curriculum reform, or developed as a result of an in-service or professional development activity. Rather, their professional learning was as a consequence of choosing to consistently pursue deeper levels of understanding of science with their students, and sharing, documenting, and reflecting together on their efforts whilst also seeking evidence of quality learning from their students. In a real sense, they came to learn more about their skills as teachers and what to do to enhance those skills in strengthening the relationship between teaching and learning.

Moving beyond activities

One of the major changes associated with developing views of teaching, that seems important in the type of shift that both Hoban (2002) and Berry and Milroy (2002) reported is linked to a recognition that teaching is much more than just having a "kit of good activities". Although it is important to have some routines in teaching, when teaching becomes "routinized", elements of quality teaching (e.g. engagement, enjoyment and intellectual challenge) can be dramatically diminished; or worse, absent all together. Therefore, developing helpful routines whilst not allowing teaching to become routinized is a tension that many teachers experience; a similar situation is equally pertinent in terms of learning.

It is not difficult to see how there can be a natural tendency for teachers to incorporate a range of teaching procedures (e.g. concept maps, Venn diagrams, role-play, interpretive discussion, etc.) into their practice in order to break-up the "normal routine". However, the use of teaching procedures simply to break up the normal routine is not the same as choosing to use a particular teaching procedure for a particular pedagogic reason. This issue goes to the heart of what it means to be an expert pedagogue: one who chooses to use a particular teaching procedure at a particular time for a particular reason, because, through experience, that teacher has come to know how teaching in that way enhances student learning of the concept(s) under consideration. Such pedagogical reasoning is important because it is the thinking central to creating a path through complex teaching and learning situations. It is a window into the thoughtful and skilful act of practice that is responsive to the given context, i.e. there is not the assumption that the same thing works the same way all of the time. The ability to adapt, adjust and make appropriate professional judgments, then, is crucial to shaping the manner in which teachers teach and respond to their students' learning.

Clearly then, understanding teaching as complex, interwoven, and problematic is at odds with transmissive views of teaching which inevitably trivialize and undersell the skills, knowledge, and ability evident in the practice of expert teachers. The use of a range of teaching procedures to break up the normal routine, even though at times apparently effective (because of the break from the predictable routine), does not in itself mean that transmissive views of teaching do not still dominate a teacher's practice. The shift to understanding teaching as problematic, and practising it that way, involves much more than "pulling out something different from a bag of teaching tricks". This point is perhaps best demonstrated through the work of PEEL (Project for Enhancing Effective Learning) teachers.

PEEL (Baird & Mitchell, 1986; Baird & Northfield, 1992; Loughran, 1999) is an example of a movement in education that directly responds to teachers' concerns about students' passive learning; which itself is partly a consequence of "traditional" teaching. PEEL teachers view teaching as problematic and have become expert at developing teaching procedures that are the antithesis of transmissive teaching. The accumulated wisdom of practice evident in their work (shared and disseminated through a diverse range of meetings, conferences, and publications) is driven by their desire to challenge students' passive learning habits in order to develop their metacognitve skills, and to therefore become more active, purposeful learners. As a consequence, PEEL teachers' knowledge of teaching is such that it demonstrates how thinking about teaching as something more than the delivery of information, is a foundation to strong, ongoing professional learning.

As an experienced PEEL teacher, Rosemary Dusting (2002), offered an extensive examination of her efforts to move from *teaching as telling* to *teaching for understanding*. In so doing, she captured the essence of the challenge associated with genuinely confronting, and moving beyond, transmissive approaches to teaching.

The method I adopted to teach Mathematics was the same as I experienced at school. ... Therefore, on my first school appointment, no option for teaching Mathematics had been demonstrated to me other than the traditional exposition model – the teacher in total control of all the knowledge. ... I suppressed memories about how certain teachers made me feel idiotic if I ventured a response that was incorrect, or how others barely even noticed whether there were students in class ... Initially I tried to perfect the exposition style and to develop a repertoire of methods to keep students quiet whilst I told them what they needed to know. Thus the type of questions I asked myself about the quality of my teaching and my students' learning tended to be restricted to blaming myself – or the students – for any perceived lack of success. I had a sense of responsibility for *making* students understand and remember. It was *my* problem. I had to show them what to do. If I did not show them properly, then they would not learn and I would have failed. (Dusting, 2002, pp. 174 – 175, emphasis in original)

In the first instance, Rosemary was confronted by the incongruity of her teaching and her expectations for students' learning, and so found the use of engaging teaching procedures as helpful in breaking her students' passive learning routines. However, over time, she also came to see the need to go beyond teaching procedures alone and to better link her teaching to her expectations for her students' learning.

I was [now] attempting to more consistently teach for understanding ... I began to ask myself reflective questions ... [and] metacognition became important and deepened my understanding of my teaching. ... As I watched students learning this way [through PEEL procedures] I genuinely felt that I had created circumstances in which there was engagement with the task, concentration, active student involvement, risk-taking and increased interest. My teaching had shifted from me doing all the work for the students to the students now working out part of the content for themselves. They had been provided with meaningful opportunities to think and I had not taught by telling. ... My understanding of what it meant to teach students to be active learners was being developed and I valued what was happening. (Dusting, 2002, pp. 177 - 180)

In a similar way, Vivienne Sullivan (1996) came to see how the relationship between teaching and learning converged when her use of teaching procedures was carefully considered and the implications of such practice applied to not only the way she taught, but how she reflected on and planned for her teaching. With a group of others at her school, she was part of a teacher-initiated examination of the use of teaching procedures, in order to better understand how those procedures influenced students' learning, as well as their own teaching practice. What these teachers did was to adopt an approach to examining their use of teaching procedures, discussing and writing about them using a simple but powerful formula. They considered the aim of their particular lesson, the method (i.e. teaching procedure) used to implement the aim, the observations they made of their students' learning, and then evaluated the process as a whole to extract new insights about teaching and learning: they were extending their knowledge of their wisdom of practice.

In considering the use of the POE (Predict-Observe-Explain) teaching procedure in a science class, Vivienne noted that:

The "Explain" part of the exercise was well written by about one third of the students. They tackled the conceptual errors that they had experienced in the "Predict" phase, and showed some real progress in their understanding of the experiment. ... others who had predicted inaccurately wrote explanations of their errors ... The effectiveness of the exercise as a learning tool was discussed with the students and feedback sought. It was judged by the majority of the class to have required more thought on their part than if the demonstration had just been shown to them. I feel confident that this is the case. (Sullivan, 1996, p. 32)

What is clear in the extract (above) is that the manner in which her students appear to be thinking about the content is dramatically different from that which would normally be the case if the content were simply being told or "delivered" to them. Even more so, it is clear that the students are also involved in considering their own learning as tackling their conceptual errors and explaining their own inaccurate predictions, behaviours that have much more to do with constructing genuine understanding as opposed to knowing what the teacher said.

This approach to better understanding the use of teaching procedures and the articulation and development of the wisdom of practice demonstrates how understanding teaching as being problematic requires a major shift in a teacher's thinking and subsequent practice. The fundamental shift is from a view that teaching can *make* students learn, or, as Rosemary Dusting described it, 'a sense of responsibility for making students understand and remember' (p. 175), to finding ways of encouraging students to accept more responsibility for their own learning.

Accepting responsibility for learning requires students to be aware of what they are doing and why, to question their own learning, and to build their knowledge by (at least) processing, synthesizing and linking the new ideas and concepts with those they already possess. In so doing, their new knowledge is a step forward in them actively developing deeper understandings of concepts/content being studied. Such acceptance is encouraged through teaching that creates meaningful opportunities for students to be engaged in constructing and restructuring their own knowledge. By the same token, it is not difficult to see that although teaching may often be misconstrued by some as the simple delivery of information, the reality is that quality learning cannot be mandated, or as Jeff Northfield explained it when reviewing a year of his teaching of Year 7, *quality learning requires learner consent* (Loughran & Northfield, 1996, p. 124).

The expert pedagogue, then, is one that not only chooses particular teaching procedures for particular reasons, but is also constantly developing their knowledge of practice in ways that allow them to see into teaching and learning with new eyes, and to articulate the insights from so doing for others. Without doubt, such teachers have a strong grasp of the notion of professional learning through actively developing their pedagogy.

Developing pedagogy

Pedagogy is a term that is used in education in a variety of ways and, to some, can appear to be a buzz word, or a form of jargon, designed to make talk of teaching appear more sophisticated and remote from real world practice. In many instances (particularly when considered in places such as the U.S.A., Canada, U.K., and Australia) it is often used as a synonym for teaching. However, using pedagogy in that way weakens the real meaning of the term.

Drawing on the European tradition, pedagogy has more to do with understanding the relationship between teaching and learning in ways that foster children's development and growth. Van Manen(1999) eloquently describes pedagogy:

> As a practice, pedagogy describes the relational values, the personal engagement, the pedagogical climate, the total life-worlds and especially the normativity of life with children at school, at home, and in the community. And as an academic discipline, pedagogy problematizes the conditions of appropriateness of educational practices and aims to provide a knowledge base for professionals ... Central to the idea of pedagogy is the normativity of distinguishing between what is appropriate and what is less appropriate for children and what are appropriate ways of teaching and giving assistance to children and young people. (p. 14)

Therefore, in considering carefully what *developing pedagogy* might mean for teachers, it becomes immediately apparent that it entails considerably more than accumulating a "bag of teaching tricks". Although there is clearly a need for teachers to be familiar with, and capable of using, a range of teaching procedures, it is equally important that their use alone is not seen as an end unto itself. Hence, in developing their pedagogy, teachers are working as professionals to better understand, create and respond to the appropriate conditions through which educational practice might be enhanced and through which their professional knowledge might grow. In all of this, a concern for students and their learning is at the heart of the endeavour.

Viewed from this perspective, telling is not teaching and listening is not learning. Rather, the fluency with which teachers adopt, adapt and adjust practices to create conditions for learning matters in creating strong and meaningful links between teaching and learning that highlight the real meaning of pedagogy. And, for teachers who approach their work in this way, development of pedagogy is an ongoing aspect of their professional life. As briefly noted earlier, Jeff Northfield demonstrated such an approach in his examination of his teaching of Year 7. In so doing, he sought to learn from his experiences.

Learning from experience

Jeff Northfield, an experienced teacher, teacher educator and educational researcher, wanted to experience what it was like to be a PEEL teacher in a school. He therefore chose to stand aside from his teaching and research responsibilities at a university for a year in order to pursue his ambitions for his high school teaching. In so doing he accepted a teaching allotment that allowed him to teach the same class (Year 7, first year of high school) for science, mathematics and home group. Through the possibilities inherent in such an allotment, he was able to examine his understanding of developing pedagogy and to create possibilities for learning from experience in ways that created new insights into teaching and learning for him and substantially shaped his professional learning.

One of the insights that Jeff gained was about the notion of "breaking set". He used the term to:

> ... describe the acceptance of the adjustments and changes he needed to make as a teacher as he learned to teach in a different context. Breaking set was part of his need to accept responsibility for what the class did and how they did it. ... he recognized that the students had a view of classrooms, what they had to do and how they had to do it and it was one with which they were comfortable – it was generally teacher centred. Students listened, did what was necessary, and the proceedings

would come to a halt at the sound of the bell. Any departure from the 'set' could lead to a favourable response if it was an enjoyable variation from the 'set', but for the students this could not become part of the set as it did not constitute real school learning; it was viewed with some suspicion. Jeff's concern was to find the right time and level of trust to introduce activities which required thinking and encouraged acceptance of responsibility for their own learning. He found it difficult when he moved from the 'set' (expected classroom approach) … 'breaking set' placed him in a less certain classroom environment, yet one that he was in fact seeking. (Loughran & Northfield, 1996, p. 32)

An important insight into the notion of breaking set is that it applies equally to both teacher and students. Routinized practice quickly becomes the "set" in teaching and so "breaking set" can create unforeseen challenges as the teacher moves from a sense of confidence in, and knowledge of, particular practice to a riskier situation characterised by uncertainty and a heightened consciousness of learning about practice through a new situation.

For students, the same obviously applies. The sense of comfort and confidence that comes with knowing the routine can quickly dissipate when the expectations for learning shift as a consequence of teachers using approaches to teaching with which students are unfamiliar. The change in expectations associated with changes in teaching and learning can therefore be quite unsettling for some and engender a response of covert resistance.

For a teacher attempting to change the expectations of, and conditions for, learning in the classroom, this resistance may be misinterpreted as students lacking the ability to work in a given way or for the quality and/or quantity of their perceived learning to be diminished as a result of 'breaking set'. However, what Jeff came to understand about this type of situation was the need to respond appropriately to the changes in expectations so that both the teacher and the students were clear about the shift in the purpose of learning. From his experience, he recognized that students needed to understand what it felt like to be active rather than passive learners, and as a teacher he needed to feel what it was like to persevere with teaching procedures that impacted the status-quo.

Success could only really be achieved when both the teacher and the students accepted that 'breaking set' led to positive learning outcomes, and that entailed more than simply enjoying the experience or having fun. Genuine quality learning was recognized as requiring effort and was very different from the 'busy work' that is stereo-typical of regular school learning.

Recognizing and responding appropriately to the issues associated with breaking set then becomes important in coming to terms with the ongoing effort and commitment necessary to teach (and learn) for understanding.

Jeff Northfield's journey offered him substantial opportunities for professional learning that, of themselves, could not be created or delivered through traditional professional development or in-service activities. Professional learning was about learning from, and building on, experiences and involved sustained reflection on practice, and a search to understand and construct new meaning by looking into situations from different perspectives. This ability to frame and reframe (Schön, 1983) is important for seeing teaching as problematic and for instituting ways of approaching practice that will challenge the view of teaching as telling and learning as listening. It is enmeshed in searching for multiple paths, and purposefully developing different entry points into learning through a dynamic interchange between knowledge and the process of building knowledge, as opposed to delivering static information.

WORKING FOR CHANGE

Many teachers experience the sense of unease or dissatisfaction in their teaching when they feel as though they have taught something well but their students do not seem to have learnt it as well as they initially believed. Recognizing such situations is a reminder of the problematic nature of teaching, and can also be a beginning point for teachers choosing to challenge entrenched routines. Changing practice is not easy. However, the outcomes for professional learning can be the driving and sustaining force in maintaining the effort. And maintaining the effort appears to be linked to new ways of conceptualizing content, teaching and learning. Consequently, through professional learning the need to be better articulate one's own learning about practice encourages the development of a language for sharing such knowledge. One aspect of such language can be described in terms of pedagogical content knowledge.

Similar to the term pedagogy, pedagogical content knowledge (PCK) can at first appear to be jargon. However, through linking the construct with the actual experience of exploring and examining the relationship between teaching, learning and content, PCK not only takes on a new and significant meaning, bit also opens professional practice to scrutiny in ways that highlight the skills, knowledge and abilities of teachers who think about their teaching in ways that are purposeful, instructive and inextricably linked to understanding the intricacies of teaching and learning in specific content. The way they construct their teaching in response to these factors is then evident in the particularities of their PCK.

CHAPTER OVERVIEW

The intention of this chapter was to highlight a number of issues that we consider important in shaping thinking about teaching. In each case, although the points may at first appear relatively simple, on further consideration, the impact of each issue creates questions about the nature of teaching and learning and the way in which they might be played out in practice. These issues include:

- Teaching is not telling.
- Learning how to teach is about much more than collecting a set of activities to use in the classroom.
- The ideal teacher understands how students learn and recognizes a number of factors that impinge on the quality of students' learning; and, on the basis of that understanding, chooses and employs teaching procedures and approaches to promote learning.
- Teaching is problematic.
- Teachers who teach for understanding develop professional knowledge about teaching and improve their practice through reflecting on their practice and on the experiences and insights of other teachers. This commonly involves trying to think about teaching and learning from different perspectives in order to develop deeper understandings of teaching and learning situations.
- Teachers' professional knowledge requires a special language in order to facilitate better expression and sharing of ideas about teaching and learning.

CHAPTER TWO

PEDAGOGICAL CONTENT KNOWLEDGE

Within the category of pedagogical content knowledge I include, for the most regularly taught topics in one's subject area, the most useful forms of representation of those ideas, the most powerful analogies, illustrations, examples, explanations, and demonstrations – in a word, the ways of representing and formulating the subject that makes it comprehensible for others. Since there are no single most powerful forms of representation, the teacher must have at hand a veritable armamentarium of alternative forms of representation, some of which derive from research whereas others originate in the wisdom of practice. Pedagogical content knowledge also includes an understanding of what makes the learning of specific topics easy or difficult: the conceptions and preconceptions that students of different ages and backgrounds bring with them to the learning of those most frequently taught topics and lessons. If those preconceptions are misconceptions, which they so often are, teachers need knowledge of the strategies most likely to be fruitful in reorganizing the understanding of learners, because those learners are unlikely to appear before them as blank slates. (Shulman, 1986, pp. 9 - 10)

Pedagogical content knowledge (PCK) is an academic construct that represents an intriguing idea. It is an idea rooted in the belief that teaching requires considerably more than delivering subject content knowledge to students, and that student learning is considerably more than absorbing information for later accurate regurgitation. PCK is the knowledge that teachers develop over time, and through experience, about how to teach particular content in particular ways in order to lead to enhanced student understanding. However, PCK is not a single entity that is the same for all teachers of a given subject area; it is a particular expertise with individual idiosyncrasies and important differences that are influenced by (at least) the teaching context, content, and experience. It may be the same (or similar) for some teachers and different for others, but it is, nevertheless, a corner stone of teachers' professional knowledge and expertise.

It stands to reason that in order to recognize and value the development of their own PCK, teachers need to have a rich conceptual understanding of the particular subject content that they teach. This rich conceptual understanding, combined with expertise in developing, using and adapting teaching procedures, strategies and approaches for use in particular classes, is purposefully linked to create the amalgam of knowledge of content and pedagogy that Shulman (1986, 1987) described as PCK.

Recognizing one's own PCK is perhaps most evident when teaching outside an established area of subject expertise. No matter how capable a teacher might be when teaching his or her specialist subject, both skills and ability are immediately challenged (and typically found wanting) when teaching content with which there is little familiarity. When teaching outside one's area of subject expertise, despite having a well developed knowledge of teaching procedures (e.g. Venn diagrams, concept maps, interpretive discussion, etc.) or strong specialist content knowledge (e.g. specialist of physics or biology or chemistry, etc.) a teacher's skill of combining such knowledge of content and pedagogy in meaningful ways for particular reasons is no longer so readily apparent. Issues associated with difficult aspects of the topic, students' alternative conceptions, important big ideas, conceptual hooks, triggers for learning and so on, are not well known or understood by the teacher when rich understandings of subject content is lacking, and it is in elements of professional practice such as these that PCK stands out as different and distinct from knowledge of pedagogy, or knowledge of content alone.

Because the development of teaching approaches that respond to a deep knowledge of the content is something that is built up and developed over time, it is possible that the knowledge of pedagogy and knowledge of content may blur, making recognition of PCK difficult. But, when teaching outside one's area of subject expertise, the distinction may begin to stand out more readily because PCK cannot simply be "imported" from one subject area to another. Therefore, being able to see into science teachers' practice in ways that goes beyond knowledge of teaching procedures and content and into the amalgam that is PCK is important, if the expertise of exemplary science teaching is to be highlighted and better valued.

WINDOWS INTO PEDAGOGICAL CONTENT KNOWLEDGE

It may be possible to see into how a teacher's PCK develops by paying careful attention to how a knowledge of pedagogy and knowledge of content combine to shape the amalgam. Central to this development and foundational to PCK is that a teacher's use of particular teaching procedures with particular content is for a particular reason. PCK is not simply using a teaching procedure because it "works" and it is not just breaking down knowledge of content into manageable "chunks"; it is the combination of the rich knowledge of pedagogy and content together, each shaping and interacting with the other so that what is taught, and how it is constructed is purposefully created to ensure that that particular content is better understood by students in a given context, because of the way the teaching has been organised, planned, analysed and presented. The following section develops this idea further as knowledge of pedagogy and content are unpacked and analysed in an attempt to illustrate how insights into the nature and development of PCK might be better recognized and understood.

Venn diagrams

A Venn diagram is a teaching procedure "borrowed" from mathematics (for detailed explanation, see White & Gunstone, 1992). It is a way of illustrating relationships between things (people, organisms, events, etc.) and, as such, is an excellent teaching procedure for probing students' understanding of concepts, definitions and the relationships between members of different sub-sets of a universal set. Venn diagrams can be seen as a generic teaching procedure; however, when used in particular ways, at appropriate times, with particular subject matter content, PCK becomes apparent (as the following attempts to illustrate).

At one level, Venn diagrams as a teaching procedure can be applied as a generic approach to testing meaning of such things as definitions (see Figure 2.1 below). The simple Venn diagram in Figure 2.1 demonstrates the relationship between herbivores, carnivores, and omnivores in terms of the commonly stated definition of each. This Venn diagram (Figure 2.1) demonstrates that herbivores and carnivores have different characteristics from one another, and that a carnivore is not a herbivore, and vice versa. However, an organism that displays the features of both is classified as an omnivore (i.e. eats both meat and plants). Therefore, when teachers use Venn diagrams they may do so because, drawing on their knowledge of pedagogy, they recognize how helpful they are as a teaching procedure for bringing out salient features important to understanding particular aspects of specific content knowledge.

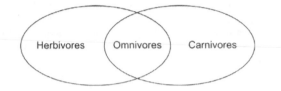

Figure 2.1: Venn diagram

Moving beyond the teaching procedure alone though, when a teacher's rich conceptual understanding of the subject content is the driving force behind the choice of the elements for students to use in drawing a Venn diagram, may well be indicative of PCK. As an important indicator of exemplary practice, PCK begins to emerge because the manner in which the content knowledge is being developed, questioned, manipulated, and tested is the driving force for the way the content and pedagogy are both shaped, and interact, in practice. Therefore, a teacher's purposeful use of Venn diagrams for developing students' understanding of differences between, and implications of, learning, in ways designed to develop richer conceptual understanding of the content beyond the basic facts, is strongly suggestive of the amalgam of content and pedagogy that is PCK.

Arguably, the type of reasoning underpinning the construction of practice (outlined above) is PCK if a teacher deliberately chooses Venn diagrams to explore terms and/or categories within a content area to challenge students' understanding and is dramatically different from simply applying a teaching procedure because it "works". In such a case, the teacher's content knowledge is important in shaping not only what terms are selected, but also, and equally important, which terms are not used. Further to this, an understanding of some of the difficulties and points of confusion that students experience with the content may well be important in the selection of the terms, when to use Venn diagrams, and how to help students move beyond knowledge as facts, in order to pursue the development of understanding. Moving beyond the simple example illustrated in Figure 2.1, consider the Venn diagram in Figure 2.2.

In this case, a Biology teacher's PCK may well be evident because the choice of these two terms (plants and animals) for students to use highlights a common difficulty inherent in the topic of classification. This seemingly straightforward Venn diagram takes on new significance when considered in conjunction with Figure 2.3 (what the teacher intends the students to construct).

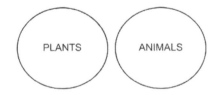

Figure 2.2: A student's initial response to the task of using 'Plants' and 'Animals' in a Venn diagram

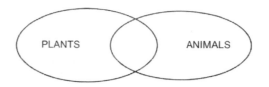

Figure 2.3: A student's deeper content understanding illustrated through the intersection of the terms

In this case (Figure 2.3), the Biology teacher's deep knowledge of the content makes the use of Venn diagrams much more valuable for learning that content than if it were applied simply as a generic teaching procedure. The use of these terms shows how the particular teaching procedure may be used with particular content at a particular time to begin to seriously develop students' understanding; as opposed to simply defining the terms.

If a student made the shift in understanding highlighted in the change from Figure 2.2 to 2.3 then the teacher would gain important indications of student learning that offers valuable feedback to the teacher not only about the effectiveness of learning, but also about the effectiveness of the teaching. (Similarly, if Figure 2.3 were the first student response, the teacher would equally be well informed about the effectiveness of the learning and further implications for teaching). In addition to this, the use of Venn diagrams in this way also creates opportunities for exploring that which might populate the intersection of both sets in ways that create a real "need to know" for students and help to highlight important aspects of taxonomic classification, its use, and ways of applying it (beyond rote learning) so that richer conceptual understandings might be encouraged. Constructing teaching in this manner is indicative of PCK and is clearly distinct from "just" applying one's knowledge of content and/or pedagogy generically.

Venn diagrams are not the only teaching procedures that offer such insights. There are many others that are equally important. For example, the use of concept maps further helps to elaborate this notion of PCK by demonstrating how the combination of content and pedagogy leads to understandings that are specific to expertise in a content field and certainly builds, in different ways, on aspects of the applicability, value, and purpose underlying the use and knowledge of practice inherent in Venn diagrams.

Concept maps

Concept maps were originally developed by Joseph Novak of Cornell University (see Novak, 1991; Novak & Gowin, 1984; Novak & Wandersee, 1991 for detailed descriptions and use through teaching and research). Concept maps are a powerful tool for organizing and representing knowledge and they emerged from his research into the development of children's knowledge of science. Like many good teaching ideas, concept maps have been used, adapted and adjusted by teachers for a considerable period of time. Although concept maps were originally designed along the lines of hierarchical representations, the way they have been refined and adapted (see White and Gunstone (1992), in particular) illustrates how, just as with the case of Venn diagrams, their use as a generic teaching procedure is nowhere near as insightful in terms of knowledge of relationships between teaching and learning in a content field, as when applied for a specific pedagogic reason.

The use of concept maps offer other ways of seeing into PCK that also helps to illustrate how PCK extends beyond knowledge of content or pedagogy alone. The concepts used (whether teacher or student generated, and why) offer possibilities for examining the reasoning underpinning such practice. In addition, the links that explain the connections of, or relationships between, the concepts offer further insights. For example, these links may vary from being relatively superficial and few in number to detailed, complex and numerous. So the value of a concept map from a teacher's perspective, beyond the understanding developed by students when constructing it (which is important in its own right), is the information that it conveys to a teacher about students' learning and about the way in which the teacher's teaching has influenced the process.

Exemplary practice, as evidenced through PCK, is highlighted, then, when concept maps are used by a teacher for a particular reason, with particular content, for a particular purpose, in contrast to being introduced to simply change the normal classroom routine. Consider, for example, the difference between the two student concept maps on the topic of plants shown in Figures 2.4 and 2.5. In considering these two concept maps, interesting questions surrounding the nature of a teacher's PCK arise. On the one hand, in terms of content knowledge, there are questions about the concepts the teacher has selected for use and why they might be important in relation to the overall topic/theme to which they pertain, or whether or not the class or individual students generated their own concepts. On the other, in terms of knowledge of pedagogy, there are interesting questions about how the students may have been instructed to approach the task: whether they worked as individuals, in pairs or small groups; whether the concept mapping exercise was a one off activity or perhaps an introduction to the unit; something to be revisited during and/or after the unit had been completed; or products to be shared, discussed and redrafted as a consequence of learning with and from others.

As the differences between Figures 2.4 and 2.5 illustrate, the use of concept maps can bring into sharp focus such things as: relationships between teaching and learning; concept attainment; misunderstandings and difficulties; such that the thoughtful use and considered timing of the teaching procedure in concert with the concepts that form the basis of the concept map, can actually illustrate how the amalgam of a teacher's knowledge of content and pedagogy that is PCK creates opportunities for valuable feedback on the essence of the teaching and learning experiences.

It is not difficult to see then how, through the use of this teaching procedure and the subsequent student responses, a science teacher might not only see into students' learning but also gain insights into issues that may need further attention, revisiting or challenging. When all of the issues and questions outlined above are considered in light of the notion of PCK, it becomes increasingly clear that exemplary practice is more likely to be realised when the specialist knowledge that teachers develop, as a consequence of their careful and thoughtful approach to developing content knowledge understanding through the use of particular pedagogical approaches, is to the fore in their thinking and their actions.

By conceptualizing practice in ways that foster the interaction of knowledge of content and knowledge of pedagogy into the type of relationship indicative in PCK, teachers can surely be described as developing and displaying their specialist knowledge and skills of teaching. Importantly, the insights into PCK that might be evident in the use of concept maps in the way we have described here begins to bring to life some of the aspects of PCK noted by Shulman (1986) at the start of this chapter, i.e. '[that] the conceptions and preconceptions that students of different ages and backgrounds bring with them to the learning of those most frequently taught topics and lessons. If those preconceptions are misconceptions, which they so often are, teachers need knowledge of the strategies most likely to be fruitful in reorganizing the understanding of learners, because those learners are unlikely to appear before them as blank slates' (p. 10). What the teacher's use of concept maps does in this case is to naturally elicit students' own views, preconceptions and misconceptions in ways that might not be so forthcoming through more "normal" classroom activities. Therefore, when this teaching procedure is used with this topic, it may well be because the teacher recognizes the importance of learners constructing and reconstructing their knowledge of particular concepts and their inter-relationships to better grasp a richer understanding of the topic as a whole.

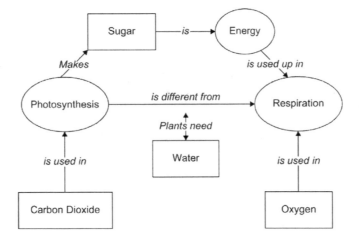

Figure 2.4: A student's initial concept map on plants

However, despite the insights into PCK that may be available by considering a science teacher's use of particular teaching procedures in a particular situation for a particular reason(s), the use of teaching procedures alone does not, in itself, capture the essence of PCK.

As much of the research into PCK has demonstrated, it is a complex constructthat, in many ways, is only fully recognized when seen through the cumulative effect of the way a teacher constructs and teaches a unit of work. Therefore, although considering a teacher's use of such things as Venn diagrams, concept maps and other teaching procedures offers helpful insights into the nature of PCK, to isolate these as PCK alone may only lead to an over-simplification of the interaction of content and pedagogy that is embodied in that which is so often tacit in a teachers' practice. And it is this tacit nature of aspects of the professional knowledge of teachers that so often overshadows the underlying knowledge and skills (for themselves and others); perhaps, as noted earlier, because development is gradual and occurs over extended periods of time.

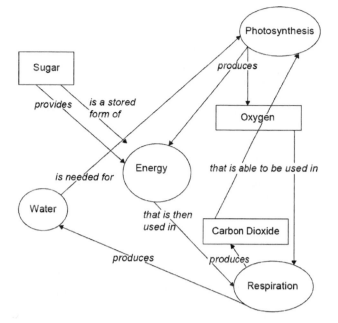

Figure 2.5: Different student understandings apparent using the same concepts

PEDAGOGICAL CONTENT KNOWLEDGE: AN ACADEMIC CONSTRUCT

When Shulman introduced PCK to the education community it was a construct that was particularly appealing to academics: 'Yet, although PCK as a construct was seductive to researchers, few concrete examples of PCK emerged in subject areas'.

As noted in Chapter 1, Mandi Berry and Philippa Milroy were confronted by the difficulties of implementing constructivist approaches to teaching (in particular when working from students' prior views and then attempting to address their alternative conceptions). They found, to their alarm, that the research literature was of little help to them in their daily attempts to change their teaching and to concurrently enhance their students' learning of science.

Just as Mandi and Philippa found, so too a similar situation applies when considering the notion of PCK, i.e. that the manner in which research into PCK has been conducted has created an impasse for teachers. The research literature on PCK is certainly extensive; however, the outcomes of such research appear to speak more to educational researchers and other such academics than to teachers who surely are not only the producers of such knowledge, but also important end users.

Although PCK offers opportunities to explore interesting ideas about that which successful teachers know in order to teach in ways that achieve student understanding, the general "fuzziness" of the concept has meant that that which is searched for and uncovered is variable indeed. In fact, in some instances, the concept has been interpreted such that some examples of PCK appear to carry little resemblance to the construct as initially conceived by Shulman.

Until recently, much of the research on PCK tended to suggest that interest in the construct was not necessarily linked with finding ways of helping teachers (whether pre-service, beginning or experienced) to improve their practice. Rather, much time and energy was expended evaluating PCK as opposed to exploring concrete examples of how teachers teach particular content topics in particular ways that promote understanding. Therefore, unfortunately, PCK has not been developed through the research literature in ways that necessarily directly correlate with enhancing the practice of science teaching. Nor has PCK research been developed in ways that might encourage it to be widely used by teachers as a central aspect of their practice; a crucial issue in making the tacit explicit and therefore leading to a purposeful refining of one's expertise i.e. professional learning.

This very point is highlighted by the work of Van Driel et al. who concluded that research on science teachers' PCK should enable useful generalizations to be made. We would agree with this view. It seems reasonable to expect that there would be some similarities in teachers' PCK if they had similar backgrounds in teaching and learning science and taught similar curriculum in similar contexts. In fact, the work of a number of researchers internationally lends support to this viewwhereby common big ideas for the topic Particle Theory (see Chapter 4 for a fully worked example) were apparent in studies in Australia and South America. This is not to suggest that all teachers' PCK in a given subject area is, or should be the same, rather that some generalizable features may well apply that are informative to subject specialists as they adopt, adapt and adjust this important feature of professional knowledge to suit their own practice in their own context.

Despite these few instances of generalizability noted above, literature of teachers' PCK based on specific topics that might be informative and applicable in the work of science teachers is largely lacking. Reasons for the sparse offerings may be related to the approach of researchers in this area.

By and large, researchers have tended to compare and contrast particular aspects of PCK of individual teachers and of groups of teachers, use case studies of novice and/or practising teachers to explore aspects of their topic specific PCK, and to explore the affect on science teachers' PCK of programs that relied on the researchers' own PCK in that particular content area. Hence, building up strong portrayals of what PCK in particular content areas might look like and how it might be enacted in practice has not been a common research agenda.

Given the potential value to teachers of some form of generalization about PCK, it is somewhat disappointing that research efforts have not yet provided detailed overviews of successful teachers' PCK so that some overarching and meaningful synthesis might be available for others to consider. One interesting exception though is the work of Van Driel et al. who offered descriptions of what teachers do to help students understand the dynamic nature of chemical equilibrium. At the heart of this concern about the research into PCK and its applicability in the work of teachers is, of course, teachers themselves.

It is an unfortunate aspect of teachers' working lives that their professional knowledge is neither overtly recognized by teachers themselves nor by others (e.g. bureaucrats, policy makers, other observers of educational processes). This is a matter of a concern, for despite the fact that knowledge, and practice, of teaching is fundamentally based on deep conceptual understandings of both content and pedagogy (which is then played out in concert with the demands of the teaching and learning context), it is not common for the majority of teachers to talk, or think about, the specialist knowledge and skills they have and continually develop (and that is encapsulated in PCK). Yet, as Shulman (1987) explains, PCK is 'the category [of teacher knowledge] most likely to distinguish the understanding of the content specialist from that of the pedagogue' (p. 8) and as such is a vital element of teachers' professional learning; something that should be recognized, developed, and valued in education generally.

PEDAGOGICAL CONTENT KNOWLEDGE: BEYOND JARGON

An issue associated with the notion of PCK that needs to be acknowledged and addressed is associated with problems carried by the stereo-typical view that some teachers tend to see academic constructs such as PCK as 'just another piece of jargon'. However, to dismiss PCK in this way is to adopt a pejorative view and is counter to some of the most recent research thathas illustrated the value of using the construct purposefully

A real and serious issue in teaching is the ability to capture, portray and share knowledge of practice in ways that are articulable and meaningful to others. Typically, teachers share their knowledge through stories, anecdotes and other forms that offer brief glimpses into their expertise and skill in the classroom. What is not always so readily apparent in this form of sharing is that teachers are in fact producers, not just users, of sophisticated knowledge of teaching and learning. And, the complex ideas associated with exemplary practice are better able to be portrayed and shared in meaningful ways if labels and descriptors such as PCK are better understood and used. Therefore, a language that comprises aspects of professional practice is central to moving knowledge of practice out from the individual and into the professional community at large. For example, in many studies by teacher researchers, language (a shared vocabulary) has been central to the development and sharing of their sophisticated knowledge of practice.

A crucial aspect of a shared language then is its ability to capture ideas and practices in ways that embrace the development of knowledge and skills and leads to a greater valuing of teachers' professional knowledge – of which PCK is an important element. It seems reasonable to suggest that a shared vocabulary (a language of teaching and learning that conveys meaning and understanding of practice), is important in teaching so that ideas, knowledge, procedures and practice can be conveyed in ways that move beyond conceptions of good teaching as the simple accrual of activities, despite the fact that teachers constantly need things that will "work in class tomorrow". It is perhaps this tension between activities that workand the underlying principles of practice, or generalizable features from specific teaching and learning situations, that masks the importance of a shared vocabulary and has been an inadvertent barrier to its development and valuing in the profession.

Mitchell, when reviewing the accumulated stories, anecdotes and portrayals of practice that PEEL teachers had published over more than 15 years, drew attention to the underlying features of PEEL teachers' knowledge as described in his Principles of Teaching for Quality Learning. What he did in articulating these Principles was to highlight that PEEL teachers had developed and gradually refined a language that facilitated the sharing of their professional knowledge in meaningful ways about: the manner in which they spoke about their students' learning behaviours; the creation and development of teaching procedures designed to enhance metacognition; and their learning through researching their own practice. When he considered this accumulated body of wisdom from a big picture perspective, some common features were evident to him which, when described as Principles of Teaching for Quality Learning were significant to PEEL teachers because of the meaning inherent in, and commonly understood, by that group of teachers.

When considering the complexity of PCK, a similar need is apparent for a language of practice associated with the ability to describe, portray and articulate pedagogical content knowledge so that others might be able to see how to develop and apply it in their own teaching and learning contexts. It seems obvious that the pedagogical reasoning underpinning particular ways of teaching particular content needs to be able to be shared within the profession. Without a language to discuss this specialist knowledge of teaching, the deep and rich skills and knowledge of practice that teachers carry will not be so readily acknowledged, shared or valued.

Just as terms such as *linking, metacognition* and *sharing intellectual control* are part of the language of teaching and learning for PEEL teachers, so too important features of PCK need to be able to be recognized, described and articulated so that PCK can be developed and shared beyond the individual. However, a cautionary note in all of this is that the use of a special language of teaching and learning may not always be well understood by others and therefore be criticized as jargon. Yet, jargon serves a very useful purpose for those familiar with the language because it carries meaning beyond the words alone; it is shorthand for more expansive and complex ideas. Therefore, although jargon may be interpreted by some as alienating or overly theoretical, it is an important basis on which the specialist skills, knowledge and practice of teaching can be shared, developed and manipulated to not only improve practice but also, to ultimately enhance students' learning.

When viewed this way, PCK and any associated language of practice that underpins it could be described as "jargon that matters". It matters for the development and understanding of teachers' professional knowledge and practice. Importantly, such jargon would be "built up from practice" and could therefore be considered as theoretically based in, and applicable to, the work of teachers. We would argue that PCK needs to be underpinned by a language developed for articulating this specialist knowledge of teaching and learning that enhances the dissemination of this rich knowledge of content specific teaching so that it is applicable to, and meaningful in, the work of teachers more generally.

The following chapter begins to explore approaches to portraying PCK and in so doing begins to develop and use a language that, we hope, helps to capture the essence of such knowledge so that it carries real meaning for others and, in so doing, moves beyond pejorative views of jargon. For example, some of the terms we introduce include:

- Big Ideas
- Frameworks
- Teacher Thinking
- Alternative conceptions
- Narrative accounts
- Representations of practice
- Teaching procedures
- Constructivism
- Ascertaining understanding
- Linking
- CoRe (Content Representation)
- PaP-eRs (Pedagogical and Professional-experience Repertoires).

In some cases, these terms carry specific meaning to particular aspects of PCK not previously developed or described. In others, language has been "borrowed" from other fields in order to import that meaning into our approach to capturing, portraying and articulating PCK so that that which is understood in one field of teacher knowledge might also be equally applicable in this field. One example is that of *alternative conceptions/misconceptions*, where the work of many science education researchers has been important in shaping the knowledge of student learning in science inherent in those apparently simple terms. Another example is that of *constructivism* which carries understandings of learning that teachers would no doubt readily identify with even if they do not necessarily use that term in their everyday conversations about practice. Clearly though, the point is that language matters and carries particular meaning and portraying (sometimes simply) very complex ideas and practices: developing a common language of PCK is then important.

The use and development of the language that occurs in Chapter 3 is designed to capture the essence of the ideas, prompts and questions about practice that we trust helps to share knowledge of exemplary practice. In so doing, we suggest that PCK as a construct can then be better understood and be more useful and applicable in science teachers' professional learning.

CHAPTER OVERVIEW

The intention of this chapter was to highlight a number of issues that we consider important in coming to understand the nature of Pedagogical Content Knowledge. These issues include the ideas that:

- Pedagogical Content Knowledge (PCK) is a notion invented by academics to describe an aspect of the professional knowledge and expertise developed *by* teachers.
- PCK refers to the knowledge that teachers develop about how to teach particular content/subject matter in ways that lead to enhanced student understanding of that content.
- PCK is not the same for all teachers within a given content area despite the fact that there are many commonly shared elements of teachers' PCK within that content area.
- Understanding teachers' practice in terms of PCK may be helpful in making explicit and refining teachers' professional learning about practice.

CHAPTER THREE

PORTRAYING PCK

[On the one hand, while] novice teachers and experienced teachers who have not taught a particular topic before may have little or no PCK in that specific content area. On the other hand, "successful" teachers in a given content area, by which we mean those whose teaching in that particular content area promotes student learning, are likely to have well-developed PCK in that specific content area. Thus the question arises as to whether it is possible to enhance teachers' topic specific PCK in those content areas where their PCK is under-developed using, in some way, successful teachers' PCK and so "prevent every teacher from reinventing the wheel" (Van Driel, et al., 1998, p. 677). This question encapsulates one of the ultimate purposes for our research ... to represent this teacher knowledge using a format which may be useful in pre-service and in-service science teacher education. (Mulhall, Berry, & Loughran, 2003, p. 1)

As alluded to in previous chapters, we believe that successful teachers have a special knowledge that informs their teaching of particular content and that special knowledge is encapsulated in PCK. We have also highlighted that few concrete examples of PCK exist in the literature. As a consequence, it is difficult for science teachers to access PCK in ways that might be meaningful for their practice. Therefore, the very notion of PCK remains somewhat elusive, and as suggested in Chapter 2, a shared language is needed to access and support the ideas foundational to PCK so that the concept (and underlying knowledge) might be better understood and valued.

If PCK as a construct is to be meaningful in science teachers' work, we would argue that it is important for concrete examples of PCK to be articulated and documented so that teachers can access and use them in shaping their own practice. However, as much of our research has highlighted, explaining what PCK is, or might look like, and then actually uncovering, describing, articulating and portraying it, is another matter all together.

Over an extended period of time, we have attempted to develop concrete examples of PCK in ways that we hope might be helpful to teachers, teacher educators and students of teaching so that PCK might be more than just another academic construct. How that work has progressed is explained in detail in the remainder of this chapter and, we trust, establishes sufficient understanding of our conceptualization of PCK for the reader to make the following chapters (which are based around examples of subject specific PCK), accessible and useable.

SHAPING FACTORS IN CAPTURING AND REPRESENTING PCK

The manner in which we have come to develop our approach to capturing and representing PCK is based on the view that it is important to recognize and acknowledge that there are many successful and effective ways for teaching particular science content. Teacher thinking about teaching is complex, and it is important to promote ways of sharing teachers' professional knowledge of teaching to further enhance understanding of teaching and learning in science.

Teaching and learning in science

Over the last 20 years, there has been much research into students' alternative conceptions/ misconceptions about science ideas (see, for example, Pfundt & Duit, 1994). This research generally draws on personal and social constructivist ideas, i.e. that students' learning is influenced by their own personal cognitive frameworks which they have developed as a consequence of their prior experiences and by the ideas of the culture in which they live (Driver, Asoko, Leach, Mortimer, & Scott, 1994). Clearly then, from this perspective, effective or successful science teaching places the teacher in the role of mediator of learning, as opposed to being a transmitter of knowledge (Tobin, Tippins, & Gallard, 1994). Thus, effective science teaching is more likely if the teacher is not only knowledgeable about common student alternative conceptions/misconceptions, but draws on this knowledge to shape teaching. In so doing, successful teachers monitor students' understanding in ways that allow them to be responsive to students' learning and create opportunities that help them to more fully grasp the concept(s) under consideration. Obviously, this cannot be achieved by simply telling students what they should think and why. Finding ways of influencing the understandings that they construct and challenging students' alternative conceptions is at the heart of such teaching. Therefore, as opposed to telling, it is crucial that teachers create meaningful and engaging activities, practices and discussion between students and/or between teacher and student(s) about science ideas and the ways these differ from everyday understandings (Driver, et al., 1994; Hollon, Roth, & Anderson, 1991; Leach & Scott, 1999; Tobin, et al.,

1994). However, as many teachers readily acknowledge, such teaching creates a tension because although they might value such an approach, they also know that it takes longer to move through the prescribed curriculum than would be the case if using more "traditional" teaching approaches. The dilemma, then, is that although students' conceptual understanding may well be richer, the amount of content covered is likely (at least, initially) to be much less than that which might normally be achieved (Hollon, et al., 1991, p. 149).

In the development of our work in PCK, we have drawn on this constructivist perspective so that one aspect of PCK which we have paid particular attention to has been related to the nature of teachers' knowledge that helps them to develop and apply teaching approaches that promote student learning in ways other than "teaching as telling", i.e. seeking to better capture and "unpack" constructivist approaches to teaching.

Teacher thinking

The research literature has long recognized that teaching is a complex activity. Good teaching is not the implementation of a number of standard steps or protocols that can be passed from one teacher to another in some technical form (Clarke & Peterson, 1986). Teacher thinking has been highlighted as important for seeing into the complex nature of teaching by uncovering the sophisticated thinking that informs teachers' actions and decision making in particular teaching situations (Husu, 1995). Therefore, how, when and why teachers think about what they do becomes an important aspect of making the tacit explicit in attempting to capture and portray PCK.

From our perspective, whether or not a particular action by a teacher is illustrative of that teacher's PCK is dependent on the thinking upon which the teacher reasons through and develops the subsequent teaching action (or in some cases, apparent inaction, e.g. in using extended wait-times). Therefore, our representations of topic specific PCK have been developed to make explicit the nature of successful teachers' pedagogical reasoning and the associated decision making within the context of the teaching of that particular science content. In so doing, we believe that it provides evidence of teachers' use of pedagogical content knowledge (whether they explicitly describe it that way themselves or not: a teacher may have PCK without necessarily labelling it in that way).

Talking about teaching through stories

Connolly and Clandinin (2000) have highlighted the importance of teachers' stories and, in so doing, have illustrated that sharing experience through narrative is one way of accessing teachers' knowledge about practice. Teachers seem naturally drawn to discussing teaching by drawing on stories of their experiences because they include the rich detail that accompanies the context so crucial to understanding not only what has happened, but also how and why. In many ways, teachers' stories actually carry most of the important information that helps other teachers to identify with, and therefore extract their own meaning from, a given description of a teaching and learning situation.

> Through narrative we begin to understand the actor's reasons for the action, and are thereby encouraged to make sense of these actions through the eyes of the actor. This understanding constitutes an enormous contribution to learning about and getting better at teaching. (Fenstermacher, 1997, p. 123)

Conle (2003) suggested that the use of narrative is helpful for viewing, and interpreting situations, from different perspectives, and in different ways. Through narrative there is a greater possibility that the story of the writer might influence the knowledge of the reader in ways that cause aspects of the tacit to become more explicit, thus resulting in personal and professional changes in the reader, and to their '[v]isions of what can be' (p. 11). And that is at the heart of why teachers' stories are often so powerful, not only for the story-teller but perhaps more importantly, for the reader/listener.

One aspect of our representation of teachers' PCK is built around the importance of story primarily because narrative constructions can often best represent the holistic nature of a given teaching and learning experience and the knowledge of the teacher working in that situation. Good stories capture and portray aspects of the context, teachers' and students' experiences, their plans and actions, and their views and responses in ways that can carry more meaning than if such things are simply stated as "variables in a research project".

A FRAMEWORK FOR REPRESENTING CONCRETE EXAMPLES OF PCK

In order to represent and share what we believe to be science teachers' PCK about particular content areas, we have, as a result of ongoing conversations, workshops and observations over a number of years, developed a format that captures important aspects of successful science teachers' knowledge of science subject matter knowledge and pedagogy. This particular PCK format is made up of two elements. The first element is what we have called a CoRe (Content Representation; pronounced 'core') which offers an overview of the particular content taught when teaching a topic. The second element is what we have called PaP-eRs (Pedagogical and Professional–experience Repertoires; pronounced 'papers'), which are succinct, but specific, accounts of practice that are intended to offer windows into aspects of the CoRe.

PCK representations demonstrated through a CoRe (or in some cases CoRes; see, for example, Chapter 5: Chemical Reactions; Chapter 7: Force; and, Chapter 9: Genetics) and the associated PaP-eRs combine to create a Resource Folio of PCK on that given content/topic. Such Resource Folios (see the examples that comprise Chapters 4 – 9) have been constructed by using the prompts associated with a CoRe as discussion points when working with teachers to gather the data that eventually becomes the completed CoRe and associated PaP-eRs (for a full description, see Loughran, Milroy, Berry, Gunstone, & Mulhall, 2001; Loughran, et al., 2004).

The Resource Folios that are offered in the following chapters are a synthesis of our research data from both individual and group interviews with experienced, successful science teachers and from observations of their science teaching. These representations of PCK are not meant to represent a single teacher's PCK, but rather the most common and agreed upon aspects from a particular group of science teachers at a particular time. Therefore, although many aspects of the CoRe and PaP-eRs may be common to other teachers, it is not intended that these Resource Folios are the only or best PCK of that subject/topic. Rather they are illustrative of PCK for that topic more generally, so they are not "the PCK for that topic" but concrete examples of PCK within that topic.

CoRe: CONTENT REPRESENTATION

A CoRe (Content Representation) provides an overview of how a given group of teachers (those we worked with in this project) conceptualize the content of particular subject matter or topic. A CoRe is developed by asking teachers to think about what they consider to be the "big ideas" associated with teaching a given topic for a particular grade level(s) based on their experience of teaching that topic. These big ideas are discussed and refined and then, when generally agreed upon, become the horizontal axis of a CoRe (see Figure 3.1 the blank template for an example). The big ideas are then probed and quizzed in different ways through the prompts that are listed on the left hand side vertical axis of the CoRe (see Figure 3.1), so that specific information about the big ideas that impact on the manner in which the content is taught can be made explicit.

Through this process, the CoRe becomes a generalisable form of the participant teachers' pedagogical content knowledge as it links the how, why, and what of the content to be taught with what they agree to be important in shaping students' learning and teachers' teaching. In the next section, we develop this further by explaining each aspect of the CoRe.

Big science ideas/concepts

The horizontal axis of a CoRe contains the "Big Ideas" which refers to the science ideas that the teacher(s) see as crucial for students to develop their understanding of the topic. In some cases a big science teaching idea may be the same as a big science idea but the two are not necessarily synonymous, as the interaction between content and teaching impacts how teachers conceptualize these big science teaching ideas. There is no defined number of big ideas, but typically, in a given topic, we have found that teachers generally settle on between 5 – 8 big ideas. Too few big ideas suggests that too much may be encompassed in a single big idea whilst too many big ideas suggests the topic may be being "broken down" into "chunks" of information that appear unconnected. Therefore, developing the big ideas can be quite a time consuming task and requires considerable thought and debate.

What you intend the students to learn about this idea

This is the first prompt in the vertical axis of a CoRe and is a starting point for "unpacking" the big ideas. Our research suggests that experienced teachers have little difficulty in being specific about what a particular group of students should be able to learn. However, in contrast, teachers inexperienced in a given topic tend to be unsure what the students are capable of achieving. Therefore, as a beginning point in unpacking science teachers' understanding of what matters in a particular content area and why, this prompt is very helpful.

Why it is important for students to know this

In the multitude of competing curricular decisions that teachers face, deciding what to teach must be linked to why it is important to be taught. We suggest that successful teachers draw on their experience and knowledge of the given subject matter with that which they know to be relevant to students' everyday lives, so that they can create meaningful ways of encouraging students to grasp the essence of the ideas/concepts at hand. Often, though, the reason why it is important for students to know about these ideas/concepts is linked to other curricular aims.

What else you might know about this idea (that you don't intend students to know yet)

Teachers often make difficult decisions about that which needs to be included, and that which needs to be excluded, in order for students to begin to develop an understanding of the topic/theme. Although successful science teachers recognize the value in not oversimplifying content, or maintaining its complexity in order to enhance understanding, they also balance this with a knowledge that perceived difficulty and/or unnecessary confusion might detract from students' learning. This then influences their thinking in relation to the next prompt in a CoRe.

Difficulties/limitations connected with teaching this idea

As Shulman (1986) and many others have noted, teachers come to develop and respond to insights they gain about potential difficulties, when teaching a particular topic. In science, this is particularly borne out in the research into alternative conceptions/misconceptions, and the limitations of such things as models and analogies in promoting understanding or explaining phenomena. Expert science teachers use this knowledge and information to shape the manner in which they teach particular concepts and topics. Without this feature of PCK it could well be argued that teaching is not genuinely responsive to constructivist views of learning and is therefore not concerned with students processing, structuring, synthesizing and reconstructing their knowledge, but more so with adding new "chunks" of learning onto existing knowledge regardless of their existing views/understanding of the content.

Knowledge about students' thinking which influences your teaching of this idea

As an aspect of the CoRe, this prompt is important for helping to make explicit that which teachers have come to know through their experience of teaching the given topic, and how that knowledge influences their thinking about their teaching. Successful science teachers plan their teaching around that which they have learnt about students' commonly held ideas about the topic (which may not be the same as, but also include, understandings of alternative conceptions as mentioned earlier) and the manner in which students "usually respond" to the topic (including level of interest) and specific teaching and learning situations developed through the topic.

Other factors that influence your teaching of this idea

This prompt in the CoRe is aimed at unpacking teachers' contextual knowledge about students as well as their general pedagogical knowledge in order to explore how these might influence the manner in which they approach and construct their teaching.

Teaching procedures (and particular reasons for using these to engage with this idea)

Just as Chapter 2 raised the importance of a shared vocabulary in talking about teaching, so too the expression 'teaching procedures' is important in differentiating between different aspects of planning for, and the teaching of, subject matter. Mitchell and Mitchell (2005) distinguished between teaching activities, procedures, and strategies. They suggested that a teacher may well use an activity to introduce students to a topic and as such, the activity can be applied to a situation "as is". Teaching procedures, they suggest, are tactical in that teachers choose which procedures to use, when, how, and why in order to promote different aspects of learning. On the other hand, a strategy incorporates an overall approach such as 'building a classroom environment that supports risk-taking" or "sharing intellectual control' (see Principles of Teaching for Quality Learning (Mitchell & Mitchell, 1997) briefly outlined in Chapter 2).

Generally then, familiarity with a range of teaching procedures is an important aspect of PCK because 'expertise in choosing teaching procedures that are appropriate to the intended learning outcomes and knowing not only how to use them, but why, under what changed circumstances, and being able to adjust and adapt them to meet the contextual needs of the time' (Loughran, 2006, p. 49) is an indication of sophisticated expertise. Clearly, teaching procedures alone cannot guarantee learning, but informed and thoughtful use in appropriate ways at appropriate times can influence student thinking and may well promote better understanding of science ideas (Leach & Scott, 1999).

Specific ways of ascertaining students' understanding or confusion around this idea

Teachers constantly monitor students' understanding and progress (both formally and informally). This prompt is designed to explore how teachers approach this aspect of their teaching in the topic in order to gather different perspectives on the effectiveness of their teaching as well as adjustments to their thinking about the same, or similar, situations in the future.

Overview of the CoRe

When creating or working with a CoRe, it is important to recognize that some sections may contain more detail than others. It is not intended that a CoRe should have a prescribed amount of information or ideas.It contains only the amount of information and ideas proposed by those involved in its formation and, in some cases, some of the boxes may well be left empty. However, because of the form of representation that a CoRe takes, it allows for changes and/or additions to be made as further insights are gained, or as issues are further clarified and refined. Obviously then, there is not one CoRe for each topic. Different groups of teachers may develop different CoRes for the same topic, as other things, not least being experience and contextual factors, inevitably influence teachers' understandings of, and actions in, practice.

The CoRe enables a solid base around which an overview of teachers' PCK for a topic can be articulated, and provides insights into the decisions that teachers make when teaching a particular topic, including the linkages between the content, students, and teachers' practice.

A CoRe, despite containing valuable information and possibilities for understanding PCK, is of itself not PCK because the information represented in a CoRe tends to be propositional in nature, and is thus limited in terms of providing insight into teachers' experiences of practice. For this reason we developed PaP-eRs (Pedagogical and Professional–experience Repertoires), which, for all intents and purposes, are windows into PCK that bring to life science teachers' practice, thinking and understanding of teaching particular content in particular ways at particular times.

PaP-eRs: PEDAGOGICAL AND PROFESSIONAL-EXPERIENCE REPERTOIRES

A PaP-eR is a narrative account of a teacher's PCK that highlights a particular piece, or aspect, of science content to be taught. (In some cases, PaP-eRs can be constructions that draw on more than one teacher's PCK even though it may be represented as an individual's PCK.) A PaP-eR is designed to purposefully unpack a teacher's thinking about a particular aspect of PCK in that given content, and so is largely based around classroom practice. PaP-eRs are intended to represent the teacher's reasoning; that is, the thinking and actions of a successful science teacher in teaching specific aspects of science content.

As narrative accounts, PaP-eRs are meant to 'elaborate and give insight into the interacting elements of the teacher's PCK in ways that are meaningful and accessible to the reader, and that may serve to foster reflection in the reader about the PCK under consideration, and to open the teacher reader to possibilities for change in his/her own practice' (Mulhall, et al., 2003, p. 9).

The "voice" of a PaP-eR varies depending on that which is being portrayed. For example, some PaP-eRs are drawn from a student's perspective, others from that of the teacher, some take the form of an interview, others a classroom observation or the thinking inherent in a teacher reflecting on the problematic nature of a given concept, while others highlight particular curriculum issues or concerns. As a consequence, the format of a PaP-eR is responsive to the type of situation it is attempting to portray. Some use call-out boxes to elaborate on particular points or to draw attention to specific instances that might otherwise be easily overlooked.

A PaP-eR is generally introduced to the reader using an overview that is in a different 'voice' to that of the PaP-eR itself. This overview is designed to offer the reader quick and easy access to the ideas and approaches that are elaborated within the PaP-eR.

Overall, a PaP-eR is one of many in a Resource Folio for teaching about a particular science topic, each designed to link to one or more specific aspect(s) of the CoRe in the relevant content area, but each focussing on different aspects of successful teachers' PCK. Together in a Resource Folio, PaP-eRs bring the CoRe to life and offer one way of capturing the holistic nature and complexity of PCK in ways that are not possible in the CoRe alone. A number of PaP-eRs focus on how teachers come to see teaching and learning situations with new eyes as they 'reframe' (Schön, 1983) their practice in response to new insights gained from questioning the taken-for-granted in the teaching and learning of particular science concepts. We suggest then, that in so doing, the total package of a Resource Folio (specifically those examples that are Chapters 4 – 9) gives the reader access to the process of development of teachers' pedagogical content knowledge in that particular science topic.

CONSTRUCTING AND USING CoRe(s) AND PaP-eRs

Figure 3.1 is a blank CoRe or template that demonstrates the major components that comprise this particular aspect of a Resource Folio including: (a) the Important Science Concepts/Ideas, i.e. the big ideas for teaching that particular topic; and, (b) the prompts for unpacking the big ideas, e.g. what you intend the students to learn about this idea, etc.

As the template illustrates, the variety of ideas and information developed in a CoRe covers a range of important aspects of the teaching and learning of specific content/concepts. Even though this template is spread over a double page, as will quickly become evident in the following chapters, it is not possible to neatly confine a CoRe to such an orderly space. However, for the purposes of constructing a CoRe, the layout demonstrated is helpful in terms of managing a visual representation of that which is involved in developing and working with a CoRe.

In our work with science teachers, we have consistently found that using a blank CoRe on a double sheet, such as that in Figure 3.1 is significant for helping participants to negotiate different regions of the CoRe and to move freely from one area to another as their ideas and thoughts progress.

With each group of teachers, a different pattern emerges for responding to the big ideas and associated prompts. In some instances, teachers prefer to work through one big idea, moving from the prompt at the top of the page down to the final prompt at the bottom of the page. Others work across the pages following an individual prompt across each big idea, one at a time. Not surprisingly, others randomly move across the whole CoRe, initially responding to those spaces that most capture their attention and then working their way back to those areas that require more time and energy. However, the last two prompts tend to draw out the richest detail as they tap into teachers' stories of their classroom practice and encourage the sharing of narratives. It is from these instances that ideas for PaP-eRs are usually first able to be encouraged and also become a catalyst for further PaP-eRs across different fields of the CoRe.

As explained earlier, there is no set amount of information or given number of big ideas that must be completed in order to "finish a CoRe". Working on a CoRe creates a sense of professional learning and sharing of the expertise of teaching that, for many teachers, is considerably different from what they have previously experienced. In discussing, debating, and articulating the aspects of the different spaces that eventually become a given CoRe, science teachers quickly develop ways of discussing their practice that make that which is normally implicit, private, and individual, explicit, clear and meaningful for themselves and their colleagues; some of these approaches have been important in shaping the language we have used in representing our conceptualization of PCK. For example, the very notion of "big ideas" and the nature and wording of the prompts appear to make sense to teachers and have been created by working closely with them. As a result, we have found that through this language, teachers do not become embroiled in some of the more common arguments that revolve around questions such as: 'what content has to be in this topic?' Rather they reflect on the importance of the concepts that are crucial to understanding the topic, as opposed to stating the propositional knowledge alone.

The template in Figure 3.1 is a good starting point for re-examining the way in which particular topics are taught and for refocussing attention on the skills, knowledge and expertise that is so often overlooked in the normal routine of teaching.

OVERVIEW OF CoRe AND PaP-eRs

A Resource Folio of a given content area contains a CoRe(s) and the associated PaP-eRs which together create complementary representations of successful teachers' PCK about teaching particular subject matter, to a particular group of students in a particular way for very important pedagogical reasons. A CoRe is a holistic overview of teachers' pedagogical content knowledge related to the teaching of a given topic, and the associated PaP-eRs are narrative accounts designed to purposefully offer insights into specific instances of that PCK. A Resource Folio is therefore a collection of two specific interactive elements that together represent that which is PCK, as developed and articulated by a given group of science teachers that, in some cases, have constructed joint understandings (more common in the CoRe), and in others, individual illustrations of specific practice (more common in PaP-eRs). It therefore seems reasonable to suggest that Resource Folios are generalisable (while still being complex and quite specific) instances of teachers' pedagogical content knowledge about teaching particular science content and offer other science teachers new and valuable ways of accessing that aspect of the knowledge base of teaching.

There is little doubt that much of that which comprises teacher knowledge is implicit. Teachers are rarely afforded the opportunity to reflect on their practice in a formalised or sanctioned manner, i.e., it is not part of their allocated teaching duties. More than this, curriculum documents usually represent topic specific teaching as "blocks of content" to "be delivered" by teachers to students in the hope that learning might occur. Sometimes, activities and teaching procedures might be suggested but such advice is not usually strategic and "engagement in learning" is often a misnomer for "fun". It is little wonder that in the busy work of teaching, as Appleton (2002) observed, discussion about subject specific teaching and learning is so frequently limited to *what works*; and even more so to *what will work in my class next lesson?*

An immediate feature of the structure of a CoRe is the manner in which it encourages teachers to problematise the content and teaching. The overall impact of a Resource Folio is that it provokes thinking about what is important in the teaching of a topic and why, and, even more so, how teachers view their existing practice in conjunction with possibilities for future development.

In many ways, the combination of CoRe(s) and PaP-eRs in a Resource Folio is an invitation to teachers to begin to reflect on and identify that which they need to know and to think further about when teaching a new topic (e.g. 'What are the big ideas for teaching this topic to this particular group of students?'; 'What should I expect students to learn?'; 'Why?'; 'What teaching procedures will help this group of students to understand a particular big idea?'; and so on). Further to this, they help to bring to the front of one's thinking the value of a construct such as PCK that, when made explicit, illustrates the value of focusing on the special skills, knowledge, and ability that successful subject specialists (in this case, science teachers) possess and continue to develop. Therefore, CoRes and PaP-eRs not only represent teachers' topic specific PCK, but also act as triggers to encourage other teachers (both pre-, and in-service teachers, as well as science teacher educators) to begin to embrace the notion of PCK in their own practice.

CHAPTER OVERVIEW

There has long been a simplistic distinction made between teaching as the swampy lowlands of practice (Schön, 1983) and the ivory tower of academia that is the world of theory. As a consequence, the theory-practice gap is often cited as a reason for the lack of influence of theory on practice, and even more so, of practice on theory. However, some have spent considerable time and energy trying to link both in more meaningful ways. There is the recognition that 'teachers need help to think more complexly about their practice and the reasons behind their actions in the light of how particular pupils learn and in relationship to specific formal academic knowledge' (Bullough, 2001, p. 665), as well as the realisation that experienced teachers see into, and respond appropriately to practice because they are: 'able to make a deeper interpretation of events, [as they] interpret significant contextual clues' (Calderhead, 1996, p. 717).

We suggest that what Resource Folios (as encapsulated by both CoRe and PaP-eRs) offer teachers (pre-service, beginning and experienced, as well as science teacher educators) is a powerful, accessible and useful representation of PCK that is responsive to practice and in practice is important to a theory of teaching. This chapter has attempted to bring these often two different worlds together by explaining our conceptualization of PCK based on the following important aspect of teaching and learning in science.

- Our representation of teachers' PCK draws on constructivist perspectives of teaching and learning.
- Teachers' PCK becomes evident through making explicit the nature of their pedagogical reasoning, and the associated decision making within the context of teaching particular science content.
- Our representations of teachers' PCK use a format that is comprised of 2 elements:

    1. a content representation (CoRe) – which offers a holistic overview of particular science concepts related to a content area; and,
    2. accounts of teachers' practice (PaP-eRs) – which illustrate specific aspects of the content within the complexity of a science teaching/learning experience.

- Together CoRes and PaP-eRs combine to create a Resource Folio of PCK for a given topic/content area, that are illustrative of PCK for that science topic.
- A Resource Folio is an example of PCK for a given science topic but it is not the only, or necessarily the most correct way of representing PCK within that subject/topic: it is an example of PCK.

A Resource Folio (particularly the CoRe) is not intended as a curriculum document/syllabus although it may well shape the way curriculum/syllabus is conceptualized.

	IMPORTANT SCIENCE	
Year Level for which this CoRe is designed.	**BIG IDEA 'A'**	**BIG IDEA 'B'**
What you intend the <u>**students**</u> **to learn about this idea.**		
Why it is important for students to know this.		
What else <u>**you**</u> **know about this idea (that you do not intend students to know yet).**		
Difficulties/ limitations connected with teaching this idea.		
Knowledge about students' thinking which influences your teaching of this idea.		
Other factors that influence your teaching of this idea.		
Teaching procedures (and particular reasons for using these to engage with this idea).		
Specific ways of ascertaining students' understanding or confusion around this idea (include likely range of responses).		

Figure 3.1: CoRe template

IDEAS/CONCEPTS		
BIG IDEA 'C'	**BIG IDEA 'D'**	**BIG IDEA 'E'**

Figure 3.1: CoRe template (continued)

CHAPTER FOUR

PARTICLE THEORY

This chapter outlines a representation of Pedagogical Content Knowledge (PCK) for the topic Particle Theory. This is the first chapter offered to illustrate how the ideas of a CoRe and PaP-eRs fit together to form that which we describe as a Resource Folio. This Resource Folio Chapter (Particle Theory) has purposely been selected as the first to be offered in the book as the layout follows the standard design, of a CoRe followed by the PaP-eRs that are associated with particular elements of that CoRe, as explained in the previous chapter. (Although based on this standard layout, not all chapters fully adhere to it, as some Resource Folios have two CoRes and/or layered and sequential PaP-eRs.)

In presenting the chapter in this way, we trust it helps to illustrate for the reader the nature of the relationship between a CoRe and itsPaP-eRs; however, it is important to be reminded that there are different perspectives on the same content and that there is not one way of representing a CoRe. This CoRe, though, is one that captures the essence of what many science teachers suggest as integral to the nature of this particular topic.

REMINDERS ABOUT SHAPING FACTORS THAT INFLUENCE CoRe(s) AND PaP-eRs

As is the case with each of the concrete examples of PCK that comprise Chapters 4 – 9, we briefly offer some of the important points that shape our understanding of representing PCK. Repeating this information at the start of each of the chapters (Resource Folios) is designed to remind the reader about the nature of this form of representation of PCK and for that information to be "on hand" for each individual topic portrayed.

Therefore, some of the important points to be kept in mind when considering that which follows in this Resource Folio are that:

- It is very difficult to offer a single example of PCK that is a neat concrete package, able to be analysed and dissected, or used as a blueprint for practice by others. Therefore, our approach to capturing and portraying PCK hinges on the understanding that the teaching and the content must be represented in ways that both maintains the complexity of their relationships, but at the same time offers some way of seeing through the complexity in order to gain insight into it.
- Our approach is based on what we have termed a CoRe (Content Representation) and PaP-eRs (Pedagogical and Professional-experience Repertoire). The CoRe outlines some of the aspects of PCK "most attached to that content", but it is not the only representation. It is a necessary, but incomplete, generalization that helps to make the complexity accessible and manageable; it is neither complete nor absolute. Attached to the CoRe are the PaP-eRs, with links to the aspects of this field that they "bring to life". A PaP-eR is of a content area and must allow the reader to look inside a teaching/learning situation in which the content shapes the pedagogy.
- PaP-eRs bring the CoRe to life and shed new light on the complex nature of PCK. They help create ways to better understand and value the specialist knowledge, skills and ability of teachers thus making that which is so often tacit, explicit for others.

		IMPORTANT SCIENCE	
This Core is designed for students in Lower Secondary School, i.e. Years 7 – 9.	**A:** **Matter is made up of small bits that are called particles.**	**B:** **There is empty space between particles.**	**C:** **Particles are in constant motion.**
What you intend the <u>students</u> to learn about this idea.	If we break up substances, the smallest bit of substance we can get is a particle.	The relative distances between particles differ in solids, liquids and gases.	Particles of matter are always moving. The speed of particles can be changed (by heating/cooling, pressure change). The way particles are arranged can change when their speed changes.
Why it is important for students to know this.	Because it helps to explain the behaviour of everyday things e.g. diffusion.	Because it explains the ability to compress things and helps to explain events such as expansion and dissolving.	Because it explains what happens in phase changes, e.g. the need to contain gases is evidence the particles are moving.
What else <u>you</u> know about this idea (that you do not intend students to know yet).	At this stage 'particles' is used in a general sense without discriminating between atoms and molecules. Subatomic structure. Chemical reactions. Ions. More complex properties of materials. More complicated models of matter. Links to diffusion and thermal properties of matter.		
Difficulties/ limitations connected with teaching this idea.	Particles are too small to see. The use of particular science models is not necessary to comprehend science in everyday life. It is difficult to decide when to introduce the labels (i.e. atoms, molecules) for different kinds of particles. Substances seem to disappear when dissolved. What holds particles together? Why don't substances automatically become a gas?	There is a big difference between macro (seen) and micro (unseen) levels, e.g. wood seems solid so it is hard to picture empty space between the 'wood' particles. Students don't tend to think of gases as matter and therefore have difficulty thinking about empty spaces between gas particles.	That macro properties are a result of micro arrangements is hard to understand. The commonly used term 'states of matter' implies that all things can be discretely classified as solid, liquid or gas. It is difficult to imagine particles in a solid moving. There are problems with some textbook representations of liquid, e.g. particles are often shown as being much further apart than they are in solids. 'Melt' and 'dissolve' are often used interchangeably in everyday life.

IDEAS/CONCEPTS

D: Particles of different substances are different.	E: There are different types of small bits of substances.	F: Atom particles don't disappear or get created, but their arrangements may be changed.	G: Models are used in science to help explain phenomena. All models have limitations.
The characteristics of substances are related to the types of particles they contain.	There are two types of small bits of substance: Atoms Molecules. Molecules form when atoms combine.	Atoms don't change but molecules can. New atoms can't be made and atoms can't be destroyed (Conservation of matter).	Particle theory is an idea constructed by scientists to help us understand some aspects of the behaviour of matter. There are limitations to what particle theory can explain. Constructions are modified over time. Breaking up all substances into categories of solids, liquids and gases can be problematic.
Because it explains the observable behaviours of different substances.	Because it explains why there are a limited number of elements, but many different kinds of compounds. Because it helps organise ideas that are later developed when studying 'chemical reactions'.	Because in any reaction involving matter, all of that matter must be able to accounted for.	Because it helps students understand why the particle model is not is perfect and because it gives some insights into how science works.
(As per Big Ideas A, B & C.)	Details about ionic and molecular structures. Fission and fusion reactions.		
	Students can come to think that molecules 'disassociate' in boiling water (because of the confusion between atoms and molecules).	Atoms don't change. It is difficult to understand that different substances with the same types of atoms have different properties. Generally students have never had any cause to consider the notion of conservation of matter on a microscopic scale.	

	A: Matter is made up of small bits that are called particles.	B: There is empty space between particles.	C: Particles are in constant motion.
Knowledge about students' thinking which influences your teaching of this idea.	Many students will use a continuous model (despite former teaching).	The notion of 'space' is very difficult to think about – most students propose there is other 'stuff' between the particles. Students think that particles get bigger during expansion.	Students have commonly encountered 'states of matter' but do not understand the ideas in terms of particle movement. Students can be confused by the notion of melting and think a particular particle melts.
Other factors that influence your teaching of this idea.	Maturity – stage of psychological development, readiness to grapple with abstract ideas. Dealing with many different student conceptions at once. Knowledge of context (students' and teacher's). Using the term 'phase' suggests the idea of a continuum and may help to address the difficulties associated with the term 'state'.		
Teaching procedures (and particular reasons for using these to engage with this idea).	**Probes of student understanding:** e.g. students draw a flask containing air, then re-draw the same flask with some of the air removed.Probes promote student thinking and uncover individual's views of situations. **Analogies:** Use of analogies to draw parallels between new ideas and specific/similar situations. For example, although something may appear to be made up of one thing – like a pipe is made up of one piece of metal – it is really the combination of lots of small things. This can be analogous to a jar of sand.From a distance it looks like one thing, but up close you can see the individual grains of sand.	**POE (Predict-Observe-Explain):** e.g. squashing syringe of air (ask students to predict the outcome based on different models of matter – e.g. continuous vs. particle). **Mixing activities:** e.g. noting that the combined volume of methylated spirits and water, or of salt and water is less than the sum of individual volumes. (The outcome can be explained as due to empty space between the bits.) **Comparing models:** (e.g. continuous and particle.)	**Translation activities:** e.g. role-play, modelling, drawing. For example, my life as a Carbon Atom; or, write about what you would see if you were inside a particle of water. **Imaginative writing:** Compare pieces with & without misconceptions, i.e. share student's work around the class and encourage students' comments on aspects of understanding in them. **Using models & demonstrations:** e.g. a jar of marbles as model: packed tight to illustrate a solid; remove one & shake to demonstrate movement in a liquid. **Observation:** Dry ice sublimating - what's happening?

D: Particles of different substances are different.	E: There are different types of small bits of substances.	F: Atom particles don't disappear or get created. but their arrangements may be changed.	G: Models are used in science to help explain phenomena. All models have limitations.
Students tend to internalise a model from textbooks that shows circles all of the same size, so they think all particles are the same.	Students use the terms 'molecule' and 'atom' without understanding the difference between these concepts.They simply adopt the language.	Students believe that new stuff can appear and that stuff can disappear (e.g. when water evaporates).	It's hard for students to shift from thinking of science as 'discovered' to 'constructed'.
(As per Big Ideas A, B & C.)			This is not traditionally addressed in science curricula.
Mixing activities: It can be helpful to model the mixing of different substances by, for example, using different sized balls for the mixing of water and methylated spirits.	**POE (Predict-Observe-Explain):** e.g. What is the vapour above boiling water? Students predict what happens to hydrogen and oxygen molecules when water is boiled. Many students predict that H and O will separate. Teacher establishes test for each gas, and class explains outcome of POE using gas tests as required. (This can create a need for different kinds of smallest bits.) **Modelling with specific materials**: e.g. explore the possible combinations of atoms and molecules in new things (e.g. using different sized blocks of plasticine). [continued over]		**Historical research:** Students investigate history of ideas about atoms and atomic structure and how scientists observing nature came to different interpretations of it. Students can sequence a set of historical events including Dalton, Faraday, & Thompson's inferences and observations (i.e. progressively building on models of matter and atoms.) **Classification and Interpretive Discussion:** Ask students to classify some substances as solid, liquid, gas. Include some problematic examples (e.g. 'Oobleck', honey, sand, foam, jelly, toothpaste.) Discuss aspects that are problematic in definitions.

	A: Matter is made up of small bits that are called particles.	B: There is empty space between particles.	C: Particles are in constant motion.
[continued] Teaching procedures (and particular reasons for using these to engage with this idea). [continued]	**Linking activities:** Behaviour of everyday things, e.g. putting a marshmallow in a gas jar and changing the pressure so the behaviour of the marshmallow is affected. This helps to illustrate the point that small bits move or act differently in response to changes in conditions. The marshmallow is good to use because it is an example of something they are familiar with – it links to their everyday experience.		
Specific ways of ascertaining students' understanding or confusion around this idea (include likely range of responses).			**Concept Map using the terms:** solid; liquid; gas; particles; air; nothing.
	Questions such as, 'Explain why popcorn pops', 'Why when popcorn is pierced does it not pop?' 'Why can we smell onions being cooked when we are at a distance from them?', 'Why does a syringe containing NO_2 appear darker when it is compressed?' (Students deduce the gas particles have moved closer. Actually the gas is darker due to a chemical reaction – it is convenient to withhold this information.)		
	Explaining thinking and defending views. Making predictions about new situations. Tracking one's own learning, e.g. 'I used to think …' Asking questions such as, 'What is something that has been bothering you from yesterday's lesson?'		
	Put on your 'Magic Glasses' (which are glasses that enable you to see the particles in substances) – What do you see? (i.e. discuss what might be seen through the magic glasses), OR, Draw what you see. Then compare and discuss these drawings.		

D: Particles of different substances are different.	E: There are different types of small bits of substances.	F: Atom particles don't disappear or get created, but their arrangements may be changed.	G: Models are used in science to help explain phenomena. All models have limitations.
Concept Map using the terms: solid; liquid; gas; particles; air; nothing. (As per Big Ideas A, B & C.)	Draw a picture to show what happens to water particles when water boils.		Listening for student questions, such as 'Why doesn't wood melt?'

Put on your 'Magic Glasses' (which are glasses that enable you to see the particles in substances) – What do you see? (i.e. discuss what might be seen through the magic glasses), OR, Draw what you see. Then compare and discuss these drawings.

INTRODUCTION TO PaP-eRs ON PARTICLE THEORY

In this section of the chapter, the PaP-eRs on Particle Theory are presented. They are not organised in a specific order and are not meant to be read sequentially. Each PaP-eR should be able to stand alone and be capable of illustrating how PCK is evident in the way the individual PaP-eR brings to life specific aspects of the CoRe.

TABLE OF CONTENTS OF PaP-eRs ON PARTICLE THEORY

4.1: WHAT IS THE SMALLEST BIT?

This PaP-eR has been constructed using a teacher's journal entries in order to illustrate how she has documented her approaches and ideas to teaching this concept, and to offer insight into the manner in which she has reviewed her own learning. As this PaP-eR begins, the class have already moved through several activities and discussions that have helped them to consider the ideas that matter is made up of tiny, tiny bits, and that these bits have nothing between them. They have started to consider that these particles (the smallest bits possible) are moving and, hence, have a particular arrangement, and that these factors help explain what phase a substance will assume. Here the teacher attempts to create a need for different kinds of particles, by asking students to explain (using different media) what happens as water boils. The teacher knows that often students find the terms 'atom', 'molecule' and 'particle' interchangeable, not clearly understanding the concepts as they perceive no real need to distinguish between them. This teaching sequence also revisits and reinforces the content ideas already covered.

PART 1

The abstract (though familiar) representation for the arrangement of particles in water translates to multiple representations in students' minds.

Teaching journal entry

On to the need for molecules ...

Found a POE[1]designed to help students understand the structure of water. It seems perfect for differentiating between particles generally, and atoms and molecules.

The teacher asks the class of Year 9 students if they know what the chemical shorthand for water is. A number call out, they have all heard it before, and the class quickly settles on H_2O. What does that mean? Easily the class agrees that it means water is made of H and O and that there is twice as much H as O.
The teacher then asks them to draw a super-magnified picture of how a beaker of water might look if we could see how the H and O are arranged in it. Students think and quietly draw their own pictures. As they work, the teacher walks around and asks several students if they would like to put their diagrams on the board. The teacher is careful to select so that there are a range of ideas shown.

Teaching journal entry

Nearly everyone knew that water is H_2O and had constructed some vague idea of what that means, even if just that it's made of hydrogen and oxygen.

---

[1]**Predict-Observe-Explain.** This teaching procedure requires students to make a reasoned prediction in advance of a given event, then explain any differences between the prediction and what they observe of the event after it has occurred.

What is amazing to me is their different constructions of what water being H_2O, and so made of two parts hydrogen to one part oxygen, means. This is the best lesson I've ever had about the variety of interpretations that can fit one piece of information!

I'm always a little bit nervous asking them to bare their ideas on the board, but lots of people were very willing.

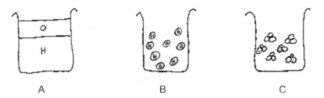

People were pretty strong on the idea of ratio – it was important to them that it was two parts hydrogen to one part oxygen. (Is this just the power of the annotation – because the formula says so??). I'm still amazed at the first picture – after all the work we (they!) have done with particles..... Several students commented on this: 'It can't be that – it has to be made of particles'. Picture A (and to some extent picture B) was challenged by asking what would happen if we tipped some of the water out of the beaker. There was some debate as to whether it could "even itself up" but it generally offended their notion of the 2:1 ratio. After some discussion we could eliminate A. A few were still undecided about B. But in the end, most of the class were happy with picture C as the best representation of water, so I moved on and asked them to work out how we could draw a picture for steam.

PART 2

Through class discussion, the teacher comes to see how students' confusion about particles can be unintentionally reinforced through commonly used science language and activities. She identifies the need to introduce more specific ways to describe particles to help lead her students to develop more meaningful understanding of such concepts as molecule and atom.

The teacher then invites the students to look at a beaker of water boiling at the front of the class, and to imagine the steam above the beaker. They are asked to draw a second picture, this time a 'super-magnifier' representation of the arrangement of H and O in boiling water and steam. As before, several students are invited to draw their pictures on the board for discussion.

Of course all those who drew the H and O as separates in liquid water were separate in gas (how would I handle this if they weren't!?). From those that had drawn molecules of liquid water, only Carolyn and Polly kept the molecules together in the gas, the rest had them separating into hydrogen and oxygen.

The teacher asks the class how they could find out whether boiling water really does separate into hydrogen and oxygen as it boils. When students suggest somehow testing to see if those gases are there, the teacher is ready to produce, and then demonstrate the presence of, hydrogen in a test-tube. She asks the class what it will mean (in terms of choosing the best picture) if they do find hydrogen above boiling water, and what it will mean if they don't.

Teaching journal entry

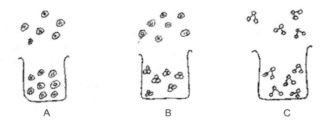

Teaching journal entry

Demonstrated hydrogen test – they loved it (I have to be careful that the 'pop' isn't the only thing they remember). Sarah nervously tested the water vapour for hydrogen. Nothing happened of course, so no hydrogen present.

Next point they said that the H stays behind and O is given off!

Kylie: Maybe it separates into the H and O gases then recombines again and that's why you feel the water droplets on your hand if you put your hand over it.

Steph: But when we see the pictures in the book it says solids 'break up' into liquids, so then the liquid also 'breaks up' into a gas, therefore H_2O breaks up into H + O.

Bron: Yeah, and when we did the role-play about ice melting and water boiling we all had to break apart and run around the room then (she looked pretty smug). [A problem with that role-play I'd never thought of before but which seems pretty obvious now it's pointed out.]

There wasn't time to work through all of this but what I LOVE is that they are fighting for those models, and coming up with ideas to defend them as hard as they can. LOTS of thinking ...

Next lesson I need to:

1) show O_2 test and test boiling water, and then ask which is the most likely model?

2) acknowledge Kylie's observation and deal with it (no H or O found by testing).

3) introduce the term 'molecule' as the smallest bit of water and link that back to the role-play (i.e., acknowledge Bron's point and help them understand that the people (particles) were molecules/smallest bits of water, and not atoms).

In the following lesson, the teacher demonstrates a test for oxygen and a student applies a glowing splint to the space above the boiling water. Via a great deal of class discussion consensus is reached that picture 3 is the most suitable one to represent water as liquid and as 'steam'. (The teacher is comfortable that for now, students interchangeably use the terms 'steam' and 'water vapour'). Students draw diagrams again in their books, and write down how they know that the hydrogen and oxygen stay together as water boils. Their next writing task asks them to apply the new terms 'atom' and 'molecule' in describing water (and some other substances).

PART 3

The teacher knows that asking students to manipulate arrangements of particles by using drawings and models, and to apply newly learnt terms during this activity, will help to develop their useful understanding of what these concepts really mean. Rather than just knowing an exemplar, they will have a more honed understanding of the concepts.

For the next lesson the classroom is set up with a beaker of water boiling out the front.
Students, with a partner, are asked to:
    draw big pictures that show what happens as water boils;
    be ready to demonstrate their understanding to the teacher using some pieces of Lego.

Teaching journal entry

The girls worked in pairs with marker pens and butcher's paper. They started off working on their explanations on large sheets of paper but eventually everyone had their Lego going to help them work out what the pictures actually should be. I'm sure it helps their thinking to be able to manipulate a model while they are trying to put snapshots of it down on paper. I'm sure that's a big problem with lots of the diagrams showing phase change that they get to see – it's hard to think about what's happened for one diagram to move on to the next.

The best bit was working through the boiling water scenario with particular pairs of students. Tammie and Nat were struggling & that led to me asking them to use the Lego to show the smallest bit of water they could possibly get, then asking which of the terms (atom, molecule, compound, element) we could use to describe it. It was REALLY POWERFUL for several students.

I asked 'Is this still water?' or 'What have I got now?' when breaking up the molecule. 'Show me an atom of water' '... a molecule of an element' '... an atom of a compound' '... the smallest bit of an element' etc. It was easy to see which bits particular students were having trouble with, and to work through it with them then and there.

It seems this idea of "the smallest bit" is really the important idea to come to. It would have been confusing talking about atoms and molecules to start with. And it takes lots of manipulating and shifting around from one level of representation to another, playing with the concepts I guess, to really get straight what we mean by them.

4.2: TEACHING ABOUT THE CONCEPT OF NOTHING

PART 1: THE IDEA OF 'NOTHING' IS PROBLEMATIC

This PaP-eR portrays how a teacher links her experience of teaching about the idea of empty space with the history of the idea of empty space/aether/vacuum. This helps her understand why the idea of nothing in the gaps between gas molecules is difficult for her Year 7 students to grasp.

The students were busily making models to show how they thought the particles were arranged in solids, liquids and gases. Prior to this class they had learned that the particles in a solid are packed closely together in a regular pattern, that in a liquid they are still close together but the arrangement is not regular and has spaces which enable the particles to slide over each other, and that in a gas the particles are far apart with no pattern at all.

Hannah, one of the more able students, raised her hand:

'Ms. Smith, you know how particles are further apart in a gas – what's in the gaps?'

Ms. Smith had been waiting for a question like this. If it had not come from one of the students she would have raised it herself. It was only after she had been teaching for some years that she had begun to realise that the answer to this question was a difficult one for many students to imagine. Each time she taught the Particle Theory she found that even when students "knew" from their lessons that nothing was between the spaces in a gas, they said or asked things which indicated that they actually thought there was something in the gaps.

Ms. Smith told the class:

'Let's think about Hannah's question. Put on your magic glasses[2] and tell me what you see when you look at a gas?'

'Gas particles with big spaces between them!'

'What do you see when you look at the big spaces?' Ms. Smith asked.

'Lots of tiny air particles!' was the reply.

As Ms. Smith had often reflected, in many ways this kind of response was not surprising. If we poured all the water out of a jug, we would say it had nothing in it. Yet we would understand that it contained air. Thus, in everyday life, "nothing" was often a synonym for "air".

But the problem went deeper than that. Looking back over the history of scientific ideas about the world, humankind had often struggled with the idea of "nothing", of a void. There had been a number of different kinds of "something", or aethers, which had been proposed as filling the spaces in which there was no matter. These had been postulated in order to explain various scientific phenomena such as how particles could affect each other's behaviour without touching and the wave-like nature of light, questions that were still being grappled with by modern physics. However, Ms. Smith did not discuss these ideas with her students – the ideas were complex and required a level of scientific knowledge that was well beyond that of her students at this stage. But they helped Ms. Smith to understand that Hannah's question was not a trivial one, that it was worth spending some time developing an understanding of the scientific idea of 'nothing'.

PART 2: DEVELOPING STUDENTS' UNDERSTANDING OF THE
DIFFERENCE BETWEEN AIR AND NOTHING

Students in the early years of secondary school often hold the belief that air is nothing, which is a barrier to understanding the particulate nature of matter. In this part of the PaP-eR, the teacher uses a POE[3] to challenge this and at the same time to develop her students' understanding of the idea of empty space.

Ms. Smith: 'Yesterday when we were thinking about the way particles are arranged in solids, liquids and gases, Hannah asked, 'What's in the gaps between the gas particles?' Many of you thought that there would be tiny air particles. Let's explore this a bit more. I'm going to blow up a balloon. I want you to predict what will happen to the weight of the balloon.'

---

[2] These are described in the PaP-eR: *Seeing things differently.*

[3]Predict–Observe–Explain. This teaching procedure requires students to make a reasoned prediction in advance of a given event, then explain any differences between the prediction and what they observe of the event after it has occurred.

As the students indicated their predictions, Ms. Smith recorded them on the white board:

After it is blown up, the balloon will weigh:	MORE	9
	LESS	3
	SAME	4

The balloon was blown up and its increase in weight was noted.

A student raised her hand:

'So air particles actually have weight?'

'Yes,' Ms. Smith replied, 'air particles have weight so air actually is something! Now let's think again about Hannah's question about what's in the gaps between gas particles. If you could look at the spaces between gas particles with your magic glasses[4], what would you see?'

One student called out: 'Other little air particles!'

Hannah raised her hand: 'No, I disagree. Air is something and is made up of particles so there can't be air between gas particles – if there were, you would always have particles between particles and so you would never have a gas!'

'Yes, so what would you see if you could look at the spaces between the particles in a gas?' Ms. Smith asked.

'Nothing!' a number of students chorused.

Later Ms. Smith reflected that at least some students were starting to get the idea of empty space between gas particles. In the following lesson she planned to use some follow up questions to help promote student understanding of "nothing". These were:

1. Explain what we did with the balloon. Why did we do this?
2. Why do we think air is nothing in everyday life? Why isn't it OK to think this way in the lessons we have been having about the Particle Theory?

Reflection and discussion by the students about these questions would help reinforce the idea that there were empty spaces between gas particles.

PART 3: ASSESSING HOW STUDENTS INTEGRATE THE IDEA OF NOTHING INTO THEIR
UNDERSTANDING OF THE PARTICLE THEORY

This part of the PaP-eR portrays one way of assessing the impact of teaching which seeks to develop students' understanding of the concept of empty space between particles.

Ms. Smith followed up the preceding POE (see Part 2) with a number of other activities designed to reinforce the idea that there was nothing in the spaces between gas particles. At the end of the unit she asked the students to work in pairs and draw a concept map with the terms solid, liquid, gas, particles, air, nothing.

After a while, Ms. Smith wandered around the classroom looking at the students' maps. Most students had 'particles' in the centre but she noticed that some had "nothing"'also centrally located. Most maps had links from solids, liquids and gases to particles, with the better ones having writing on the links referring to the spacing of the particles.

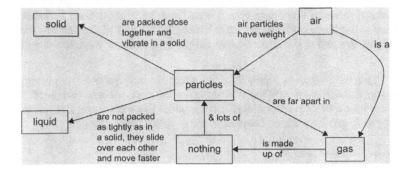

---

[4] See PaP-eR: Seeing things differently

Two groups had links which caught Ms. Smith's eye. One group had made the link 'Air isn't nothing'.

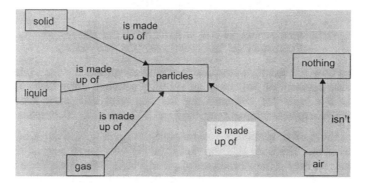

And the other group had 'Gases have lots of nothing'.

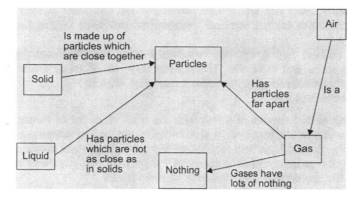

Once Ms. Smith would have regarded these links as trivial, but not any more …

4.3: PLAYDOUGH BALLS: CONCRETE MODELS OF ABSTRACT IDEAS

Many students in the early years of secondary school have difficulty grasping the abstract ideas of the Particle Model of matter. Providing students with concrete models which they can manipulate can be effective not only in promoting their understanding but also in enabling the teacher to diagnose possible sources of student misunderstanding. The parts that comprise this PaP-eR portrays how and why a teacher uses physical models with her class.

PART 1: THE PARTICLE MOVEMENT DURING PHASE CHANGES NEEDS TO
BE MADE EXPLICIT TO STUDENTS

While students may know how the particles are arranged in solids, liquids and gases, they do not necessarily make the link that there must be particle movement to achieve a phase change. Recognising her students' difficulties in understanding particle movement as matter changes phase, the teacher responds by asking the students to make and manipulate model particles.

As she went through the Year 8's homework about solids, liquids and gases, it became clear that many of the students didn't really understand what it was that we were representing. They could draw dots as they were arranged in each phase, but I didn't feel they had a sense of the change, the transition between the phases.

So we all rolled little balls of playdough (that I had ready for the next part of the lesson). On a piece of butcher's paper divided into three sections, each pair needed to be able to demonstrate how the balls, "particles", would be arranged in each phase. As I came around I asked them to show me what happened as the substance changed from a liquid to a gas, or from a liquid to a solid. Thinking in terms of the particle model is such an abstract exercise – I think it benefited several students to actually manipulate the "particles". They had to show how they move; how they move more as they are heated; and how this results in the particles breaking away[5] from one another and moving further apart. It's like the

_____

[5] See PaP-eR: What is the smallest bit? Part 2

roleplay[6] that students often take part in, but here they worked through it themselves to gain a sense of the transition between the states they see represented in their textbooks.

PART 2: DISTINGUISHING BETWEEN THE PARTICLES IN ELEMENTS, COMPOUNDS AND MIXTURES CAN BE CONFUSING FOR STUDENTS

This Part illustrates how one teacher's careful selection of an activity for her students that requires them to show the arrangement of particles in an everyday solution, using their playdough models, helps to serve as the basis for distinguishing the important difference between fixed ratio arrangements of atoms in a molecule and compound and the loose ratio of compounds in a mixture.

I gave the class a definition of an element and some examples (hydrogen, oxygen, chlorine and sodium) with their chemical symbols. The main idea was that all of the 'bits' in an element are the same as each other. Each pair of students used different coloured playdough balls to represent these elements.

Then I put the names and symbols for two compounds (water and sodium chloride (salt)) and a mixture (salty water) on the board and asked the students to use the playdough to work out models for these.

Different groups showed their representations and we used these to build up definitions for compound and mixture. Importantly, pairs had different proportions of salt and water in their salty water. So we could bring out that mixtures are not chemical arrangements and don't require fixed amounts of each particle.

The concepts of element and compound, represented using the playdough balls, required us to differentiate between atoms and molecules. The students then moved on to a worksheet that clarified these four concepts using nonsense examples and non-examples of each.

Three things I'd like to mention:

- I was not intending to make much of a link with the work on states of matter. It was interesting, however, that a number of students thought about whether the various substances were solids, liquids or gases, and tried to show this, as well as whether they were elements or compounds. On reflection I can see how using the same materials to represent the particles is a good way to reinforce that this model applies to all of the ways we ask them to think about matter.
- A few students had separated the sodium and chloride in their salty water. If they had also separated the hydrogen and oxygen then I knew that they didn't have the compound part right. If it was only the NaCl then I said something like: "You've shown what actually does happen to the salt in the water, but for now we want to keep the compounds together and show how the two compounds are mixed up." This is an example of where we teach misconceptions in order to get the concepts straight[7].
- Underlying all this is my belief that to grasp complex abstract ideas, students need to revisit them from different directions and manipulate them in different ways. If they just spout back the words that you give them—for example, just tell you back what an element is—then you can't be sure that they've learnt anything at all.

4.4: CAREFUL CHEMICAL REACTIONS

This PaP-eR illustrates the teacher's recognition of the importance of linking students' prior knowledge of particles with their new experiences of learning about chemical reactions. Through a role play of chemical word equations, the teacher is able to help the students in her Year 9 all-girls' class begin to see how particles can become rearranged to form a new substance during a chemical reaction. Using words rather than chemical formulae for the equations is an important part of the teacher's approach since she has seen that students often struggle to manipulate symbols and formulae which can hinder their understanding of the process of particle rearrangement.

The class is recalling and thinking about some chemical reactions that they have experienced in previous lessons (rusting steel wool; burning magnesium; magnesium in hydrochloric acid). Pairs of students volunteer to re-demonstrate the second and third reactions to the class, and the students are encouraged to think about which of these they think is most closely linked to the first.

Ms. Stephens asks them to consider word equations for each of these reactions. (Last lesson they revisited the rules for writing these and the reasons for these rules). The first two seem fairly straightforward to translate into a word equation, while the third needs a lot more thinking about ...

(Ms. Stephens writes on the board):

---

[6] In the roleplay, a group of students is asked to show how they would be arranged if each of them was a particle in a solid. They are then asked to show what they would be doing if they 'formed' (1) a liquid (2) a gas.
[7] See PaP-eR: Careful chemical reactions

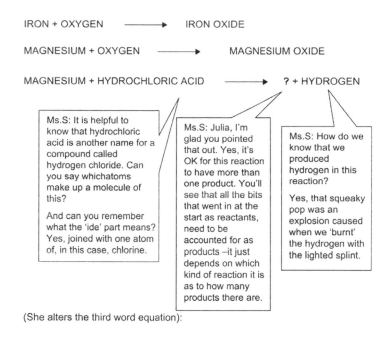

(She alters the third word equation):

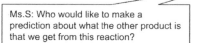

Three or four students put their hands up. A couple of them are enthusiastically bobbing up and down. Ms. Stephens says she is pleased that no-one is calling out as it gives everyone a chance to think actively about the answer in their own way.

Ms. Stephens: 'We need to look at this again a different way to give more people a chance at working out what they think the product is. Three volunteers up the front please.'

Valerie, Yasmin and Petra stand in front of the bench. Ms. Stephens asks Yasmin and Petra to link arms. 'You two are a hydrogen atom and a chlorine atom linked together to make hydrogen chloride. Valerie, you are a magnesium atom.' As she speaks Ms. Stephens lifts the name of each atom from the board and seems to place it above the three girls.

'Now Magnesium, I'm afraid you're a bit of a bossy boots and when you meet these two you just muscle on in and push that hydrogen atom out of the way. We already know we have hydrogen on its own afterwards.'

She gets Yasmin to move over and stand in front of the word hydrogen. 'Bossy magnesium has linked up here instead. So have a bit more of a think about the other product …'

This time at least three quarters of the class put their hands up. A few struggle with names, but all are clear that it is Valerie and Petra with linked arms – magnesium chloride.

After the class, Ms. Stephens explains:

I know that Magnesium and Chloride are joined in a lattice rather than a 1:1 linkage but I don't worry here about that or getting the charge right or the actual formula right. What is more important to me at this stage is helping my students to get the idea that different atoms rearrange their groupings to form new molecules, and that is what a chemical reaction is. Sometimes it is ok to teach "wrong" science if it helps to illustrate an important concept. In junior years complicated and abstract chemical reactions are often thrown at students. I wondered for a while whether they should be thinking about them at all. I think though that if they are explored simply and carefully then, rather than being confusing, they can help to reinforce students' understanding of particles.

4.5: QUESTIONS AND ANSWERS

This PaP-eR illustrates the questions asked by a Year 7 class during lessons about the Particle Model and the teacher's responses. Importantly it provides insights into one or two aspects of the complex thinking behind the teacher's responses.

Questions the students ask.	Teacher's response.	Teacher's thinking.	
Where do particles come from?	The $64,000 question. Scientists don't know for sure but they think they are star dust.	The $64, 000 question. Scientists don't know for sure but they think they are star dust.	
Where do our particles go to when we die?	Teacher talks about the role of decomposers such as bacteria in the disintegration of dead bodies. Particles from dead and rotting things go into the soil, air and water and so end up in other living and non-living things. There are only a certain number of particles in the world and these are continually being re-arranged to make new things. 'It's a bit like having a bucket of Lego: you can build lots of different things but you only have a certain number of Lego pieces to do it with.'	This explanation is brief but if I provide too much detail about decomposition and food webs, the point I am making about particles being recycled may get lost. So I don't provide any more information than is necessary to satisfy the students' questions.	
What are particles made of? –And what are atoms made of? –And what are protons, neutrons and electrons made up of?	'Atoms.' 'Atoms are made up of protons, neutrons, and electrons.' 'Protons and neutrons are made up of things called quarks, and electrons belong to a group of particles called leptons. Scientists are still finding out all the different particles there are.'	I just give a straightforward answer without further explanation. If students press for more detail, I keep reiterating that that there are limitations to the "Particle Model" which I am giving them and that in later years they will learn about more accurate models. From previous experience I know that the "complicatedness" of the science can't be simplified enough for students at this level.	
Do individual particles melt? Is a particle a solid?	'The particles themselves don't melt—the melting is the particles moving apart.' 'That's a hard question. Think about a class of students. We normally don't think of a class with one student as being a class.'	It's important to pay attention to these questions because the ideas are so abstract. These questions are reasonable if we are thinking about particles, in the everyday sense they are macroscopic objects, e.g. a particle of dust. It's important to stress that the particles we are talking about in the particle theory are much tinier than this and quite different to "everyday" particles.	
Is toothpaste a solid or a liquid?	'It's both—it's a liquid with solid bits in it.'	This kind of question tells me that the student is trying to link the ideas we have been talking about (viz. the three phases) with their everyday experiences.	
Can wood be changed from a solid to a liquid to a gas?	'No it can't. That's one of the limitations of our model. All scientific models have their limitations. Our particle model is good at explaining some things but not others. In later years you will learn about ways of modifying the model so it explains more things.'	These are typical questions where students are dissatisfied with my answer. Once I would have tried to elaborate on ways of modifying the model but this just confused the students.	My focus in this unit is on developing a particulate view of matter in my students. I don't dwell on the fact that the idea of 'states of matter' itself is idealised.

Questions the students ask.	Teacher's response.	Teacher's thinking.	
If people are made up of particles, how come we don't melt?	'Again this is a limitation of the particle model.'	I now know this is an area where the complexity of the science can't be simplified enough to make it understandable to students at this level.	And nor do I talk about the difference in the nature and types of particles in the toothpaste, wood and people when I answer these questions.
You know how the particles are further apart in a gas, what's in the gaps?	Teacher explores students' perceptions of what is in the gaps: many think there are tiny air particles and that this is what is meant when scientists say there is nothing in the gaps. Teacher develops a number of activities to develop the idea of "nothing".[8] 'This is a hard idea to understand'.	The idea of "nothing" or empty space is difficult for many to comprehend and indeed throughout the history of science, scientists have often wrestled with this idea.[9]	

4.6: SEEING THINGS DIFFERENTLY

This PaP-eR illustrates how important the teacher's understanding of the content is in influencing how she approaches her teaching about the Particle Model of Matter. In this PaP-eR, an interview with a teacher called Rhonda, the teaching unfolds over a number of lessons and is based on the view that understanding how a model can help to explain everyday phenomena requires continual revisiting and reinforcement with students. The PaP-eR closes with an illustration of how inherent contradictions in teaching resources need to be recognised and addressed in order to minimise their level of interference in learning specific concepts and how important that is in teaching about models.

Rhonda is a Chemistry major with a commitment to making science meaningful for her students. She enjoys teaching about 'States of Matter' and has developed a number of important frames for approaching the content so that her students will better grasp the ideas rather than simply learn how to "parrot" the appropriate "science" responses in a test.

Rhonda's framing in the interview: The content

At Year 7 level it really is only a very limited particle theory that I teach - I don't go into atomic structure in any serious way. I try to introduce the students to the idea that everything around them is not continuous, but is made up of small particles that fit together. I don't try to give any detail about how they fit together, but I do talk with them about the particles being roughly spherical objects that are very, very, very, very tiny.

I know that getting students to use a particle model is not going to fully happen: they will revert to a continuous model when they are pushed. But it is important to start moving them some way along the path – to get them to consider that there may be another way of looking at the things around us. The ideas of the particle model also need to be linked to what is happening during phase changes (melting, freezing etc.) and that link needs to be at the very tiny level rather than at the macroscopic level. So these two ideas influence how I approach the teaching.

It's important to continually remind yourself that particle theory at Year 7 and 8 needs to be presented in helpful ways. I believe that maturity plays an important part in what students can actually grasp at a certain age. It's easy, as the teacher, to forget how conceptually difficult and conceptually abstract this topic is. It is an important topic to teach about, though, because it's one of those building blocks of chemistry which you can build on in layers over the years in science classes rather than trying to do it all at once. It's conceptually meaty so I enjoy teaching it!

---

[8] See PaP-eR: Teaching about the concept of nothing: Part 2
[9] See PaP-eR: Teaching about the concept of nothing: Part 1

So what do I do? Well I suppose the first issue is helping the students to start thinking differently about what they're looking at. It's important to help them realise that although the things they are looking at appear to be made up of one thing – like a piece of pipe is made up of one piece of metal – you can break it down until it is made up of lots of small things combining together. A simple analogy is a jar of sand. From a distance it looks like one thing, but up close you can see the individual grains of sand.

From this, you can begin to explain the behaviour of everyday things in terms of movements of particles. This is a big shift in thinking for students. Again, you can play with this idea by getting something like a marshmallow and putting it in a gas jar and changing the pressure so the behaviour of the marshmallow is affected (this behaviour is described later). It helps to illustrate the point about small bits moving or acting differently in response to the conditions. The marshmallow is also good because it is an example of something they are familiar with – it links to their everyday experiences and that really matters. I've built up quite a few of these examples in my teaching over the years; it's good fun, too.

The other idea to try and aim for is the idea of space, nothing, between the particles: it's really hard. One way of helping to address this is by using the demonstration of mixing water and methylated spirits. You add equal volumes of them together, if each liquid is one big block of water or methylated spirits, then the volume should be double, but it isn't so – how come? That helps to make the point about the spaces, so that in this case things can fit between the spaces.

So overall I suppose, really, I'm only concentrating on three things:

- Things are made up of tiny little bits.

- There is space between the tiny little bits.

- You can use the model to explain phase changes, etc.

But I don't mean to make it sound as simple as that because really what I do is respond to what's happening in the class. Last year I went "down the density path" even though I wasn't intending to. But, because it was students' questions that took us there, I let it go on and followed it for longer.

The point really is that the use of the particle model is a way of thinking and it's something that the students have to be reminded of so that they think about things from that perspective, rather than reverting to their continuous model perspective.

Rhonda's framing in the classroom: 'Imagine'

The unit starts with Rhonda asking the students to imagine that they have been shrunk down so that they are very tiny and then they fall into a droplet of water on the lab bench. They have to imagine what the droplet looks like from the inside, and then they write a short adventure story and draw a picture of what they can see. The students' pictures show a range of responses, a handful contain dots but most of these are explained as being 'the dirt and stuff in the water'.

Through a number of activities and discussions over several lessons Rhonda introduces the class to the content ideas that she outlined in the interview.

Then Rhonda gets all of the students to make a pair of cardboard glasses. They decorate these in whatever way they wish. She encourages them to use their imagination in designing their "magic glasses". Putting the glasses on is a cue for them to think in terms of particles.

One of the problems I find is that they easily revert back to a continuous model, so putting them in a situation where they wear the glasses and look at something helps them to better understand how the model works to explain what they are seeing. You can get them to put them on at different times throughout the unit and it helps them make the transition to particle model thinking.

In one lesson Rhonda fries onions on the front bench in the laboratory. The students call out from their seats when they start to smell the onions. They track the progress of the smell towards the back of the lab. Rhonda asks them to put on their glasses and look around the room. Can they explain the smell through particle theory?

She asks them to think about when they mixed the methylated spirits and water together. With their glasses on they need to describe what is happening as the two liquids combine.

Rhonda shows the class a marshmallow inside a gas jar. By reducing the air pressure in the jar she causes the marshmallow to swell up and then eventually collapse. She asks the students to think about the air inside the marshmallow. If they could 'see' it through their glasses how could they explain what was happening to the marshmallow?

The class revisits their shrinking adventure in the drop of water. Rhonda asks them to think carefully and draw what the inside of a drop of water would be like with the 'magic glasses' on.

Later in the unit, Rhonda will introduce a new activity based around the way that textbooks represent water as a liquid.

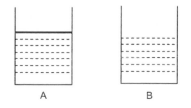

A   B

If you look at the pictures in books they often show liquid as particles but the liquid is capped by a continuous line (diagram A), which inadvertently undermines what we're trying to get students to understand by these representations of a particulate model. The students end up thinking that the water is the clear stuff and the particles are just dots in the water.

Rhonda decides that this year she will ask the class to look at a beaker of water through their glasses and to decide which of the two diagrams best represents water and why they think so.

If the students are wearing their glasses when they look at a beaker of water they should see diagram B rather than diagram A. And be able to explain why they do!

4.7: PROBING STUDENTS' VIEWS

This PaP-eR describes a probe designed and used by one teacher to explore her students' ability to visualise what happened at the microscopic level when a change occurred macroscopically. Linking these two levels was essential for understanding chemical ideas. The teacher reflects on the probe, its insights and limitations.

What was the probe?

I provided the students with a diagram of some sugar being added to a glass of water. I asked them to imagine that they had shrunk down so that they could fit inside the glass and could see the particles of sugar and water. Their task was to draw what they thought they would see, using an   to represent water particles and **o** to represent sugar particles (at the time I didn't give much thought to this way of representing particles, but I came to regret this, as I acknowledge later).

How did you come to design this probe?

I had been thinking a lot about the way much of chemistry involves thinking simultaneously about the behaviour of matter at two levels: macroscopic and microscopic. At the time I was teaching a chemistry unit to Year 8 and wanted my students to think beyond what they observed (e.g. something disappearing when it dissolved) — I wanted to make them aware of the microscopic world of matter and how our model of this was useful for explaining macroscopic behaviour. So the probe was to see what prior views, if any, the students had about what happened at the microscopic level in a common, everyday experience of a physical change.

Later I used the probe with a Year 9 and Year 10 class for the same reasons.

What did the probe show?

Well, first of all I'd like to say that on reflection I wish I had been able to interview the students about their diagrams so I could be sure that my interpretations were correct!

Drawings A to N show the different types of responses the students gave. Above each I've shown how many from each class gave that response. There were 30 students in each class.

Quite a number of students seemed to think that the sugar just disappears when it dissolves (Drawings A & B). I wonder if the students actually thought this or whether they were thinking of the sugar particles as the small crystals they see in a teaspoon of sugar and the water particles as water droplets. If the latter was the case, the diagrams would be reasonable.

In four of the diagrams it looks like the students think that the water particles are a kind of bag which the sugar particles enter when they dissolve (Drawings C, D, F, G). Again here my instructions about the relative sizes of the circles may have been a problem, which I talk about later.

I think that some of the diagrams with sugar at the bottom (Drawings D, F, J) were perhaps the result of students knowing that when you add sugar to water it sits at the bottom of the container and slowly disappears.

And some of the diagrams are just too hard to interpret (Drawings B, H, L, M, N) — several appear to have been influenced by pictures students have seen in textbooks and on lab walls.

And of course some of the diagrams seem to be consistent with a scientific viewpoint (Drawings I, J, and L — if the ordered arrangement of particles is ignored).

So what did you learn about students' ability to visualise what happened at the microscopic level when sugar dissolved in water?

Up to 40% of some classes appeared to think the sugar particles just disappeared—interestingly, in my small survey, this view was still prevalent with older students, e.g. Year 10. And up to 20% in the Year 10 class seemed to have ideas about sugar particles going into the water particles which contradict the scientific idea of particles being the smallest things in substances—it makes me wonder if students who verbalise that particles are the "smallest thing" actually realise the consequences (e.g. that you can't go inside one).

What were the limitations of the probe?

As I said earlier, the main one was that it would have been more informative to have actually interviewed at least some of the students about their diagrams rather than just speculate on what they meant.

And I was probably promoting a misconception with the sizes of the circles I gave them to represent the water and sugar particles. The sugar molecule is in fact bigger than the water molecule. It would have been interesting to see how/whether students who thought the sugar particle went inside the water one would have shown this if I had given them more accurately proportioned circles to represent the particles with.

Chemistry at the Microscopic level *(Response of year 8, year 9 and year 10 students. 30 students at each level)*

Q. *Complete the diagram of what happens to the sugar and water particles after the sugar has been stirred into the water*

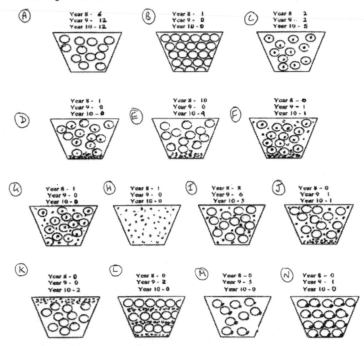

NB. Large circles represent water particles and small circles represent sugar particles.

Has using this probe changed the way you think about teaching about the behaviour of substances at the microscopic level?

Despite its drawbacks, the probe has made me realise that it is a mistake to think that students will automatically link changes at the macroscopic level with behaviour at the microscopic level in the same way that scientists do. For me it has also reinforced that as teachers we need to spend a lot of time probing and challenging, if necessary, students' ideas. Importantly we need to provide them with many opportunities to interpret everyday events (e.g. 'Why can I smell some onions cooking?' 'Why do dust particles in the air move?' 'Why does popcorn "pop" when heated?') in terms of the behaviour of microscopic particles. Then we can perhaps progress to talking about atoms, molecules and chemical reactions.

What advice would you give to other teachers who are considering using this probe?

The most important thing is to explore what the students' responses really mean. If it's not possible to do this with each student, then a sample of students should be interviewed individually. I'd say something like, 'Tell me what you were trying to show in your diagram' and depending on what the response is ask, 'Why do you think that?/Tell me what is happening with the sugar particles/Tell me what is happening with the water particles etc.' The other thing is to give careful thought to the wording of the question and check that the students understand what it is that you are asking them to do.

4.8: GOOD VIBRATIONS

This PaP-eR is designed to illustrate one way of helping students come to better understand the abstract notion that particles vibrate and that particle vibrations and the distance between particles change with change in state. Using a model constructed from everyday materials and a teaching sequence carefully designed to link the model and the concept, the teacher makes the concept of particle vibration more concrete for her students. At the same time, the teacher challenges the students to reconsider their often superficial notions about the nature of phase change in matter.

Over the years I have noticed that there are some particular misunderstandings about particle behaviour that Year 9 students commonly share. These are that:
- Students find it hard to believe that the particles of a solid are actually moving.
- Students think that as a solid heats up (particles have more energy), the particles themselves get bigger, rather than the distance between the particles themselves increases.
- Students generally do not have a well formed mental picture of phase change; they tend to think that matter is arranged in 3 "states" which are discrete and readily identifiable rather than understanding that these states are parts of a continuum of particle movement.

Text book diagrams often serve to reinforce these simplistic notions about matter. Traditional representations show three separate boxes each with a clearly different arrangement of particles, labelled solid, liquid and gas. It is hardly surprising then that students tend to think that matter exists in these states only, that it is easy to identify each "state" and that there is only one kind of arrangement that comprises that "state". The language of the science classroom also serves to reinforce these ideas as teachers and students talk about the 3 states of matter, as though they are always obvious discrete categories. In addition, the idea that particles in a solid are actually vibrating just doesn't seem plausible to students because it doesn't reconcile with their experiences of everyday life.

That's why I like using the "speaker" demonstration. It lets them see something that is not always easy to visualise and as such it becomes a useful anchor for the development of the students' understanding of particle theory. More generally, I find that I can use this demonstration to promote students' thinking about models. I think that too often science teachers expect students to be able to understand things at a microscopic or submicroscopic level, without explicitly 'showing' them to students or unpacking the notion of a model with them.

To start things off, before I begin the demonstration, I ask students to tell me what they know about solids, liquids and gases, and more generally about the particles in them. During this stage, as students offer their ideas, I gently probe their thinking with questions such as 'What are the particles in a solid doing?' 'What are the particles in a liquid doing?' 'What happens to the particles when a substance changes from a solid to a liquid?' However, it can be quite difficult to push students to explore their understanding of particle behaviour. They often feel as though they have "got it" and don't need to revisit these ideas because they have successfully reproduced the required information in their previous years of schooling for their other science teachers.

Next, I introduce (or re-introduce) the idea that individual particles are moving, although this means that now I need to bring in the idea of energy, (which is a very difficult concept to understand). In fact, because energy is in the story, I try to be careful how I use the word and avoid as much as possible getting side-tracked to explain what it is. At this stage, what is most important for students to know is that energy exists and it causes things to move.

I place an old speaker on the bench in the middle of the lab. I connect the speaker to a power supply then fill the speaker full of small polystyrene balls (0.25 cm diameter work really well). The balls form a neat cone shape on the inside of the speaker and I turn the speaker on low, just rumbling. The balls begin to move a bit, but maintain the same shape. (It is not easy to see that the balls are moving when the speaker is on low – you have to look really hard.) I ask the class to think about how the balls might be like particles in matter. Somebody usually says, 'This is like a solid isn't it?' As different ideas come out I will invite students to "say a bit more" about their thinking, but I don't push for detailed explanations because at this stage, I am most interested in encouraging as many students as I can to engage with the model, and to begin to make links with their ideas about particles. Later on, I will be asking students to explain their thinking in more detail.

Then I turn the speaker up just a little and the balls start to move around more noticeably. This is an important part of the demonstration. As the movement gradually becomes more noticeable I link this increase in movement to increasing energy in the particles. I do this by talking about turning up the speaker volume as being similar to heating the "cone of particles".

Obviously, the more the volume of the speaker is increased, the more the kids love it, as the balls begin to bounce out all over the place – but that's not really the point. Not just yet, anyway.

I then ask them to tell me what they have seen – to give me the chain of events that has occurred since the speaker was switched on. I don't ask them specifically to describe their observations in terms of particle theory, though students usually choose to use this language in their explanations. For any contribution that is made, I try to give non-judgemental responses, so that more students might feel inclined to share their thoughts. This often brings out some subtle differences in their observations, for instance in the way in which the balls/particles are moving or even that they are moving during the initial part of the demonstration. These kinds of comments are helpful to refocus students' attention and to build links with particle theory as I prepare to begin the demonstration again.

This time, to help make the observation of movement observable at the individual "ball level" as the volume changes, I take one ball out, write a letter on it and replace it, so that it clearly stands out from the rest of the balls. I turn the speaker volume on low, again. Now it is easy to see that this ball is slowly vibrating and although it maintains its position relative to the other balls, it actually rotates and moves around a bit, so more students are able to see the movement that perhaps they had not detected earlier.

As I gradually increase the volume, one ball will occasionally jump up a bit from the rest. I invite students to describe what they see, as they see it, and to use some language of particle theory. Usually at this point, someone will say that this is the 'solid cone' starting to melt. If no one mentions melting, I may leave it at that for a while or try to quiz and probe in ways to help them make the link:

'What makes the balls move in the model?'

'What makes the particles move in a real substance?'

I can also start to confront ideas about particle expansion with heating. I ask students to tell me what they notice about the size of the balls as more energy is put in. Clearly, the particles themselves stay the same size, with only the distance between them changing.

Then I increase the volume steadily until it blasts the balls out everywhere – voila, evaporation! Students quickly make the link between this term and the event, as they call out for less melting and more evaporation!

Following this, I ask them to describe in pictures and writing what they have observed during the second demonstration with the marked ball as the volume is increased. This time, I encourage students to use as much of the language of particle theory as they can. I also ask the students to write a list of things that surprise or puzzle them about particles from the demonstration. One thing that regularly comes out of this is that many students find it hard to believe that solids aren't just sitting there 'solidly'. Seeing the marked ball moving when the speaker is making a low hum is an important way to highlight for them that there is low level movement even when the particles are packed together in a solid – something that they have 'learned' in previous years but have not often found plausible until this demonstration. For homework, I usually give students some textbook diagrams of different phases and ask them to consider the following questions:

- What did the demonstration show about phase change?
- What do the diagrams show about phase change?
- What can the diagram show that the demonstration can't, and vice versa?

The central idea that I am wanting students to think through here is the notion of particle movement existing along a continuum that is not obvious in text book diagrams. I am also anticipating that some students will begin to see that each type of representation has limitations. Some consideration of these ideas at least means that they will be better prepared to consider a further, final aspect of the demonstration.

In closing this activity with my students I think it is important to make a distinction between the model and the concept that it is illustrating. All models have limitations – some models may even cause students to develop wrong ideas, so it is important for me to ask, 'How might this model be different from how particles behave during phase change?' This question often challenges even the most able students (I find it challenging myself), so I usually pose it with plenty of thinking time, and we revisit it in later lessons. However I am not so concerned that they come up with these actual differences as much as recognising that there are differences between the model and the concept.

I think that using this sort of approach really matters because, as I mentioned earlier, it is important to challenge the superficial views of particles held by students. Through engaging their thinking with a simple model, students can deepen their understanding of particles at the same time as recognising a bit more of the complexity of these ideas.

CHAPTER FIVE

CHEMICAL REACTIONS

This chapter outlines a representation of Pedagogical Content Knowledge (PCK) for the topic Chemical Reactions. However, one important difference in this chapter compared with that of the topics of Particle Theory (Chapter 4), Circulatory System (Chapter 6), and Electric Circuits (Chapter 8) is that we offer two CoRes as opposed to the single CoRe approach of the other topics. The reason for the production of two CoRes in this chapter is a result of our work with science teachers whereby we found that two different approaches to the construction of a CoRe for Chemical Reactions. Therefore, the format for this chapter is a little different to that of the other topics, as it includes the first CoRe followed by the PaP-eRs attached to the first CoRe, then the second CoRe, with a brief introduction highlighting its conceptual basis.

The use of two CoRes is not meant to suggest that one is more correct than the other, but rather to highlight that two very different and distinct perspectives on this topic were readily apparent amongst the science teachers with whom we worked. As noted earlier, it could easily be that alternative CoRes could be developed for the other topics as well; however, in this instance, the difference in conceptualizations through the CoRe was so striking that we felt it important to include both.

In presenting the two CoRes in this way, we trust it also helps to illustrate for the reader the importance of different perspectives on the same content and to reinforce the notion that there is not one way of representing a CoRe.

REMINDERS ABOUT SHAPING FACTORS THAT INFLUENCE CoRes AND PaP-eRs

As is the case with each of the concrete examples of PCK that comprise Chapters 4 – 9, we briefly offer some of the important points that shape our understanding of representing PCK. Repeating this information at the start of each of the chapters (Resource Folios) is designed to remind the reader about the nature of this form of representation of PCK and for that information to be "on hand" for each individual topic portrayed.

Therefore, some of the important points to be kept in mind when considering that which follows in this Resource Folio are that:

- It is very difficult to offer a single example of PCK that is a neat concrete package, able to be analysed and dissected or used as a blueprint for practice by others. Therefore, our approach to capturing and portraying PCK hinges on the understanding that the teaching and the content must be represented in ways that both maintain the complexity of their relationships but at the same time offers some way of seeing through the complexity in order to gain insight into it.
- Our approach is based on what we have termed a CoRe (Content Representation) and PaP-eRs (Pedagogical and Professional-experience Repertoire). The CoRe outlines some of the aspects of PCK "most attached to that content" but it is not the only representation. It is a necessary but incomplete generalization that helps to make the complexity accessible and manageable; it is neither complete nor absolute. Attached to the CoRe are the PaP-eRs, with links to the aspects of this field that they "bring to life". A PaP-eR is of a content area and must allow the reader to look inside a teaching/learning situation in which the content shapes the pedagogy.
- PaP-eRs bring the CoRe to life and shed new light on the complex nature of PCK. They help create ways to better understand and value the specialist knowledge, skills and ability of teachers thus making that which is so often tacit, explicit for others.

This Core is designed for students in Middle Secondary School, i.e., Year 10.	**A:** **In a chemical reaction (one or more) new substances are produced.**	**IMPORTANT SCIENCE** **B:** **Chemical substances can be represented by formulae.**
What you intend the <u>students</u> to learn about this idea.	A chemical reaction involves an input (reactants) and an output (products – which have different chemical properties). Chemical reactions are all around us.	The formula of a substance reflects what it 'looks like' at the atomic level. A particular chemical always has the same formula regardless of where it comes from. The way of writing formulae is universal amongst chemists. **Rules of the game:** Some elements are represented as if they are single atoms (e.g. metals such as zinc, which is Zn) and others are represented as molecules (e.g. oxygen, which is O_2). Compounds are represented by the molecules they contain (e.g. water, which is H_2O) or by the combination of charged atoms ('ions') they contain (e.g. salt, which is Na^+Cl^-). All substances are made up of zillions of atoms. When you breathe in oxygen, you are breathing in zillions of O_2 molecules.
Why it is important for students to know this.	It enables an understanding of real life situations (e.g. as reported in newspapers) and personal experiences: e.g. environmental issues (such as pollution), corrosion, analysis of bottled water, cooking a cake, lighting a match, effervescent powder, BBQ. It helps develop an understanding of consumer chemistry, e.g. ammonia in floor cleaners.	Formulae are part of the language of chemistry. The ability to communicate the structure of a substance through writing its formula is a vital precursor for further studies. To understand chemical reactions in Year 11 (Upper High School) students need to understand the order of magnitude of numbers of particles involved.

IDEAS/CONCEPTS		
C: **Equations describe the reactants and products in a chemical reaction.**	**D:** **There are patterns to many chemical reactions.**	**E:** **Organic chemicals contain carbon.**
Equations are a form of chemical communication — for a particular reaction, the same equation applies in all parts of the world. The learning of more able students may be extended to include: • The equation represents the proportion of reactants needed and of the products produced. • When writing equations: 1. It is necessary to use correct formulae for reactants and products. 2. Equations need to be balanced because mass is conserved.	Classifying reactions enables one to predict products. As with much of chemistry, this predictability is not perfect: although you can write an equation, the reaction does not always happen at all, or happen according to prediction. An understanding of (and ability to correctly use) useful terms like acid, base, salt, combustion, precipitation etc. is important. Students should understand the 'well behaved' reaction types, e.g. acid-base, acid-carbonate, acid-metal, precipitation, combustion, synthesis/decomposition.	Organic chemicals contain carbon. Carbon atoms can form 4 bonds with other atoms. This means that they can form an infinite array of compounds. Many of these compounds contain long chains of carbon atoms to which hydrogen and other atoms are linked. Most of the chemicals in the world around us (and inside us) are organic. Organic chemicals can react to make molecules which we can use (e.g. glucose, carbon dioxide – the latter is not always considered 'organic').
Equations form the language used to explain chemical reactions.	Categorising reaction types provides students with reasonable measures for making predictions about products. If an experiment does not proceed as anticipated, students need to appreciate that they should consider the possibility that there is something that they have not taken into account (rather than assume something is wrong with their observations).	There are lots of organic chemicals all around us.

	A: In a chemical reaction (one or more) new substances are produced.	B: Chemical substances can be represented by formulae.
What else <u>you</u> know about this idea (that you do not intend students to know yet).	Not all reactions are complete (e.g. some biological reactions & some industrial processes) – this is not addressed unless it is raised by a student. The chemical equilibrium constant is a guide to the extent to which a reaction proceeds. Chemical reactions involve the breaking of existing chemical bonds and the formation of new ones.	States of matter are usually indicated. Complex formulae are left out as they are too confusing for students (e.g. toluene).
Difficulties/ limitations connected with teaching this idea.	The explanations of what is occurring are quite abstract. This is compounded by the fact that the scale is so small in comparison to the macroscopic level at which the students are working. Thus it is difficult for students to make links between the macro and micro-scopic levels of behaviour of chemicals.	If students cannot write the formulae of substances then further work (e.g. on equations) is difficult. Teachers can provide a technique for struggling students of swapping valencies and writing them as subscripts: e.g. $Pb^{4+} PO_4{}^{3-}$ $Pb_3(PO_4)_4$ This works without understanding but can lead to problems later (e.g. Mg_2O_2).
Knowledge about students' thinking which influences your teaching of this idea.	Teachers can get a "feeling" of the general interest level of the class by the links the students are making to other ideas and experiences.	Formulae are often taught in Year 9 (Middle High School) but always require revising. This also applies to ionic and covalent compounds. To work out the starting point for teaching, it is important to determine students' ability level by getting them to write formulae/equations as this helps teachers to understand how students are thinking about these operations. Students tend to think that a formula only represents one "lot" of that substance, e.g. H_2O means just two H and one O.

C: Equations describe the reactants and products in a chemical reaction.	D: There are patterns to many chemical reactions.	E: Organic chemicals contain carbon.
Chemical equations involving half reactions, redox reactions, and ionic transfer are complex and can be too confusing at this level.	Although most reactions **are** predictable, there are rare exceptions, some of which are the consequence of important rules met in Senior Chemistry (e.g. why Zn reacts with dilute acid, but Cu does not – a Redox reaction). While combustion at this level refers to combining with oxygen, in fact something can be burnt in anything in which it can oxidise, e.g. chlorine, fluorine.	There are more organic chemicals than all the others put together. At this level we hardly scratch the surface beyond seeing that organic chemicals react too.
Too much emphasis on the microscopic behaviour can detract from development of knowledge and understanding of the macroscopic behaviour of substances.	This topic is so broad that one can only deal with a few types; on the basis of safety and those which are available in the school laboratory. It is difficult to generate many examples that are related to students' everyday experiences because what happens in the lab is oversimplified and specialised. Students have to accept "in good faith" a teacher's explanation of the details of a reaction. Teachers' concern for management and safety often creates a dilemma for the construction of good learning episodes.	It is always difficult to know whether or not one should teach functional groups, which are the basis of lots of organic reactions. It is difficult to provide suitable experimental work because most organic chemicals are flammable, toxic or both! Bonding is central to developing an understanding of organic compounds, but is a difficult concept for students to grasp at this stage.
Students usually demonstrate a superficial acceptance of Conservation of Mass. It is a difficult concept for them to grasp so understanding their thinking beyond superficial responses matters. At this stage of their development, students are often particularly interested in environmental issues. Ideas about chemical reactions can be made relevant by linking them to such issues.	It is often hard to convince students of the value of their observations and of experiments that do not work according to the rule, and that one can learn a lot about chemistry from one's observations. Students often think that an experiment is wrong if it does not get the results expected and therefore do not interrogate the ideas or their approach to the experiment seriously enough.	

	A: In a chemical reaction (one or more) new substances are produced.	B: Chemical substances can be represented by formulae.
Other factors that influence your teaching of this idea.	The idea of chemical reactions is introduced in early secondary years so this would be revisiting the concept. In particular they have already seen some chemical reactions and are familiar with tests for carbon dioxide, hydrogen and oxygen. If students do not make the links that teachers want them to then there is a need to help them by asking 'leading' questions (e.g. to help them see patterns in acid/base reactions). Because of safety considerations it is difficult to provide meaningful opportunities for practical work which will engage students in designing their own experiments.	Students often enjoy working out formulae using a given table of valencies. Expecting students to remember valencies can lead to rote learning rather than understanding.
Teaching procedures (and particular reasons for using these to engage with this idea).	Practical work can be presented in the form of a problem to be solved (e.g. in a forensic science context students have to identify the nature of some mystery powders). This helps develop 'a need to know' using a real world context and helps develop knowledge about the properties and behaviour of substances. It also provides an opportunity for students to practice writing formulae and equations. Most students enjoy the activity and are able to achieve a reasonable level of success.	**Chalk and talk:** Often effective for those who grasp ideas easily. **Making models:** Making models of molecules and ionic substances using Playdoh provides a sensory and visual aid to understanding formulae. **"Dirty tricks":** To help promote understanding about how formulae are written, ask which is right: 1. NaOH or Na(OH) [teacher may need to point out that brackets are not needed here] 2. $CaNO_{32}$ or $Ca(NO_3)_2$ [students often realise there is something wrong with the first of these]. **Linking:** To explain why we write $Ca(OH)_2$, it may be useful to make links to maths – where a mathematician might write $2(x+1)$ the chemist would write $(x+1)_2$.

C: Equations describe the reactants and products in a chemical reaction.	D: There are patterns to many chemical reactions.	E: Organic chemicals contain carbon.
More able students often enjoy balancing equations. Discussion of the importance of predicting correct proportions to minimise costs and unwanted environmental effects in industrial processes can be useful in generating a 'need to know' amongst students.	Students are probably familiar with terms like acid, base, salt, combustion (or 'burning'). Students enjoy practical work and like 'playing' with chemicals and apparatus. Practical work is also appealing because it is a sensory experience. Students are not expected to remember reaction types at this level as this would lead to cognitive overload. However, given the categories of reaction types they should be able to make reasonable predictions about possible products. Reaction types covered (see first box in this column) are interesting for students but not too dangerous.	Organic chemistry is more important and relevant for students than inorganic (e.g. hard to justify the importance of learning about $ZnCl_2$ for most students) but is much more complicated and dangerous.
Practical work involving a range of different reactions where students identify as many products as possible. Results are discussed as a whole class leading to the writing of equations as words, then as symbols. Algorithmic skills can be developed in more able classes bypresenting students with a page of equations of steadily increasing difficulty. The challenge is to see how many they can correctly balance.	**Forensic science:** Identification of unknown ionic compounds through practical work (using flame/precipitation etc. tests previously derived by testing known substances) and using semi-micro test tubes (for safety): • gives students control; • provides a real-world application; • creates motivation; • helps students to remember reactions and understand equations. **POE (Predict-Observe-Explain):** To emphasize predictability is not a guarantee of what happens, and that observation is the key to chemistry, the following POE is useful. Ask students to predict what happens when $CaCO_3$ (as marble chips) is added to H_2SO_4, and then perform experiment. There appears to be no reaction (actually it bubbles a little bit and then stops because the $CaSO_4$ formed is insoluble, forms a coating over the unreacted $CaCO_3$ and stops the reaction). Ask students to explain their observations.	Students make models of molecules of some familiar chemicals (e.g. petrol, nail polish remover) with Molymod™ kits (which are designed so that they closely replicate the exact shape of the actual molecule). It is useful to have as many actual samples of these chemicals in the lab. to help emphasise that the models are of real molecules in real things. This also provides the opportunity for students to become familiar with some of the physical properties of these chemicals (e.g. smell, appearance etc.). Soap making.

	A: In a chemical reaction (one or more) new substances are produced.	B: Chemical substances can be represented by formulae.
Specific ways of ascertaining students' understanding or confusion around this idea (include likely range of responses).		**"Dirty tricks":** The teacher deliberately makes mistakes and waits for students to notice (e.g. write $CaOH_2$ instead of $Ca(OH)_2$

C: Equations describe the reactants and products in a chemical reaction.	D: There are patterns to many chemical reactions.	E: Organic chemicals contain carbon.
Write the formulae first, then get students to balance the equation – this shows whether or not conservation of mass is obvious to students. **POE (Predict-Observe-Explain):** Get students to weigh a piece of Mg, then predict the weight of the product after it burns, measure this weight (i.e. observe) and explain the result. This POE offers evidence that the burning of Mg involves an "adding on" to the Mg. It also helps to make an abstract equation real.	See POE in box above	

INTRODUCTION TO PaP-eRs ON CHEMICAL REACTIONS

In this section of the chapter, the PaP-eRs offered have been organised and separated into two different sections. In the first section, the PaP-eRs have been developed around the idea of developing a unit of work, and are designed to illustrate how PCK is evident across the extended processes so common to developing a unit of work. In so doing, they illustrate how linking the teaching of particular content with pedagogy in a purposeful manner is important in conceptualizing a unit of work as a whole, rather than as discrete and individual lessons/activities.

As a consequence, the PaP-eRs that make up this first section more broadly address a range of aspects of the (preceding) CoRe rather than focussing on one or two specific features.

The second section of PaP-eRs reflects the approach to PaP-eRs evident in the previous chapter (Particle Theory) i.e. non-sequential and, as such, offers insights into specific aspects of the CoRe.

TABLE OF CONTENTS OF PaP-eRs CHEMICAL REACTIONS

SECTION ONE

A Series of PaP-eRs exploring an approach to teaching about chemical reactions:
PaP-eR 5.1A: Creating a unit of work.
PaP-eR 5.1B: Glimpses of a unit of work.
PaP-eR 5.1C: Background to murder mystery unit.
PaP-eR 5.1D: Students love a murder mystery.
PaP-eR 5.1E: An annotated syllabus.

SECTION TWO

PaP-eR 5.2: Understanding what substances are.
PaP-eR 5.3: What are the differences in the ways metals react?
PaP-eR 5.4: Introducing reaction types: Less is more.
PaP-eR 5.5: The limitations of predictability of chemical reactions.
PaP-eR 5.6: Probing students' ideas: Insights into teacher change.
PaP-eR 5.7: The increase in mass through combustion.

READING THESE PaP-eRs

All of the PaP-eRs that make up both sections have purposely been placed between the two CoRes that have been developed for this chapter so that the links between both CoRes might better be explored when reading.

Again, as in the case of all of the concrete examples of PCK that are illustrated through Chapters 4 - 9, although the PaP-eRs are offered in a particular sequence, it is not intended that this be seen as the only way to read them. The PaP-eRs link to the CoRe(s) in a variety of ways and should be delved into, cross-linked, and referenced in ways that the reader feels appropriate in coming to better grasp the essence of PCK as portrayed through this work.

As is immediately evident, the PaP-eRs in this chapter illustrate a variety of formats each designed to capture and portray particular and distinctive aspects of PCK. With each of the portrayals offered we encourage readers to seek to identify with the given situation and to reflect on their own approach to such work. By so doing, we hope that these PaP-eRs help to create new ways of framing existing understandings of the pedagogy, content and context, that impact the teaching of chemical reactions and from which science teachers are able to draw new meaning.

SECTION ONE

A SERIES OF PaP-eRs EXPLORING TEACHING ABOUT CHEMICAL REACTIONS

This series of PaP-eRs is designed to illustrate how a unit on chemical reactions might be explored through the context of a Murder Mystery. The PaP-eRs, all based on the work of one teacher, together form one way of considering aspects of the unit of work in order to give insights into some of the features of this unit. They do not attempt to cover every issue within the unit. The PaP-eRs are purposely combined as a sequence in order to help illustrate some of the issues that are central to approaching chemical reactions in this way.

5.1A: CREATING A UNIT OF WORK IN CHEMISTRY

Many students begin their science courses excited at the prospect of doing interesting experiments involving mixing chemicals. However, they often become quickly disinterested because the experiments that they do are too prescriptive and seem to reinforce the "prac. as a recipe" approach. Therefore, students are inadvertently caught up in a process whereby they complete these experiments without thinking much about what is happening and why. While ideally students should be allowed to design their own experiments, as is often the case in other areas of science, this is not necessarily possible in chemistry as teachers' concerns for safety naturally impact on what they will allow their students to do.

One way of dealing with this difficulty is to embed chemistry problem solving tasks into the course. This is what has been done in the 'Murder Mystery' unit. There are three murder mysteries presented at different stages in the unit, each requiring students to analyse a mystery substance found at the scene of the crime. To solve each mystery requires knowledge of some of the chemistry covered up to that point in the unit. The task also develops students' problem-solving and observation skills as well as their ability to logically plan and perform experiments. The PaP-eRs that follow in this series illustrate different aspects of the unit.

Glimpses of a unit of work

Offers insights into the content and structure of the unit's beginning lessons.

Background to Murder Mystery unit

Illustrates some of the thinking for adopting a Murder Mystery approach.

Murder Mystery PaP-eR

Illustrates how the Murder Mystery scenario is offered to students.

Annotated Syllabus Outline

Highlights some of the thinking (over time) that has influenced the way the syllabus has been organised and why, as well as some of the issues and concerns that have shaped the way I have organised the unit.

All of these PaP-eRs have something different to offer in terms of the nature of teacher thinking and how it has influenced the way this unit has been developed. The PaP-eRs should be able to be read as stand alone items; however, they have been grouped in order to show the thinking and actions associated with looking into Chemical Reactions through a unit of work approach.

5.1B: WHAT IS A CHEMICAL REACTION - GLIMPSES OF A UNIT OF WORK

This PaP-eR is designed to offer a brief insight into some of the features of the early lessons in the Unit on Chemical Reactions.

Objectives

To help students to develop:

• an understanding of atomic theory & bonding;

• an ability to observe chemical reactions and write correctly balanced equations;

• investigate practical skills;

• an appreciation of the importance of chemical analysis;

• an ability to conduct qualitative tests for various gases, acids & metals.

Unit Content

Lesson 1:

This lesson is designed to create a situation whereby students have the opportunity to investigate the way in which metals react with oxygen gas. A worksheet is used for students to make careful observations during the demonstrations conducted by the teacher. The students will explicitly describe the properties of metals and begin to investigate issues associated with metallic bonding.

Lesson 2:

In this lesson students will investigate how metals react in water. A worksheet is used for students to record their observations from the demonstrations, by developing and using appropriate language that conveys understandings of the different types of reactions in ways that allow them to compare and recognize these in different contexts. The students will also begin to develop word equations for the reactions of the metals with water and oxygen.

Lessons 3 & 4:

These lessons build on the ideas developed in the previous two lessons as students embark on solving a Murder Mystery.

Element	Reaction Observation
Ca K Na	All burn very vigorously. Solid oxide forms. Oxide soluble in water giving basic (alkaline) solutions.
Cu	
P	
S	
C	
Zn	
Mg	
Fe	
Pb	

Reactions of Metals with Oxygen

Observe the reactions performed by the teacher. Complete the table below.

Questions:

List the metals and non-metals in the table.

Which elements react vigorously/slowly with oxygen?

Which elements form solid oxides, which form gaseous oxides?

Which oxides dissolve to form acidic solutions, which form alkaline solutions?

Reactions of metals:

Metals and Water (observe the reactions performed during class and record your observations)

Sodium & water: What is the gas produced? What indicator was used? What was the colour change of the indicator? What else is produced? Use a word equation to write the reaction.

Calcium & water: What gas is produced? What else is produced? Use a word equation to write the reaction.

Magnesium & cold water: List your observations for this reaction.

Murder Mystery:

Crime Scene: A victim has been found in a park apparently bludgeoned to death with a blunt instrument. Forensic experts have collected metal shavings from the deceased for analysis.

Task: Identify the metal used in the crime.

Materials: Zn, Pb, Cu, Al, Mg, Fe, Forensic Sample, H_2SO_4, HCl, NaOH, tongs, test-tubes.

Safety: In a forensic laboratory labcoats and goggles must be worn.

Forensic Report: Must include the tests conducted, the observations made, a table of results, conclusion.

5.1C: BACKGROUND TO MURDER MYSTERY UNIT

This PaP-eR is designed to offer access to some of the teacher's thinking that underpins the purpose for a Murder Mystery approach to chemical reactions. It examines the dilemmas faced by the teacher when trying to organise work that is both interesting and fun for students while at the same time trying to make clear the importance of the content knowledge to be explored.

The main purpose: Developing the concept of a chemical reaction

The underlying theme of this unit is the idea of a chemical reaction. Students will have been introduced to this term in earlier years, but it has become increasingly clear to me that it takes a long time for them to really grasp the concept. In this unit, I keep coming back to the idea that in a chemical reaction, the reactants join together in a different way to form products that have different properties and that the differences in these properties are observable.

It is sometimes hard for me to accept that although many of the students will have a reasonable conception of a chemical reaction by the end of the unit, only a few will be able to explain (i.e. by writing a chemical equation) what happens at the microscopic level in a chemical reaction.

Another purpose: Giving students experience/knowledge

Teaching science is often easier in areas with which students have some familiarity from their everyday life.

One of the difficulties we face when teaching chemistry is that often the chemicals we use in the laboratory are not indicative of those that students have much (or even any) experience with in their everyday life. We use these chemicals because they are often less complex and it is therefore easier to understand these chemicals' behaviour; or maybe we are just accustomed to using them because of our chemistry training.

Therefore, one of the purposes of this unit is to give students experience of some of the substances that they will encounter if they continue with their studies in chemistry. This is done by continually using the same metals (e.g. Zn, Pb, Cu, Al, Mg, Fe) throughout the unit, but with a changing focus: for example, we look at their physical properties and also at some of their chemical properties, such as combustion in oxygen and reactions with water and acids. In this way students get a chance to know what these metals look like, some of the different behaviours they can exhibit, and, in particular, differences in the nature of their reactivity.

Students also acquire other incidental knowledge. For example, because acids and alkalis are used several times, they learn about them as liquids (they do not yet realise they are solutions) and, again, that they behave differently.

I believe that an important part of chemistry is its language. Not only does the unit provide students with some knowledge of, and physical experiences with, these chemicals, it also tries to help familiarise them with chemical language. This is done informally through the labelling of substances in the laboratory that show both the chemical name and formula, and by having the periodic chart on the wall and posters showing different important reactions and their chemical equations.

Constant exposure to such chemical names and symbols helps render them a little less mysterious when I am discussing them more formally in class. It is also helpful to use the periodic chart to illustrate how it helps us to organise our understanding of characteristics of chemicals and to have the laboratory as a place for easy access to examples of these chemicals.

5.1D: STUDENTS LOVE A MURDER MYSTERY ... BUT DO THEY THINK ABOUT THE CHEMISTRY?

A popular problem solving task used in middle school chemistry classes involves students adopting the role of forensic scientist to analyse and identify several unknown materials. The purpose of the task is for students to learn about and apply approaches to chemical analysis; however, it can be easy for students to become caught up in the excitement of the story rather than thinking about the relevant chemistry.

This PaP-eR is designed to illustrate how sometimes attempting to make science relevant and applicable to everyday situations can be a good motivating tool for students, but can also inadvertently mask the intended content learning. Despite the appearance of engagement in learning, student understanding may not be developed.

Setting the Scene

The night was cold and the autumn leaves swirled around in the breeze casting shadows over the ground as Michele raced through the park on her way home. If only she'd left 10 minutes earlier she wouldn't have missed the last bus. She hated going through the park late at night like this and purposely kept her gaze straight ahead, not wanting to see what else might be around her.

As she turned the corner she could see the last two cabs at the taxi rank with their drivers standing around talking. It made her feel safe to see them so she decided to take the short cut through the garden to get to the cabs quickly. She moved steadily on her path through the trees, regretting her decision almost immediately as her left foot sank into the thick gooey mud that oozed up through her open toed shoe. Moving on she looked down, kicking the mud from her foot and losing sight of the cabs for just a moment.

Suddenly she fell to the ground. It felt as though everything was happening in slow motion. She saw the taxi drivers look up as she heard her own scream ring out through the park.

She lay on the ground looking into the blood spattered face of another person. She had fallen over what must've been a dead body.

The forensic scientist

The students love the story that sets the scene for this unit. They jump quickly into the role of the forensic scientist and soon begin talking about the crime scene and the evidence that they might look for and find. It is the discovery of the small fragments of metal that is the main clue they will work with. The victim has been bludgeoned to death with some form of blunt instrument. Their task is to determine what type of metal has been extracted from the corpse's battered skull.

Over the past few lessons, the class have been building their collective knowledge of different tests that offer insights into the nature of metals. They have examined a variety of reaction types (metals with acids, flame tests, combustion in oxygen, metal oxide in water, etc.) and attempted to learn how to distinguish between different metals through a growing knowledge of these reactions. I want them to be able to draw on this knowledge as they work towards solving the murder mystery.

The problem solving task certainly generates a great deal of interest and sustains student engagement over an extended period of time as they 'play' with the chemicals. However, as I listen to students' conversations and observe the ways in which they work, I have come to pay careful attention to what they actually learn from the experience; it is something I am continually listening for. It goes like this:

'This is a great way to get us used to doing experiments. It's so much fun', I heard Jodie say to her prac partner.

'Yeah, finally we get to do some real science working with all these chemicals. What test are you doing now?'

'Umm, number 4. Look, it turned blue. Write that in the table.'

'Ok, sample 4, blue. Are you sure that's right?'

'I dunno! Go check with Kim's group, they usually get it right. And you'd better hurry up, 'cos we want to finish first.'

Hearing conversations such as this one (above) reminds me of the importance of keeping students' thinking focussed on the chemistry of the reactions they are observing.

Too often it seems that students' thinking about the chemistry content gets lost as they whizz through the work to solve the mystery and the information that they gather is simply part of the task, rather than helping them to develop their understanding of chemistry.

Recognising this as a limitation of the Murder Mystery unit approach has led me to try out some different ways of refocusing students' attention on the chemistry of the metal samples.

For instance, one approach I use is to ask students (as they work in their groups) to tell me what they know about each of the metals "so far". I encourage them to go beyond simply describing what happened in each reaction to interpreting the meaning of the information they have gathered.

Other times, I have set up a mock courtroom scene following the testing which requires a group of students to explain how they could identify the metal of the murder weapon from the samples tested. It becomes a cross-examination of the expert witness and helps to get them to think a bit more carefully about what they have found out and how to justify their answers.

Overall though, I find it really hard to strike a balance between students having fun, doing a task and them really learning something. In fact, sometimes I wonder if they really see what the chemical reactions are all about in this unit. It is a real dilemma for me.

5.1E: AN ANNOTATED SYLLABUS

In organizing a unit on chemical reactions it is important for teachers to be able to see into the thinking that underpins the structure of the syllabus and the different activities that are associated with the content. This PaP-eR is designed to illustrate the thinking that influences the ideas, actions and why, when considering what is in the syllabus. In this PaP-eR, parts of the syllabus are explored in ways that begin to show the teacher's thinking about the importance of particular aspects of the work.

Chemical Murder Mystery Syllabus

Learning outcomes/objectives
For students to develop:
- an understanding of atomic theory and bonding;
- an ability to observe chemical reactions and write correctly balanced equations;
- investigative skills;
- an appreciation of the importance of chemical analysis; and,
- an ability to conduct qualitative tests for various gases, acidsand metals.

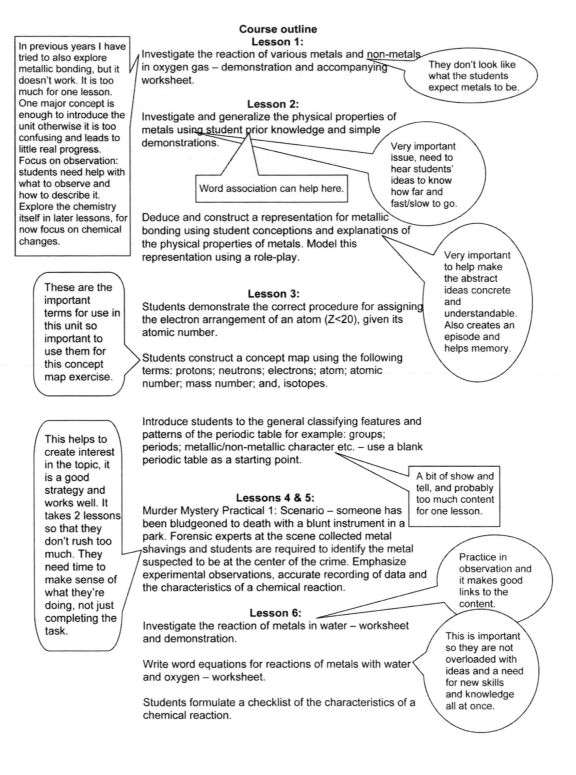

Course outline
Lesson 1:
Investigate the reaction of various metals and non-metals in oxygen gas – demonstration and accompanying worksheet.

In previous years I have tried to also explore metallic bonding, but it doesn't work. It is too much for one lesson. One major concept is enough to introduce the unit otherwise it is too confusing and leads to little real progress. Focus on observation: students need help with what to observe and how to describe it. Explore the chemistry itself in later lessons, for now focus on chemical changes.

They don't look like what the students expect metals to be.

Lesson 2:
Investigate and generalize the physical properties of metals using student prior knowledge and simple demonstrations.

Word association can help here.

Very important issue, need to hear students' ideas to know how far and fast/slow to go.

Deduce and construct a representation for metallic bonding using student conceptions and explanations of the physical properties of metals. Model this representation using a role-play.

Very important to help make the abstract ideas concrete and understandable. Also creates an episode and helps memory.

These are the important terms for use in this unit so important to use them for this concept map exercise.

Lesson 3:
Students demonstrate the correct procedure for assigning the electron arrangement of an atom (Z<20), given its atomic number.

Students construct a concept map using the following terms: protons; neutrons; electrons; atom; atomic number; mass number; and, isotopes.

Introduce students to the general classifying features and patterns of the periodic table for example: groups; periods; metallic/non-metallic character etc. – use a blank periodic table as a starting point.

This helps to create interest in the topic, it is a good strategy and works well. It takes 2 lessons so that they don't rush too much. They need time to make sense of what they're doing, not just completing the task.

A bit of show and tell, and probably too much content for one lesson.

Lessons 4 & 5:
Murder Mystery Practical 1: Scenario – someone has been bludgeoned to death with a blunt instrument in a park. Forensic experts at the scene collected metal shavings and students are required to identify the metal suspected to be at the center of the crime. Emphasize experimental observations, accurate recording of data and the characteristics of a chemical reaction.

Practice in observation and it makes good links to the content.

Lesson 6:
Investigate the reaction of metals in water – worksheet and demonstration.

This is important so they are not overloaded with ideas and a need for new skills and knowledge all at once.

Write word equations for reactions of metals with water and oxygen – worksheet.

Students formulate a checklist of the characteristics of a chemical reaction.

Lesson 8:

Investigate the physical properties of ionic solids using simple demonstrations and the section on ionic solids in the Saunders Chemistry CD ROM.

Describe ionic bonding and the properties of ionic compounds. Students construct a model of an ionic solid for a homework exercise.

Write chemical formulae for ionic compounds, given the formulae and charges of the ions involved – worksheet. Use the internet sites: Anions1; Anions 2; Cations 1; Cations 2; and, ionic formula at teacher's discretion.

Lots of new information needed, they need time to work on it; maybe it needs to flow into homework if they are to get the drift of the ideas.

This is hard for them to do but important to try to get a concrete picture of what is going on.

Visual representation can help beat the 'task only' approach.

A lot to do.

Lesson 11:

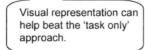

Engage students in generating and constructing definitions of acid, base, salt, neutralization and pH based on their prior knowledge.

Compile a list of the properties of acids and bases.
List the common acids and bases found in the laboratory.

Ask students to predict the pH of common household materials and then demonstrate the use of a pH meter for this purpose.

Explain and demonstrate the use of indicators and test strip for determining the strength of acids and bases. (Show use of pool test kit and range of pool chemicals - good for discussion and placing it in context).

Real world examples, it makes a big difference.

Important for them to test their own ideas.

Lesson 12:

Students complete Metals and Acid experiment on prepared pro-forma.

Students construct an order for metal reactivity (most reactive to least reactive) based on the reactions of various metals with oxygen, water, acids and displacement reactions.

Nice way to give creativity and freedom to their processing and synthesizing of ideas and information. Can be a good assessment piece because it illustrates a valuing of different approaches to assessment procedures.

Starts to synthesize previous ideas and begins to build the idea of recognizable patterns.

Lesson 19 & 20:

Descriptive writing piece on a 'murder mystery'. This could be scheduled earlier in the unit and the format is open to individual teachers, their interests and expertise. Perhaps the myriad of internet sites on this area may assist with a starting point.

SECTION TWO

The second section of PaP-eRs although organised numerically, can of course be read in any order as they are designed as "stand alone" items in their own right; more so than was case the for the way the first section was developed and organised.

5.2: UNDERSTANDING WHAT SUBSTANCES ARE

This PaP-eR discusses the importance of students developing an understanding of the idea of a substance and how substances differ, as a precursor to recognising and understanding chemical reactions.

Chemical reactions tend to be presented to students as processes in which new substances are formed. Teachers often consider this idea to be unproblematic for students and tend to focus, instead, on developing student understanding of scientific explanations for the behaviour of a reaction at the atomic level. But I have noticed that students often are not sure what a substance is and find it hard to decide if a chemical reaction has occurred: when they see a chemical reaction taking place, they do not automatically see that new substances are formed because they do not think this way about matter.

Over the years I have often heard the following types of conversations between students in prac groups as they are doing an experiment:

Pat: (recording the group's notes about the prac): What happened?

Kim: It went fizzy.

Pat: Did you see any new substances?

Kim: Nope.

Sam: What shall I write down was formed?

Chris: A blue colour.

While students such as these see bubbling, they do not make the connection that a new substance (gas) is formed. They may see a colour change but not that a different substance (powder) is now floating around in the test tube. So I spend a lot of time trying to develop students' awareness of substances. I do this by trying to develop their awareness of the ways in which *stuff* differs. In chemistry terms that means considering the physical and chemical properties of a piece of stuff although early on I do not worry about this distinction.

We do a lot of activities where basically the task is for students to try to describe as accurately as possible a number of different substances. I pick out a few substances that have a similar property (for example, colour) and ask how we know they are different.

Sometimes it's hard to be sure (unless we perform a chemical analysis – and that is a long way down the track for these students), but the important thing is to start students thinking about the differences between things and what makes one substance different from the rest.

It's really important to have some pure powders among the examples students have to consider and some whole pieces of the substances that these powders come from, such as a piece of iron and fine iron filings: this helps them to realise that powders are the same stuff or substance as the thing they came from, and that size is not a good way of distinguishing substances.

When I think they have the idea, I push them further to start considering situations where a new substance may have been produced.

Of course this is getting into chemical reactions, but I do not use that term yet. I am still focussing on the idea of substance and whether students can distinguish between different substances.

I give students the following handout to discuss in small groups.

IS A NEW SUBSTANCE BEING FORMED HERE?	
The event	Group decision (with reason)
The foul smell of food gone bad	
The rusting of a nail	
Cheese being grated	
Baking a cake	
A tree growing from a seed	

As the discussions progress, I wander around and listen. Conversations like the following tell me they are getting the idea.

Gina: Well grated cheese looks the same as the block of cheese it came from.

Teresa: Tastes the same too – yum!

Tom: Yes, it's just smaller bits of the big cheese but still the same stuff.

Hugh: Of course a cake is a new substance!

Con: Yeah, looks and feels totally different to the eggs, butter, flour and sugar.

Tim: In fact you can't even see them anymore.

If I hear an observation like Tim's, I store it in the back of my mind for the next lesson when I want to develop the idea that when new substances are formed, the original ones disappear. For the moment though I am pleased that the students can recognise when new substances are formed. (The tree growing from a seed is a tricky one – the leaves look new but what about the bark? There are often arguments between the students about this – what's important here is not the actual decision that students make but their reasoning and I like to emphasise that it is situations like this, where scientists are not sure of the answer, that often lead scientists to doing further experiments.)

Ultimately I want students to see things they have seen before, both in the world around them and in the lab, in a new way so that the conversations in the lab I mentioned at the start runs like this:

Pat: What happened? (Pat asked while recording the group's notes about the prac.)

Kim: It went fizzy.

Pat: So a gas was produced?

Kim: Yes.

Sam: What shall I write down was formed?

Chris: A blue substance.

Exchanges like this between students tell me that they are starting to look at the world through the lens of *substance* rather than just properties (e.g. colour) and behaviour (e.g. bubbling). Soon they will be ready for the concept of chemical reaction.

5.3: WHAT ARE THE DIFFERENCES IN THE WAYS METALS REACT?

This Pap-eR illustrates one teacher's approach to helping her students build their understanding of the properties of metals. Through carefully organising a series of demonstrations showing the combustion of different metals in oxygen, then repeating these demonstrations, the teacher helps her students to focus on one aspect of the intended learning at a time. In this way she attempts to navigate the layers of complexity in the learning by reducing the amount of cognitive overload experienced by her students. The Pap-eR is presented as an annotated lesson plan illustrating both the teacher's intentions for the lesson and some of the thinking behind these intentions.

LESSON PLAN:

Teaching about the reactivity series of metals.

Purposes for the lesson, to:

- Build students' knowledge of the properties of different metals;
- Help students learn to distinguish between different metals based on their properties;
- Recognise that metals can be organised into a reactivity series based on how vigorously they react;
- Help students learn a predictable chemical pattern, that metals react with oxygen to form metal oxides. (This helps to lay a foundation for writing chemical equations.)

What I plan to do	The thinking behind what I do
Begin the lesson by revising with students the idea that elements can combine chemically to form compounds.	While the students appear to have no difficulty with this idea in theory, I have found that many of them do not readily transfer this knowledge to a new (in this case, laboratory) situation. Reminding them at this point helps me to establish the main idea for the lesson. I will be revisiting this idea at different times during the lesson.
Explain that I am going to show a series of demonstrations using the same element (oxygen) combining with a collection of different elements (all metals). This is one way that chemists can use to identify unknown metals in a sample. Students are to observe and compare the intensity of each reaction and to consider what might be the new compound formed in each case.	One immediate problem is that not all these samples match students' expectations of what metals 'should' look like (eg. soft sodium). Organising the curriculum so that students have already had some experience of different metals is important.
	In the past I felt it important to use the 'glowing splint' test to convince students that oxygen is contained in the glass cylinders that I use for this demonstration; however, I have found that this test can become time consuming and unnecessarily distracting. Students tend to confuse the oxygen test with the metal reactivity tests. Now I simply tell students that the cylinders contain oxygen. If they are sceptical/interested to follow up, I can do this later. Even though I am asking students to think about what new compound is formed I will not revisit this until later in the lesson. However, some of the more able students enjoy the extra challenge at this stage.
Ask students to use a page from their notebook and draw a line extending from the top to the bottom of the page. Write the words 'most reactive' at the top of the line and 'least reactive' at the bottom. Hand out to each student a set of 10 cards. Each card has the name of one metal printed on it. Explain to students that their task will be to arrange the cards along the line on their page from most reactive to least reactive metal, based on their observation of the demonstrations (and some further follow up work).	Having the cards seems to be a helpful way for students to flexibly organise and reorganise their thinking as they observe the different demonstrations, more so than keeping a written list. After I have demonstrated a few samples, I ask students to guess in advance about the comparative reactivity of the next sample. (How do they think this might compare to what they have seen?) While I don't expect that anyone will know enough about the samples to make a real prediction, guessing has useful engagement value as students are often keen to know whether their guess is correct, and all students can easily participate.
	Not all the metals printed on the cards will be demonstrated (e.g. gold, copper). I ask students to check out their list for homework, find out about the missing metals, then add them to the list, each in the appropriate place.
Begin demo by igniting a piece of iron (steel wool) and lowering it into a flask of oxygen. (The steel wool flares up in a brief intense reaction.) Tell students that combining a substance with oxygen is called combustion, and that heating is a way of speeding up the combustion reaction, to make it easier to observe. Ask	Choosing which metals to use has been a real challenge. There are only a few different examples of metals that can usefully demonstrate combustion in the lab. Either the metals are too reactive and are therefore unsafe (for instance sodium and potassium) or they are so unreactive that there is little for students to directly observe and they quickly lose interest (e.g. copper).
	I used to worry about students being confused about why I was using steel wool as an example of iron. I thought they would say, "how can steel be iron?" especially since we have not yet dealt with alloys. However, it is not something that seems to trouble them. One reason for this seems to be that many students seem to think iron and steel are the same thing.
	I think it is important to introduce appropriate terminology (e.g.

What I plan to do	The thinking behind what I do
students to keep a "mental video" of that reaction before proceeding to the next sample, magnesium, so that they can compare the intensity of its combustion.	combustion), and I want to help them to know why we are heating the samples, but I don't want to overload students' thinking. Focussing on the way that each metal reacts with oxygen is the most important part at this stage. I mention combustion, knowing that we will revisit it later when I repeat the demonstrations.

I also want to help students recognise combustion as a naturally occurring everyday process as metals combine with the oxygen in air, but again I hold back — it is not necessary yet.

Confusion can also be created for some students in this demo because a few of the samples are heated while others are ignited. |
| Following magnesium and steel wool demos, show video clips of sodium, potassium and calcium combusting in oxygen. | I use a mixture of video clips and 'live' demos to provide variety and try to organise the demos so that students can clearly distinguish between some samples but not others. This gets some good discussions going between students as they try to sequence their cards. I don't tell them that they have to agree on the sequence, but because they often ask to know the 'right answer', I can use this opportunity to tell them that some samples are very hard to distinguish between and ask them how scientists might decide. I can also introduce the idea at this point that we can use the reactivity series to make sensible predictions about the way that some metals will react with oxygen, but not others e.g. sodium would be more reactive with oxygen than copper but it is difficult to compare sodium and calcium. |
| Ask students why do they think that some metals seem to combine more vigorously with oxygen than other metals? | This is a very challenging question because it has to do with how the electrons are held around the nucleus of different atoms. I am not expecting them to be able to understand this in any detail, just start to recognise a pattern. Sometimes I don't ask this question - it depends on student readiness to grapple with these ideas. I use the periodic table to see if students can find each of the metals we have used. They generally find that the more reactive metals are on the left hand side of the table and have lower (atomic) numbers, although the small number of samples used "rigs" the results somewhat! |
| Tell students that each of the demonstrations will be repeated and this time they need to think about what new compound is being produced from the combination of the metal with oxygen. | I used to do the demos only once until I realised just how much information I was expecting students to process in one "hit". A second run allows them and me to focus our attention at a different level. It also gives them a chance to check through their cards, although the idea of this lesson is not for students to be able to remember the reactivity series of metals, but to establish the idea of differences between metals and to set in place a pattern that metal combusts with oxygen to form a metal oxide. Although combustion occurs with gases other than oxygen, I choose not to mention this. I reintroduce here the idea of element + element → compound.

One of the problems with this combination reaction is in demonstrating the presence of an oxide. The test itself can become time consuming and confusing for students because, in some cases, a solid oxide is formed, in other cases the oxide is a gas; some oxides dissolve to form acidic solutions, whereas others give basic solutions. |
| Revisit idea of combustion as a combination with oxygen and that some metals, when heated strongly in oxygen, burn to form metal oxides. Other metals do not burn readily in oxygen, but react with it | Instead of worrying about proving that an oxide is present, I use the second round of demonstrations to reinforce the idea that a combination resulting in an oxide has occurred. |

What I plan to do	The thinking behind what I do
on heating to form oxides.	
	I am aware that what happens in the lab can be easily separated from students' real life because of the specialised equipment that we use. There are lots of everyday examples of the corrosion of metals through combustion with oxygen in air, but at this stage I am not choosing to focus on this aspect.
Give students a chance to work out what the likely oxides are for each of the demonstrations	
Ask students to find out for homework the position of the metals that have not been demonstrated from their card pile.	

5.4: INTRODUCING REACTION TYPES: LESS IS MORE

Teachers often underestimate the difficulty of the ideas that they are teaching in science. And because they are so familiar with these ideas, they tend to chunk them in their teaching, rather than breaking them down into smaller bits for students to understand. This PaP-eR offers insights into the ways a teacher has modified her teaching of reaction types to make the learning tasks more manageable and effective.

Q. How do you introduce the concept of reaction types?

My approach used to be to get students to observe a large number of different reactions and try to work out as much as they could about the products using different tests and their knowledge of the formulae of the reactants. My purpose was for them to see that there were patterns to these reactions – such as acid and carbonate gives salt, carbon dioxide and water. However, they needed a lot of help from me to work out the products. For example, in the acid-carbonate reaction, while they might get the carbon dioxide "bit" they usually did not get the salt or water "bits" and I would introduce the idea of chemical equations to "show" them that these would also be produced. This worked for some of the brighter students but the rest would often ask how we "know" how to write the products of a chemical reaction. It was clear they did not "get" the idea of reaction types and see the patterns that I hoped they would see (e.g. hydrochloric acid and metal reactions are similar; hydrochloric acid and carbonate reactions are also similar; hydrochloric acid and carbonate reactions are different to hydrochloric acid and metal reactions). I began to understand that I was expecting too much: the task of seeing similarities and differences between different reactions was too difficult when students were still grappling with the ideas behind chemical equations.

Now my approach is to introduce one reaction type at a time. I begin with a leading question: 'Can anyone tell me what happens when we mix an acid and a base in a test tube?' Usually someone remembers from work the previous year that the result is a salt and water. While I intend to unpack this reaction later, I just accept the answer at this stage and tell them we are going to see if we can find some patterns in other types of reactions. It's important to establish what actually is observable in a given reaction type before getting into the theory of what happens at the microscopic level, because students often forget that these ideas about atomic behaviour are attempts to explain macroscopic behaviour. That is, chemical reactions become, in the minds of students, microscopic processes that can't be seen rather than processes that are actually observable (in the school laboratory at least) involving forms that change.

I begin with metal – acid reactions because these are relatively straightforward to investigate and explain. I introduce this reaction type with a practical activity in which students have to add different metals to different acids. Students enjoy mixing chemicals so don't need much motivation to perform this task. However the danger is that this becomes a 'fun' activity with no real learning occurring. Hence I constantly emphasise the importance of thinking about: (1) what is being mixed; and, (2) what is the result of that mixing. The task I set the students is to record their results and try to work out what was formed using their observations, and tests on products. Most students only manage to work out the name of the gas that is produced – hydrogen – but a challenge I may set for the brighter students is to see if they can work out other possible products by looking at the formulae of the reactants.

Q. What do students already know that enables them to observe what you want them to observe?

We do some revision of chemical reactions from previous years and I get them to brainstorm the things they might see happen when chemicals are mixed. I write their responses on the board. Because they've already got some experience of mixing chemicals they offer responses like 'colour changes', 'fizzes', and 'disappears'. I usually explore their responses with further questions exploring their understanding ('What does a fizz tell us?') and seeking examples ('When have you seen a fizz?').

Q. What do students have to already know to make sense of their results?

The students have used a range of tests in the past to help the identification of the products. However, students don't tend to consider the possibility of links between their current work and previous work so they won't necessarily think of using tests they've used before. So I spend a bit of time reminding them about these tests – for example, the use of litmus with acids, the 'pop' test for hydrogen, limewater turning 'milky' for carbon dioxide and the reigniting of a glowing splint for oxygen. While this might seem like information overload, it starts to make sense to the students once they have started to do the actual experiments and are trying to identify the products.

Q. What do you do after the students have completed the task?

When they have finished we discuss their results as a class. I'll say, 'Can anyone sum up for me what you observe when you add an acid to a metal?' Most students, if not all, will say there is a gas produced because there is a fizz. Many will also have worked out that it is hydrogen from the "pop" test.

So I sum up on the board:

acid + metal → hydrogen

Then I do a bit of "teaching as telling". I remind students that the reaction between acids and bases, which they studied in an earlier unit could be summarised as (and I'll write this on the board).

acid + base → salt + water

From experience I know that at this point a little bit of "side teaching" involving revision of 'salts' helps students to make sense of the rest of the lesson. Lots of students associate 'salt' with sodium chloride or table salt so I remind them that in chemistry we use the term as a descriptor for a whole class of substances formed in acid/base reactions. I don't dwell on this but I do give some examples, drawing comparisons between potassium chloride, formed from the reaction between hydrochloric acid and potassium hydroxide, and sodium chloride, formed from hydrochloric acid and sodium hydroxide. I also talk about the salts formed if we use a different acid with these bases.

When I think that students have got the idea of salts, I tell them scientists have found out that they are also produced, along with hydrogen, when acids are added to metals. (And I'll add to the plausibility of this statement by actually demonstrating that when some solution left over from one of these reactions is heated, the liquid evaporates leaving behind a powder.)

So I add 'salt' to the acid/metal reaction:

acid + metal → hydrogen + salt

And this is the point of the lesson. If students grasp this, I am pleased. I don't expect them to see this statement as anything more than a summary of what happens because I have not introduced the idea of a chemical equation. At this stage I don't expect them to be able to name the salt.

Q. What happens in the next lesson?

In the lessons that follow, students learn how to identify the names of salts from the name of the acid involved in the reaction (e.g. chlorides are formed when the acid is hydrochloric, sulfates from sulfuric acid etc). This involves a lot of teacher talk, but I am constantly writing formulae on the board to make my arguments plausible, e.g. if we add magnesium to sulfuric acid, whose formula is H_2SO_4, the hydrogen given off comes from the acid and leaves 'SO_4' which joins to the magnesium, so we get $MgSO_4$ or magnesium sulfate (which I emphasise is a 'salt'). I'll actually have written on the board:

magnesium + sulfuric acid → magnesium sulfate + hydrogen
[A SALT]

$$Mg(s) + H_2SO_4(aq) \rightarrow MgSO_4(aq) + H_2(g)$$

While I am actually writing chemical equations on the board, I don't expect students to remember them or work them out themselves. Some of the brighter students will do this, but for the majority of the class the equations serve merely to show that the explanation for the products that form is reasonable.

Eventually after plenty of class discussion about examples like this, most students get to the point where they can correctly predict that the products of a reaction involving a metal and an acid will be hydrogen and a salt, with many actually able to provide the name of the salt.

5.5: THE LIMITATIONS OF PREDICTABILITY OF CHEMICAL REACTIONS

The concept of reaction types is a powerful tool that helps students make sense of the many different chemical reactions they encounter. However, students tend to regard generalized patterns of behaviour for given chemical types as rules that must always be obeyed. Situations where reactions between certain chemicals don't 'work' as expected provide an opportunity for teachers to demonstrate the value of careful observation and a development of an understanding of scientific processes.

Mr. Lee was reviewing the recent lessons on Chemical Reactions with his Year 10 science classes. One of the big ideas of chemistry that made teaching and learning about the topic manageable (possible even), given the myriad combinations of chemicals that react with each other, was the concept of reaction types – that is, there is a recognisable and logical pattern to chemical reactions. Mr. Lee's students had spent some weeks mixing a range of chemicals and exploring the nature of the products (if any). They were now familiar with a range of reaction types (acid-base, precipitation, combustion) and, judging from their responses to a series of exercises which he had given them, were able to use that knowledge to correctly predict the products in reactions they had not observed.

'Now,' thought Mr. Lee, 'It's time to upset the apple-cart ...'

The next lesson Mr. Lee passes around some marble chips on a watch glass and tells the students its chemical name is calcium carbonate, which, although it looks different, is the same chemical as that which comprises chalk.

'Now, what do you think will happen when I add some sulfuric acid to the marble chips which I've placed in this conical flask? ... I'll give you a few minutes to talk about it in your groups.'

While the students discuss their ideas, Mr. Lee writes on the board:

$$\text{calcium carbonate (marble chips)} \quad + \quad \text{sulfuric acid} \rightarrow$$

$$CaCO_3 \quad + \quad H_2SO_4 \rightarrow$$

'Okay, now what did you decide?'

Hands shoot up in the air.

'We think that since there's an acid and a carbonate, there will be some bubbling because the gas carbon dioxide will be produced.'

'Our group also predicted water will be formed.'

'Our group worked out that there would be a salt which was a sulfate formed, but we couldn't decide what its name would be.'

'We decided that because the CO_3 in the calcium carbonate reacts with the H_2 in the sulfuric acid, that would leave Ca and SO_4 so the salt is $CaSO_4$ or calcium sulfate.'

Mr. Lee: 'Does anyone think that something else might happen?'

'Nooo,' the class choruses.

Mr. Lee: 'Let's check that everyone in the class thinks the same. Hands up if you think carbon dioxide will be produced … who thinks water … who thinks calcium sulfate. Okay, it looks like everyone thinks that all three would be formed.'

And he adds these three products to the right hand side of the equations on the board:

**calcium carbonate + sulfuric acid → calcium sulfate + carbon dioxide + water
  (marble chips)**

$$CaCO_3 \quad + \quad H_2SO_4 \rightarrow CaSO_4 \ + \ CO_2\uparrow \ + \ H_2O$$

Mr. Lee gets the students to stand around the front bench so they can all see what happens when he pours the sulfuric acid into the flask containing the marble chips. He holds the flask up so all can see what is happening, or rather is not happening. As always happens when he performs this experiment, a murmur of disbelief echoes around the class, 'Nothing happened!'

Mr. Lee: 'In other experiments where you've added an acid to a carbonate, there's been a quite vigorous reaction. Can anyone think of a reason why nothing happened in this case?'

The students offer a variety of suggestions.

'Maybe the acid is too weak.'

'Maybe it's too cold.' And so on.

With each suggestion, Mr. Lee invites responses from the rest of the class, resisting their pleas to 'Tell us the answer!'

Eventually there is agreement that the students will repeat the experiment for themselves using semi-micro test tubes and very small amounts of reactants for safety reasons. Some astute students notice that there does appear to be a small but short lived reaction, with a few tiny bubbles appearing just after the acid is added to the test tube and but then nothing appearing to happen after that.

Mr. Lee: 'There is a small amount of calcium sulfate formed which is insoluble. It forms a coating over the marble chips which acts like a barrier to the acid and prevents further reaction … What I want you to realise is although our classification of reaction types is a powerful tool for predicting the outcome of particular reactions, it is not 100% accurate. Occasionally there needs to be something else taken into account, and observation is the best way of finding this out.'

As the class filed out at the end of the lesson, Mr. Lee chuckled quietly to himself. From experience he knows he will have to revisit this idea with his students several times in the next two years: it will take at least that long for many of them to come to grips with the idea that you can learn something from chemistry experiments that don't work.

5.6: PROBING STUDENTS' VIEWS: INSIGHTS INTO TEACHER CHANGE

Teachers often interpret students' responses to mean that they have a level of understanding that in fact they do not have. This PaP-eR illustrates how a teacher gradually became aware of this through experience and how her teaching changed in response to what she learnt about students' responses to teaching.

Ms. Ely's year 10 class are gathered around the bench at the front of the classroom. This is the third lesson on Chemical Reactions, a topic which they have encountered in earlier years at secondary school. The students have just observed what happens when a small piece of sodium is added to a large bowl of water. Over the years Ms. Ely has found that while this demonstration always impresses the students, they may not engage with what has happened at a chemical and microscopic level. Furthermore students' understanding of scientific words like 'dissolve' and 'react' is often problematic and a barrier to further learning. Ms. Ely has a number of purposes for the demonstration that she will pursue in later lessons. For the moment, though, she plans to probe students' views about what they thought happened in the demonstration: not only will this provide insight into what the students are thinking, but it will encourage them to actually think about what happened.

Excerpt from the ensuing lesson:

Ms. Ely:	What happened when I added sodium to the water?
Student:	There was a fizz.
Ms. Ely:	What does a fizz mean?
Student:	That things are dissolving.
Ms. Ely:	And what does dissolve mean?
Student:	That things are disappearing.
Ms. Ely:	So when there's a fizz you think things disappear?
Student:	No, they're becoming a gas.

Talking about this discussion later, Ms. Ely reflected on the way her approach to class discussion about chemical reactions had evolved over time in response to her experiences of teaching it. Her comments are shown in the following table.

Ms. Ely noted that it now takes longer to get to the question 'So what gas was produced?' Indeed she often spends more time on a piece of content than previously, which means in practice that she covers fewer topics in the unit. However, she believes that quality is more important than quantity when getting students to engage with ideas about chemical reactions.

What was said during the discussion.	How I would have responded when I first started teaching, and why.	How I would have responded after I had been teaching a while, and why.	How I respond now, and why.
T: What happened when I added sodium to the water? S: There was a fizz.	I would have assumed that the student's meaning for fizz was the same as mine, which was that bubbles of gas were forming. My response would have been: T: So what gas was produced?	From the kinds of things that students wrote in their books and said in class discussion I realised that students often use words like fizz in ways which are different to mine. Because I wanted them to know my meaning, i.e. the scientific meaning, I would ask: T: What does a fizz mean?	I actually try to explore that student's meaning for fizz by asking him/her further questions. This gives me insight into their thinking.
T: What does a fizz mean? S: That things are dissolving.		The student to whom I directed this second question would usually not be the same one who answered the first question. And I would have kept asking DIFFERENT students this question until I got the response that I was after, viz that it indicated there was a chemical reaction occurring in which a gas was being produced. Once a student had given this response I would assume that all students had immediately absorbed and understood this piece of information. So I would move on to ask: T: So what gas was produced?	So my second question would still be What does a fizz mean? BUT TO THE SAME STUDENT.
T: And what does dissolve mean? S: That things are disappearing.			Unpacking a student's thinking like this gives me further insight into what he/she is thinking. I know that often students use 'dissolve' to mean something quite different to its scientific meaning.
T: So when there's a fizz you think things disappear? S: No, they're becoming a gas.			It's often useful to "feed" what a student has said back to him/her as I did in this question. It gives that student the opportunity to reconsider his/her answer.

What was said during the discussion.	How I would have responded when I first started teaching, and why.	How I would have responded after I had been teaching a while, and why.	How I respond now, and why.
			While the rest of the students have not been physically involved in this discussion I know that many will have been mentally engaged with it. There will be different understandings present so I would probably next ask. T: Who agrees that a fizz means a gas is produced? Only when I think that most have the idea (this may take further teaching) would I then ask: T: So what gas was produced?

5.7: THE INCREASE IN MASS THROUGH COMBUSTION

Students sometimes find it hard to believe that when a chemical reaction takes place that the product is a new substance made up of a combination of the reactants. This is made all the more 'unbelievable' to many students when the reaction involves combustion. This PaP-eR explores one way of making it possible for students to see how the product of burning is a combination of reactants and uses the change in mass to illustrate the point.

The Magnesium Oxide POE (Predict-Observe-Explain)

This is one of those typically counter-intuitive situations that I find helps students to see and better understand things that their experience normally misinforms them about what is really happening.

I start with a crucible with a lid and then I somewhat theatrically clean some magnesium ribbon with sandpaper, fold it and place it in the crucible. Most students have seen magnesium ribbon burning before so they already have ideas bubbling up about what I am going to do.

I then ask them what to do to work out the mass of the magnesium and they easily tell me to weigh the crucible and lid, then to weigh the whole lot together and the difference is the weight of magnesium. So I do that and write up the result on the board:

Combined mass of the crucible, lid and magnesium = 24.20 g
Mass of the magnesium = 0.39 g

Prediction

I then move into the prediction part of the POE and ask them to predict what will happen when I burn the magnesium. Typically they say it will burn quickly and brightly, some say it will burn up and leave some ash; and so I need to help them focus a little on mass by reminding them about the idea of their prediction about the change in mass – they often forget this when they get caught up in ideas about burning. Most say after burning it will be lower, some say the same, but it is very rare to get any to say higher.

Observation

With the lid in place, I then heat the crucible strongly for about ten minutes using a Bunsen burner. In that time I get them to record what they think might be happening. So in one sense, the notion of observation is not really right here because they can't see what is happening, so in this case I suppose it's Predict-Hypothesise-Explain. I suppose it's one of those things you do as a teacher, adjust the teaching procedure to suit the ideas you are trying to develop.

While we wait for the crucible to cool down, I start listing on the board the students' hypotheses about what they think has been happening. These are not usually too different. They say that it probably takes a while for the magnesium ribbon to start to burn. Then that it burns brightly for a while. Then that the magnesium is burnt up and that a dust is left behind.

Importantly, I push them again to remind them about the mass, and now most students say that the magnesium is burnt up so that there must be less mass. Some may stick to their prediction of the same, but there is a definite shift to less mass as the outcome.

Explanation

After the crucible has cooled I then weigh it again and we record the results on the board:

The new mass = 24.39 g
Gain in mass = 0.19 g

I then (again quite theatrically) remove the crucible lid so we can see the contents. These typically consist of a white powder with some greyish material encrusted onto what appeared to be fragments of the original ribbon.

Therefore, the experiment showed that the combustion of magnesium involves an addition of mass and the only source of this new mass was air. You can imagine the discussions that follow that help the students come to understand how the mass has increased.

One time, a really persistent student pushed me to repeat the experiment. Although it was going to use up the remainder of the lesson I thought it was worth it so we did it again.

In the repeat experiment the mass of magnesium was again 0.39 g and the mass added as a result of heating was 0.18 g[10].

She then further pushed for me to do another round of heating, cooling and weighing of the same product but it produced no further change in the mass indicating either that the reaction was complete or that remaining metal was protected from the air by the crust of oxidised material. She was very happy with this opportunity to push the ideas further.

This is one of those POEs that I think is really helpful in showing a fundamental idea of two substances combining to make a product and the change in mass that would be expected for such a situation. In this case, it shows how it applies even though it is not what students expect, but it confirms the fundamental idea really well.

---

[10] According to the chemical equation 0.39 g of magnesium (0.016 moles of Mg) should have reacted with 0.26 g of oxygen (0.008 moles of O_2), suggesting that the reaction had not gone to completion.

PREFACE TO SECOND CoRe

Introduction

As noted in the introduction to this chapter a CoRe is not meant to represent the only way in which content might be understood and represented. The CoRe that is represented on the following pages (the second CoRe for this topic of Chemical Reactions) offers another way in which the topic of Chemical Reactions has been portrayed to us by science teachers and we offer it here to further reinforce this notion of multiple perspectives on a given topic.

The CoRe that follows is conceptualised through the big ideas that:

- chemical reactions involve a rearrangement of atoms;

- determining whether a chemical reaction has occurred requires a search for evidence; and,

- a special language that has its own symbols is used to represent chemicals and chemical reactions.

In conceptualising chemical reactions in this way it is also important to be reminded of the view that models and other representations in chemistry have been created by humans in an attempt to explain observations pertaining to chemical reactions. Further to this, there is also a notable point of difference in the conceptualisation of science teachers' PCK on this topic. It is apparent that there is a shift from a view that the teaching of chemical reactions revolves around the ability to balance equations and apply algorithms in chemistry (and, therefore, the development of a range of teaching procedures to aid in this skill development) to that of the notion that chemical reactions is based on an understanding that atoms are conserved and molecules are changed through chemical reactions.

This shift in understanding seems to be based on the recognition that teaching the algorithms, and therefore completing appropriately a large range of worksheets that reinforce the use of the algorithms, is not necessarily helpful in developing students' understanding of chemical reactions at a deeper level – yet teachers may well "choose" to view teaching of this topic solely as skill development in that sense. There is also recognition that many of the reactions and examples used in chemistry to portray particular situations are hardly ever seen outside of the chemistry laboratory and is a further point of divergence in the teaching of chemical reactions.

Those teachers who see this is an issue in their teaching of chemical reactions tend to be concerned that students' understanding of chemistry (and chemicals) is based solely on the labelling of jars and containers housed in the Preparatory room of the laboratory. Therefore, engaging with chemical reactions beyond the laboratory is an important issue that shapes the PCK of some science teachers and is a catalyst for considering issues related to everyday science - the use of substances and reactions that are apparent in the world around us and, addressing the perceived dichotomy of physical versus chemical change.

Overall, then, an issue about chemical reactions for some science teachers is how to represent a topic that has an array of messy variables in a holistic manner such that students can engage with the ideas of chemistry, rather than just perform the skills necessary to manage stoichiometry. The following CoRe offers insights into some of these issues.

This Core is designed for students in Middle Secondary School, i.e. Year 10.	**IMPORTANT SCIENCE**
	A: **Chemical reactions involve a rearrangement of atoms.**
What you intend the <u>students</u> to learn about this idea.	1. A chemical reaction is a process involving an input (reactants) and an output (products – which have different chemical properties). 2. The same atoms are present at the end of a reaction as at the start but they are rearranged differently. Hence atoms are conserved in chemical reactions. 3. Chemical reactions are all around us. 4. Chemical reactions and physical reactions are not dichotomous: some reactions are not clearly one or the other.
Why it is important for students to know this.	1. Understanding that it is a process is important because when chemical equations are introduced, students can confuse these with mathematical equations in which both sides are equal. 2. This idea is at the heart of explanations of chemical reactions and equations. 3. Students can use their knowledge of chemical reactions in their everyday lives, e.g. when deciding how to remove grass/dirt stains from clothes; understanding the list of ingredients on the packaging of processed food; deciding what may be substituted for a missing ingredient when cooking. 4. Physical reactions may also involve rearrangement of atoms.
What else <u>you</u> know about this idea (that you do not intend students to know yet).	Not all reactions are complete (e.g. some biological reactions & some industrial processes) – this is not addressed unless it is raised by a student. Chemical equilibrium. Why some reactions don't occur.
Difficulties/ limitations connected with teaching this idea.	The treatment is difficult to "contain" – where do we stop? The explanations of what is occurring are quite abstract. This is compounded by the fact that the scale is so small. It is also difficult to teach if students don't have a particulate model of matter.

(NOTE: within each column, statements preceded by the same number or symbol (e.g. *) are linked.)

IDEAS/CONCEPTS	
B: **To determine if a chemical reaction has occurred it is necessary to look for evidence.**	**C:** **A special language which has its own symbols is used to represent chemicals and chemical reactions**
There are certain indicators that a chemical reaction might be occurring (e.g. bubbling, temperature change). There are practical tests that can be used to identify products, e.g. gases (CO_2, H_2 etc.), colour indicators. It is not always possible to decide whether or not a chemical reaction is taking place or will actually occur, especially in the school laboratory. Instead looking at trends in the behaviour of similar kinds of reactants (based on previous experience) can be helpful in deciding the likelihood of a reaction and its products.	Chemicals are represented by symbols, with different chemicals having different symbols. A particular chemical is always represented by the same symbols regardless from where it comes. Chemists everywhere use the same symbols to represent a particular chemical. Equations are also a form of chemical communication - for a particular reaction, the same equation applies in all parts of the world. The equation represents the proportion of reactants needed and of the products produced. When writing equations: a) It is necessary to use correct symbols for reactants and products. b) Equations need to be balanced because mass is conserved (i.e. the number of atoms is conserved).
Because often it is not possible to provide direct evidence for chemical reactions occurring.	Being able to use the language is important for further studies.
It can be difficult to explore a diverse yet credible (i.e., ones that the students are familiar with) range of reactions.	*Students may ask where valency tables come from. It is difficult for the teacher to provide a satisfactory explanation at this stage but it is important to tell students that there is one.

(NOTE: within each column, statements preceded by the same number or symbol (e.g. *) are linked.)

	A: Chemical reactions involve a rearrangement of atoms.
Knowledge about students' thinking which influences your teaching of this idea.	Students already are familiar with a lot of chemical reactions from their everyday life. Students like learning how to explain these experiences. Most Year 10s have a particulate model of matter (but this needs to be checked).
Other factors that influence your teaching of this idea.	A belief that students should be learning something that is useful to them in their everyday lives. **An overall emphasis** in the teaching of this topic is that atoms, models etc are human-made ideas that have been created to explain chemistry.
Teaching procedures (and particular reasons for using these to engage with this idea).	Text books tend to oversimplify the differences between physical and chemical reactions. In fact there is not a clear cut dichotomy between them. This idea can be brought to the fore by confronting students with a range of situations and asking them to explain whether there are chemical or physical changes occurring in each case. Examples: • Methylated spirits and water. • A metal ball which just fits inside a metal ring. The ball is removed from the ring and heated and attempts are made to reinsert it into the ring. • 'AlkaSeltza' and water. • Sand and water. The discussion also enables the teacher to judge whether the students have a particulate model of matter.

(NOTE: within each column, statements preceded by the same number or symbol (e.g. *) are linked.)

B: To determine if a chemical reaction has occurred it is necessary to look for evidence.	C: A special language which has its own symbols is used to represent chemicals and chemical reactions
The idea that chemical reactions are predictable (based on one's previous practical experience/knowledge of trends) is not obvious to students, at least initially.	Visual learners pick up these ideas much faster than non-visual as they recognise patterns more quickly. Such students are often good at algebra as well and good at finding embedded patterns in a list of symbols (e.g. word finds). Non-visual learners take more time to grasp the ideas of a chemical language; it is important that the teaching allows for this. Teachers can help by breaking the ideas up into steps using activities like 'bingo', role plays, flash cards etc which encourage use of/recognition of symbols. *In relation to valency tables, students already have some notion of charge from everyday experiences (e.g. combing hair). They need only be told there are two types (+ and −) and that equal numbers of each give zero charge.
An expectation that students won't accept things on blind faith. Explanations about 'why' are only explored if prompted by the students.	Even if students are not intending to continue with chemistry it is worth spending time on this, as it enables an understanding of the labelling of ingredients on processed food and household chemicals.
An overall emphasis in the teaching of this topic is that atoms, models etc. are human-made ideas that have been created to explain chemistry.	**An overall emphasis** in the teaching of this topic is that atoms, models, etc. are human-made ideas that have been created to explain chemistry.
Lots of practical work and discussion leading to an appreciation of the trends in certain reaction types (e.g. acid/base, acid/metal etc.). Students should be encouraged to use a range of tests to identify some of the products. The remaining products in these reactions can be proposed once students have been acquainted with chemical formulas and equation.	A useful introduction is for the teacher to write a number of chemical formulae on the computer and then change the font to 'Wingdings'. Students can then be given the task of finding similarities and differences in the Wingdings version of these formulas. The teacher can then point out the usefulness of using letters that are more easily drawn and recognised. Chemical equations can also be treated similarly. This forces students to look for how the substances in the equation are being changed.

(NOTE: within each column, statements preceded by the same number or symbol (e.g. *) are linked.)

	A: Chemical reactions involve a rearrangement of atoms.
Specific ways of ascertaining students' understanding or confusion around this idea (include likely range of responses).	Most Year 10s have a particulate model of matter but the discussion above will check that this is the case for this class.

B: To determine if a chemical reaction has occurred it is necessary to look for evidence.	C: A special language which has its own symbols is used to represent chemicals and chemical reactions
Look for indications that students are processing the lesson content by listeningto what they are asking or saying in class discussion and to each other during prac: 'What about if we do this …' 'When I did this at home … so what if …' If they are not, the teacher needs to use prompting strategies: e.g. 'What's similar about this?' etc.	

CHAPTER SIX

CIRCULATORY SYSTEM

This chapter outlines a representation of Pedagogical Content Knowledge (PCK) for the topic Circulatory System.

REMINDERS ABOUT SHAPING FACTORS THAT INFLUENCE CoRe(s) AND PaP-eRs

As is the case with each of the concrete examples of PCK that comprise Chapters 4 –9, we briefly offer some of the important points that shape our understanding of representing PCK. Repeating this information at the start of each of the chapters (Resource Folios) is designed to remind the reader about the nature of this form of representation of PCK and for that information to be "on hand" for each individual topic portrayed.

Therefore, some of the important points to be kept in mind when considering that which follows in this Resource Folio are that:

- It is very difficult to offer a single example of PCK that is a neat concrete package, able to be analysed and dissected, or used as a blueprint for practice by others. Therefore, our approach to capturing and portraying PCK hinges on the understanding that the teaching and the content must be represented in ways that both maintains the complexity of their relationships but at the same time offers some way of seeing through the complexity in order to gain insight into it.
- Our approach is based on what we have termed a CoRe (Content Representation) and PaP-eRs (Pedagogical and Professional-experience Repertoire). The CoRe outlines some of the aspects of PCK "most attached to that content" but it is not the only representation. It is a necessary, but incomplete, generalization that helps to make the complexity accessible and manageable; it is neither complete nor absolute. Attached to the CoRe are the PaP-eRs, with links to the aspects of this field that they "bring to life". A PaP-eR is of a content area and must allow the reader to look inside a teaching/learning situation in which the content shapes the pedagogy.
- PaP-eRs bring the CoRe to life and shed new light on the complex nature of PCK. They help create ways to better understand and value the specialist knowledge, skills, and ability of teachers thus making that which is so often tacit, explicit for others.

This Core is designed for students in Middle Secondary School, i.e. Year 10.	IMPORTANT SCIENCE		
	A: It is useful to explain the circulatory system using the model of a continuous closed system.	**B:** The circulatory system functions to service the needs of individual cells.	**C:** Body systems are very dependent on each other for their proper functioning.
What you intend the <u>students</u> to learn about this idea.	The blood circulatory system includes the heart, blood, and blood vessels. Blood is contained within closed vessels. A closed system enables fast and efficient transport of blood to specialized organs.	All living things require a means of transporting nutrients to, and wastes away, from cells. Individual cells each require nutrients (e.g. oxygen, sugars) to do work. The functioning of cells will be impaired if waste products (e.g. carbon dioxide, urea) are not removed. Waste materials must be transported from cells in order to be disposed of.	Body parts and systems are interdependent. Damage to one system/part will affect, to some extent, all others. Exchange occurs between the circulatory system and other systems e.g. the respiratory (oxygen/carbon dioxide); digestive (products of digestion) and renal systems (metabolic waste).
Why it is important for students to know this.	Increased understanding of body processes is likely to lead to increased personal responsibility for particular behaviours, (e.g. relationship between diet and artery thickening.) Through improved personal knowledge students may make more informed choices about health issues.	Because cell life and death affects the whole organism. The links between the circulatory system and cells underscores the need to look after one's circulatory system to maintain the health of the rest of the body.	Even though the blood circulatory system is a 'closed circuit', it requires exchange with other systems for 'life' to be maintained. This emphasizes a need to maintain all body systems.

IDEAS/CONCEPTS			
D: Blood is a complex substance	**E:** The heart is a pump that maintains the movement of blood around the body.	**F:** Different types of blood vessels perform different functions.	**G:** Membrane permeability enables diffusion for supply and removal of materials to/from cells.
Blood is composed of cells, cell fragments, liquid plasma and dissolved substances. Blood is not a uniform substance. Different types of blood cells have different functions e.g. white cells act in defence against disease, red cells carry oxygen, platelets function in clotting of blood. Water is a major component of blood.	The heart is a muscle. The heart is a double pump which pushes blood along two different pathways: heart→ lungs→heart; heart→body→heart The human heart consists of 4 chambers that each receives blood in turn. The pumping of blood through the heart maintains movement of blood and maintenance of blood pressure around the body. The flow of blood is unidirectional.	The composition and thickness of various blood vessels is related to their function, e.g. thicker walled, muscular arteries are flexible to accommodate changes in blood flow directly from the heart. Valves are present in veins to prevent the backflow of blood.	Cell barriers (membranes) are permeable and, therefore, tiny 'bits' can move into the cell. Small blood vessels (e.g. capillaries) are permeable under normal circumstances. Larger other vessels are generally impermeable. Diffusion allows delivery of nutrients and removal of metabolic wastes. This depends on the difference in concentration inside and outside the cell.
Blood is a medium for carrying nutrients into cells & waste away from cells. Health implications of giving/receiving different body fluids e.g. transfusions.	The heart is required because it is important to maintain continuous movement of blood around the body. It is important to maintain muscle health for adequate health of the circulatory system.	The transport system needs to reach every corner of the body. Different kinds of blood vessels enable servicing of all parts of the body. Understanding the relationship between diet and artery thickening promotes good eating behaviours. Exercise promotes efficient blood flow.	This knowledge enables understanding of how materials enter the circulatory system and enter/leave every cell. Whatever goes into the body can affect all cells, not just those at the point of entry.

	A: It is useful to explain the circulatory system using the model of a continuous closed system.	B: The circulatory system functions to service the needs of individual cells.	C: Body systems are very dependent on each other for their proper functioning.
What else you know about this idea (that you do not intend students to know yet).	Details of the circulatory systems of other kinds of living things e.g. insects, plants. Details of the lymphatic system.	Details of the supply of energy through chemical reactions in cells. The complexities of surface area : volume (sa/vol) ratio for cells.	
Difficulties/ limitations connected with teaching this idea.	Models and drawings (e.g. cells/systems) are idealized representations. Limitations of the 'closed-system' model need to be acknowledged, because in fact, some materials pass (in and out) across barriers.	There can be confusion about what "waste" means e.g. CO_2 is not generally thought of as a waste. The idea that individual cells supply body needs is difficult for students to grasp. Students tend to think more on a 'macro' level and hence don't see the significance of many tiny cells.	How 'smaller' systems link together to form bigger systems (e.g. excretory and digestive system). Barriers are not always barriers! Students must understand that barriers are actually permeable and therefore tiny or appropriately 'carried' bits can get through (i.e. diffusion). Students may not have a lot of knowledge about other body systems.
Knowledge about students' thinking which influences your teaching of this idea.	Students don't often have a sense of continual movement of blood. Even with knowledge of capillaries, they often don't realise they are connected in a circuit. Students don't have much prior experience of a closed system.	Ideas about 'waste' are more likely to be connected with digestive system. Students do not think of gases as possible wastes.	

D: Blood is a complex substance.	E: The heart is a pump that maintains the movement of blood around the body.	F: Different types of blood vessels perform different functions.	G: Membrane permeability enables diffusion for supply and removal of materials to/from cells.
Details of production of blood cells. Details of different types of blood cells.	Understanding of the pump mechanism e.g. what keeps the heart pumping (electrical impulses, respiration). The heart requires its own blood supply.	Probably avoid lymph vessels.	Details of osmosis e.g. osmotic pressure. Details of chemistry of cellular respiration. Details of processes that require energy to transport materials against a concentration gradient (e.g. active transport)
Blood parts and types are made in different parts of the body. The idea that nutrients and waste are carried in solution can be difficult for students to appreciate because it depends on understanding of particle theory, dissolving, etc.	The heart requires its own blood supply. It is difficult for students to get the idea of two different simultaneously functioning circuits. The heart tends to dominate student perceptions of the circulatory system. Students often attribute other functions to the heart beyond it being a pump.	Students must have a strong understanding that an organism is made up of cells that have needs for the delivery and exit of nutrients and wastes. The cell membrane as a permeable barrier. Understanding of surface area /volume ratio is needed to understand how capillaries function. It is difficult for students to understand that blood vessels are able to transport vessels that supply cells with what they need, because these vessels themselves are made up of cells.	Students' lack of knowledge of cells and particle theory can make explanation in this area difficult. Osmosis and diffusion create difficulties for students' understanding yet at the same time enable them to understand how an individual cell 'knows' what it needs.
Students may often only be aware of the existence of red blood cells. Sometimes students know about blood cells that 'fight disease'.	Students tend to over-focus on the heart when thinking about the circulatory system. They do not always see that the heart is made up of cells and that it also needs nutrients supplied and wastes removed. Students don't always have a sense of the continual movement of blood in one direction. Instead they often think of blood as washing around inside blood vessels.		

	A: It is useful to explain the circulatory system using the model of a continuous closed system.	B: The circulatory system functions to service the needs of individual cells.	C: Body systems are very dependent on each other for their proper functioning.
Other factors that influence your teaching of this idea.	Students enjoy learning about themselves.		The sequence of the curriculum influences how students make links to other systems.
Teaching procedures (and particular reasons for using these to engage with this idea).	This serves as the basis for class discussion about what is known/not known about circulatory system. **Question Building** Through 1:1 discussion: Students explain to each other (in pairs) what each knows about the human circulatory system and develop a list of questions/issues they would like to know more about. The pairs then keep their list of questions/issues and complete answers to them as they are raised in lessons. **Making the microscopic meaningful:** Students describe a "bloody injury". The class (together or in small groups) develops an explanation of the consequences of the injury through a focus on blood clotting. **Roleplay& imaginative writing:** e.g. a day/week/month in the life of Robbie the red blood cell.	**Ask questions:** why do we eat/ breathe? **Students draw** onto a body outline the pathway of a marshmallow showing any changes that occur as it moves through the body. **Students draw** onto a body outline the pathway of molecules of air showing any changes that occur as they move through the body.	**Road transport analogy:** Students develop a detailed analogy of the circulatory system as a road transport system that includes important parts of other systems. For example, the road transport system involves roads, vehicles – for picking up and delivering items – and these are linked to other systems (e.g. factories, warehouses etc.). **Concept map** using terms from different systems.

D: Blood is a complex substance.	E: The heart is a pump that maintains the movement of blood around the body.	F: Different types of blood vessels perform different functions.	G: Membrane permeability enables diffusion for supply and removal of materials to/from cells.
	The availability of curriculum kits that examine issues such as transplantation, transfusion, heart surgery etc.		
Brainstorm list of body needs for survival and then teacher provides information, or students research blood components that meet each need. **Making the microscopic meaningful:** Students describe a "bloody injury". The class (together or in small groups) develops an explanation of the consequences of the injury through a focus on repairing the damaged site.	**Heart dissection** (real or virtual). Students identify different chambers of heart, thicknesses of walls and valves for closing chambers. This physical experience supports learning. **Comparison** of real heart with idealized diagrams in books that look different to the "real thing." **Roleplays** both of whole circulatory system and of functioning heart, as blood moves through each chamber. These offer personal and concrete learning experiences. **Watching videos** that show the actions of a functioning heart, e.g. heart operation.	**Demonstration:** view live goldfish's tail under a microscope to see the movement of blood through different blood vessels. The teacher draws attention to how thickness of blood vessels is related to their function. **Detailed observation:** with a focus on structure and function, students examine the vessels in the heart during a dissection. **Revisit and Review:** with a focus on structure and function, reconsider the road transport analogy and have students elaborate the links to different road types.	**Diffusion laboratory exercises:** For example, spraying perfume in one part of the room and mapping its rate of diffusion, or place a crystal of $KMnO_4$ into a petri dish of water and observe the rate of diffusion. **'What if' Questions:** Teacher generated and/or student generated "what if" questions to probe understanding. For example, what if the veins were as permeable as capillaries? **Question dice:** using the question dice, get students to construct questions to pose to the rest of the class.

	A: It is useful to explain the circulatory system using the model of a continuous closed system.	B: The circulatory system functions to service the needs of individual cells.	C: Body systems are very dependent on each other for their proper functioning.
Specific ways of ascertaining students' understanding or confusion around this idea (include likely range of responses).	From the body map and circulatory system drawings, the teacher attempts to listen to students' descriptions of different aspects of their drawings. Students write 'agree' or 'disagree' next to statements then explain their thinking. For example, 'The blood pressure in the capillaries is lower than that in the arteries and veins because the narrow capillaries offer greater resistance to blood flow.' Or, students create their own and share these with each other to see what they think etc.	When students are discussing macro actions (eating etc.) with needs of cells, the teacher listens carefully for their ability to make links between the two.	Listening for links between digestive and circulatory system. For example, it is important to listen for evidence that students realize the digestive system is not just a tube that takes food in and sends wastes out, but also that it has an important interface with the circulatory system. Similarly student recognition of the links between the circulatory and respiratory system is important. Listening for signs that students have a well developed road transport analogy with appropriate symbols for gut, lungs etc. For example, the lungs may be described as a Park because it has lots of air around, whilst not really grasping the functional aspects of the lungs.

D: Blood is a complex substance.	E: The heart is a pump that maintains the movement of blood around the body.	F: Different types of blood vessels perform different functions.	G: Membrane permeability enables diffusion for supply and removal of materials to/from cells.
The nature of students' links between the Road Transport analogy and the circulatory system component is important. Recognising limitations of the use of symbols and analogies (see for example the RoadworksPaP-eR).	The teacher looking to see if students show through roleplay/story of blood cell that blood passes through heart twice in a circuit. Posing 'what if' questions to explain (e.g. what if a baby is born with the aorta & pulmonary artery reversed). Posing difficult questions and listening for explanations about the concepts, for example, how is the heart itself supplied with blood?	Students make appropriate physical models of simple mammalian circulatory systems showing varying vessels and the pump. In this case, the teacher is looking to see that the components of the physical model are appropriately represented.	Create different scenarios for students to explain how the scenario "plays out" in practice. It is important to listen to their explanations to see that they grasp the ideas. For example, how does a "smell" move through the air?

INTRODUCTION TO PaP-eRs ON CIRCULATORY SYSTEM

In this section of the chapter, the PaP-eRs on the circulatory system linked to the preceding CoRe are offered.

6.1: WHAT IS IT ABOUT BLOOD?

This PaP-eR comprises three separate sections, each of which is designed to stand-alone, but equally sit together to form a group of approaches to exploring the nature of blood and its actions within the circulatory system. An important issue at the centre of each of these sections is the need for teachers to be ready to recognize students' ideas (questions, issues, responses, etc.) and appropriately respond to these in ways that take into account these different views and science ideas.

PART 1: WHAT DOES IT MEAN TO BLEED?

Teacher: 'What happens when you cut your finger?'

Student: 'Duh, you bleed!'

I had been teaching for quite a few years before I realized how this seemingly simple idea - bleeding - was so often misunderstood by many of my students. It had not occurred to me that students did not really understand what happens when we bleed as I had rarely probed their responses in any depth. I had always assumed the explanation was obvious.

My view was quite straightforward. Since blood is carried in blood vessels - and that is certainly a central issue in teaching about the circulatory system - then bleeding must in some way involve breaking into one of these blood vessels so that the blood can escape. Therefore, when I asked students about bleeding, I assumed they made this 'obvious' link. However, much to my surprise, one time when a student cut herself with a broken test-tube, the conversation we had 'opened my eyes' to a different world-view of bleeding. It went a little like this.

Student: 'Miss, Miss, Jana has cut her hand. Can I take her to the sick bay?'

Teacher: 'How deep is the cut? Let me see it before you go rushing off.'

Student: 'It's only a cut Miss!" (Puzzled look. Pause) "Can we go now?'

After I washed Jana's hand it was easy to see that it was a relatively superficial cut, yet as I talked about what I could see, it brought an interesting response from Van, Jana's friend.

During our conversation it became apparent that Van seemed to believe that blood just "sloshed" around the body and that the cut simply created a way for the blood to escape by "oozing" out through the gap created by the injury. Van had this view because, despite my teaching about the circulatory system and the associated functions of blood vessels, her experiences of bleeding had always been of superficial cuts whereby blood simply oozed out of the wound. Therefore she did not really link the idea of blood travelling in vessels with the reality of her experiences of how blood escaped from the body through a wound. As the cuts she was familiar with only broke capillaries or venules, and these were not visible through the wound, it "looked" to her as though blood simply sloshed around the extremities of the body rather than being confined to blood vessels.

This realization was a great surprise to me and has influenced how I now question students' responses to even the most obvious features of a given concept. When it comes to bleeding, I now ensure that we discuss fully what really happens in a cut (that blood vessels may be damaged) and link the features of blood vessels to the roles they perform (i.e. veins and arteries) and how the outcomes of the damage depends on the type of blood vessel cut.

For me, this apparently simple issue has led to a new appreciation of the need to genuinely explore what students mean when they respond to questions and not to assume that their answer means what I think it should mean. However, there is more to the story above as the following section illustrates.

PART 2: BLUE BLOOD

As I was heading back to the staffroom at lunchtime, Van caught up with me. She had a puzzled look on her face that caught my attention.

Van: 'You know if you're right about the blood from Jana's cut, then she couldn't have cut a vein.'

Teacher: 'Why is that Van?'

Van: 'Well, if she cut a vein then she would've had blue blood coming out. But it was red blood so she must have cut an artery.'

Van had obviously been thinking about this issue and could not reconcile the new information I had offered to explain Jana's cut with another idea she had about the colour of blood in the different vessels of the circulatory system.

Teacher: 'Well, actually blood is never blue.' I started.

Van: 'Yes it is, look.' she said showing me the veins in her arms. 'Look at yours.' she continued.

I turned my wrists up and there, true enough, were blue veins.

My mind turned to the wall charts of stylised veins and arteries commonly displayed in science rooms and text book diagrams showing blue veins and red arteries. They are helpful for showing the difference between oxygenated and deoxygenated blood, but misleading for learning about the real colour of blood. Thinking about those images, and the look of veins through the skin, led me to see that Van's explanation was not surprising. Not surprising, but what was the scientific view? I'd have to read up on this. With those thoughts running through my head I responded.

Teacher: 'Well, actually, despite what it looks like here, these vessels only look blue because we are looking at them through our skin. But I'm going to have to get back to you with a reason because I'm not sure what the scientific explanation is at the moment!'

Later that night I found a research report[11] which investigated the phenomenon of venous blood appearing blue in people with light coloured skin. It seems that when light coloured skin is illuminated by white light, some of the reflected light comprises light which has penetrated the skin and been scattered back by the tissue and other substances under the skin. Above the veins, the scattered light contains less wavelengths of red light than does that from the surrounding tissue. Because of the way our eye interprets the different balances of red wavelengths relative to other wavelengths, we see these veins as blue. I thought about Van. The explanation given by the article was too complex to give her, and yet it was important to help her understand that venous blood could appear blue even though it was dark red.

Next class I set up a simple demonstration. I cut a finger off a whitish yellow rubber glove. I told the students that this represented the flesh above a vein. I showed the students a test tube, representing a vein, which contained some dark red "blood" that I had previously prepared by mixing red and blue food colouring, water, and chocolate topping. Then we slowly lowered the test tube inside the finger. The portion of the test tube inside the finger appeared bluish and contrasted nicely with the dark red liquid that could be seen in the part of the test tube above the top of the finger. While this didn't "prove" that blood

---

[11]Oxygenated and deoxygenated blood, each contained in glass cylinders representing blood vessels, were lowered into a milky liquid intended to represent the skin tissue surrounding a blood vessel. Changes in colour of each were noted. At first there was no change in colour. Increasing the depth of the deoxy blood changed its appearance to a bluish colour. At greater depths, the oxy blood acquired a bluish tinge. (There was also a minimum diameter needed for the blood vessel to appear blue: thus because arteries are generally smaller and have thicker walls they are generally not able to be seen below the skin.) Very interestingly, the analysis of light reflected by these immersed 'blood vessels' revealed that the light contained more red wavelengths than blue although the amount of red was less than before immersion. So one might expect their perceived colour would be red. However, according to a complex theory of colour perception called the 'Retinex Theory', the colour of an object depends on the relative intensities of different wavelengths compared to the surrounding area. Because the light reaching our eyes from above veins contains less red wavelengths than the light coming from the surrounding tissue, we perceive the colour to be blue. Source Reference is:

Kienle, A., Lilge, L., Vitkin, I. A., Patterson, M. S., Wilson, B. C., Hibst, R., et al. (1996). Why do veins appear blue? A new look at an old question. Applied Optics, 35(7), 1151 - 1160, Available at http://www.uni-ulm.de/ilm/litzopt/1151.pdf.

in veins under our skin isn't blue, the students did seem happy to accept the possibility that the apparent colour of the veins was because they are "in" our skin. All I wanted to do was to establish that it is plausible that blood in veins, while appearing bluish, is actually dark red. I think I found a way to do that; Van thought as much.

> Van: 'Well I guess it makes sense. If veins really are closer to the surface than arteries, I s'pose it's usually the veins that are broken when I cut myself, and now I can see why I've never seen blue blood!'

PART 3: PLATELETS – SLOWING THE FLOW

Another (seemingly) simple concept is the role of platelets in blood clotting. Although it can appear easy to explain how platelets function and therefore why bleeding slows down as a result of their action, I have found the following role-play to be a good way of illustrating the action in a concrete way.

I usually begin by asking one student to stand by the classroom door. I then ask the class to stand up and start walking around the room in the same direction, in a circuit that goes past the door. After a short while I ask the student at the door to open it and for those students closest to it to walk out through the open door as they circulate. The 'circulation' continues but some of the students easily 'bleed' out through the 'cut blood vessel' door.

We then have a brief discussion about platelets and how they work. Then, I repeat the exercise, only this time I ask a small number of students to wear a coloured band so that they look different to the rest of the class. These are the platelets and I tell them that as they pass the door they can grab onto the opening (and each other) to link up. As the 'platelet' students begin their circuit they are just part of the flow, but when the door is opened they slowly start to fill the doorway space, thus impeding the flow of students out and eventually blocking the doorway completely. The students see and feel what it is like to 'stop the bleeding' and are better able to link blood clotting and platelets in a concrete way.

6.2: NOT JUST A THING, BUT A NEED FOR A FUNCTION

Students rarely consider why we have blood circulating in our bodies. This PaP-eR illustrates how a teacher began a Year 9 unit about the circulatory system with a visualisation activity that prompted students to consider the need for a circulatory system in the human body.

Commonly, students associate blood almost exclusively with the heart, with cuts and injuries, and perhaps with a pulse rate, without ever wondering why we have blood and why it is circulating in our bodies. If they do consider the idea of the blood carrying food and oxygen "for our bodies to use", students tend to think that the heart is the source of these nutritional needs, or that they are just "in" the blood itself. Such views about the function of the circulatory system often stem from a lack of awareness of the relationship between the circulatory system and other systems. This is aggravated by the body systems commonly being treated discretely and separately in teaching.

A colleague and I decided that it was important to begin a Year 9 unit about the circulatory system with an activity that challenged students to carefully consider the underlying purpose of the circulatory system. We felt that introducing the various components and then putting them together (a common approach) was unlikely to lead to students developing a picture of the circulatory system as a functioning whole. We believed that they had to have an understanding of what the circulatory system did, so that this in turn would allow them to "see" further "needs" for the components of the system, and also for its interconnections with other body systems.

We adapted the 'Body Systems' approach[12] with a fundamental change. Rather than asking students to generate a picture of a body system first and then tracking the progress of food molecules through the body (this is useful for review and consolidation), we asked them to consider molecules entering the body with the intent of this leading them to understand there was a need for the body systems.

In the classroom

(This is based on my teaching journal: as well as describing what happened, I try to "unpack" my thinking about the lesson.)

---

[12]Loughran, J.J., & Corrigan, D.J. (1991) Do You Know Your Body: An assessment task. *Australian Science Teachers' Journal, 37* (4), 44–48.

What happened	My thinking
Quiet music playing as the girls came in and moved to their seats. Each place had a marshmallow sitting there on a serviette. It wasn't necessary to tell them not to eat it – they seemed quite reverent about it! It was quite good letting them wonder about the marshmallows as everyone arrived.	The dramatic use of music at the start of the class is intended to set up an expectation that something new and important is going to happen and helps to focus students' thinking on the tasks that followed. Hopefully this unusual use of music will help the students to remember the lesson that follows!
I asked them to have their books open to a 'thinking page' and a pen ready.	The left hand page of the students' exercise book is used as a 'thinking page' for writing ideas and questions that occur to them during the lesson. (This is an unstructured activity which serves as a means for ongoing conversations between students and the teacher. Students have been 'trained' to use this whenever they choose in science lessons.)
Me: "Look at your marshmallow. Now chew it slowly with your eyes shut. Think about what is happening to it as you swallow it. This is a silent activity." • 'Where is the marshmallow going? ... What is happening to it? Write your ideas on your thinking page – and please don't talk yet!' • 'Where will the marshmallow be in 1 hour? ... in 2 hours?' • 'What will have happened to it? Where will it have gone?' • 'How about after 6 hours? ... 12 hours? ... in 24 hours time?'	I don't want them to talk yet because I want to allow them time to become aware of their own ideas – what they really think – before we start any discussion.
They formed their own groups as I gave out huge sheets of butcher's paper and markers. They had to draw a body outline (around a volunteer) and then show the marshmallow's progress over 24 hours. After about 15 minutes I got everyone to move around the lab looking for similarities and differences. There was a fair variety in the amount of detail shown about the digestive system ('But we did this last year, Miss'), but only one group indicated that some 'nutrition' would go from the stomach "into the body". Back at their own "bodies" most changes involved improving the details of the digestive system.	This is a powerful way of exploring what they actually think. It is also a powerful learning tool because thinking about the location of the various body parts and their needs can challenge students' ideas about the process of digestion (which they have studied the previous year).
Now I started to ask the million dollar question ... Me: 'Why do we eat food? Why do we bother?'	This question is the key to getting students to think in ways that leads to a recognition of the need for a circulatory system.
'We need the food for our bodies to work.' 'It gives us energy.' 'We need energy to move.' 'We need vitamins and minerals and things like that.' 'We get the stuff for our bones and everything from our food.'	The students' answers are fairly superficial as

What happened	My thinking
Me: 'But if the marshmallow goes in here and 24 hours later it comes out here, then how can it do those things? Why do we bother eating it? (OK – besides the taste!)'	they tend to respond with ideas and issues from earlier work that are not purposefully linked to the drawing we've just done. So my question's purpose is to try to get them to think about the real links that are possible based on their careful reasoning and thinking. (Actually, I know there will be little if any waste passed into the colon from the digestion of a marshmallow – but this detail is not important at this stage.)
Some people objected to a marshmallow being food, as opposed to junk food, which caused lively discussion. 'It's got lots of sugar and the sugar gives us energy'. I told these groups to think about a pizza instead. Every group started talking about "using" some of the marshmallow. Arrows started to appear – mostly radiating from the "stomach". A couple of groups had them coming from the small intestine too. The arrows radiated out into 'the body'. Louisa even said that 'vitamins and minerals go through the villi of the small intestine', and Genwa suggested that protein came out 'because we need protein'. For a handful the details of last year started coming back. As a class we talked about the marshmallow. Yes, some of it 'went right through' and came out as waste. But what happened to the rest? The consensus was definitely that the 'good bits' of the marshmallow went through the walls of the digestive system into the body to be 'used in the cells'. Me: 'So how do they get to the cells? How does a cell in your middle toe (brain/elbow/ovary) get all the energy and nutrients that it needs to keep functioning if it is such a long way from your intestine?' 'It gets there in the blood.' 'It gets into your blood and then travels in the blood 'to where it is needed'. 'The blood takes it to all of the cells'.	Students have learned these ideas in their study of digestion the previous year but it takes a lot of discussion and probing on my part for them to make this leap.
Homework: "Go back over your thinking page and use this to write one question that you want answered about ideas arising from today's lesson."	This gives me an insight into students' understanding which helps shape what I do next in my teaching. It also encourages students to think about their understanding.
Planning for next lesson: Book drama room. Get students to lie on the floor with eyes closed. Breathe slowly and deeply. Get them to think about the breath of air – what happens to it? Why do we breathe? What do we need oxygen for? Where does the oxygen go? etc. Then get them to add their thoughts to their bodies (similar process to today).	It should be quicker because of today's lesson, although they are less familiar with the respiratory system than the digestive system.

Throughout the unit we return to these 'body pictures' to modify them as we build up a picture of the circulatory system, to think about interfaces and transfer between the different body systems, to think about waste transport, and to revise ideas later in the unit. They are fabulous for probing ideas, assessing understanding, promoting curiosity, and teaching, all at once, in a small group setting. Vitally however, we find that starting the unit with these visualisation activities helps to get prior (working) knowledge out, and provides the class with not only a 'need' to learn about the human circulatory system, but also a framework to help them make sense of its functioning.

6.3: HEART EXPLORATION

Laboratory activities that provide opportunities to examine real body parts are used in science classes so that students can see what these structures actually look like, and develop their understanding of the relationship between structure and function in organisms. However, real body parts can be surprisingly different in shape, size and organisation compared with the representations that students regularly meet in textbooks. This PaP-eR is presented in two parts. The first part highlights how one teacher comes to recognise some of the difficulties experienced by students using stylised representations to learn about a real mammalian heart, and the second part illustrates an approach that the teacher chooses to address this issue.

PART 1: RECOGNISING A PROBLEM WITH TEACHING ABOUT THE HEART

I believe that an important purpose for learning about the mammalian circulatory system is to help students develop an appreciation of how their own bodies function; for example, the role of the heart as a pumping organ maintaining the constant circulation of blood. One way of helping students learn more about their functioning heart is to give them a first hand experience of examining and dissecting a real sheep's heart. Since the anatomy of a sheep's heart closely resembles that of a human heart, this can be a useful activity for students to gain an appreciation of the size and shape of their own heart and its various structural components.

Dissection (of anything) usually generates high levels of excitement amongst students because of the opportunity to use 'dangerous' laboratory equipment, for example, scalpels; the opportunity to do something different from regular class activities; and, for some, because of a fascination with real body parts. However, I have come to learn that dissection activities do not usually result in correspondingly high levels of learning about the organ being dissected. One reason for this is that students often experience considerable difficulty locating and identifying the structures that they are asked to observe and describe. A major difficulty for students encountering a real sheep's heart is that their prior school experiences of seeing a heart have mostly been two dimensional textbook diagrams (or stylised pictures from everyday life, ♥) that bear little resemblance to the organ that they now have in front of them. This became very clear to me recently when the following situation arose in my class. The students were supposed to be carrying out a heart dissection prac that involved locating, drawing and describing different structures of the sheep's heart. I noticed that Chris, one of the brighter students, had spent little time with the sheep's heart and had turned instead to copying information and pictures to answer the prac directly from his text book. So I asked him about it:

'Chris, I see you're copying the diagram of the heart from your text book. The prac instructions ask you to draw and label what you see from your dissection.'

'I can't do that, Mr. Taylor.'

'Why not?'

'It's too hard. Look at that!' he said pointing to the sheep's heart. 'How do I draw that? I can't work out what anything is. It doesn't look like it's supposed to.'

'Supposed to? I'm not sure what you mean?' I replied.

'Well.' he explained, 'Where are the atria on this sheep's heart? Aren't they supposed to be above the ventricles or something? How can I draw what I can't see?'

I looked across to the heart Chris had newly dissected. Compared to the stylised line drawing in his textbook of two neat atria sitting above the ventricles, it was very difficult to locate the atria in this sheep's heart, let alone draw this 3D organ in a 2D picture.

I attempted to point out the atria to him.

'The right atrium is this bit here.'

'Are you sure?' he asked. 'It's so tiny!'

'Quite a bit of it is cut away when the hearts are prepared for sale.'

'So how big is the right atrium, really? And, how do you know which bit is the pulmonary artery and which bit is the atrium?'

'It is difficult,' I agreed.

I looked around the room. If Chris was struggling with identifying the heart structures then how were the rest of the class doing?

This episode with Chris led me to question my expectations for students' learning from their experience of examining a real heart. After all, from my point of view the purpose of the lesson was not simply to reproduce the text book illustrations in order to get a good prac result. I wanted students to begin to appreciate the look, feel and structure of this organ and to think about it functioning within their own bodies. However, I could see that there were considerable difficulties in achieving this learning goal. I realised that I had never previously discussed with students the reasons why diagrams of the heart (and other structures) are represented in various ways, nor the differences there might be between what students expect to observe and what they actually encounter with the real thing. I resolved to change my approach to better help my students learn about the heart as a real, living organ.

PART 2: IMPLEMENTING A CHANGED APPROACH TO TEACHING ABOUT THE HEART

As we start to investigate the heart as part of the circulatory system, I now ask students to draw a picture of what they think a real heart looks like and to label their drawing with their ideas about how they think the heart works. Some students feel uncomfortable with this activity mostly because they believe their writing and drawings must be textbook correct. So to help reassure them I gently encourage students in this task by telling them there is no correct answer, and that they will not be required to put their work on display. I find that this task is helpful because I can ask students to link their expectations of the heart with their later observations.

Then, I play a short video of a human heart operation that enables students to see a live human heart in situ. I ask them to describe what the heart looks like to them and encourage them to ask questions about what they have seen and to compare this video picture with their previous ideas of heart structure and function. I find this activity really helps students to develop their own mental picture of a real heart and, importantly, to develop a sense of the heart as a working organ. Many students are quite surprised to see the heart beating; it is a much smaller vibration than they expect it to be.

Then, each pair of students is provided with a sheep's heart to examine and a worksheet that begins by asking students to compare this sheep's heart with what they have seen on the video, and their own expectations. The worksheet tasks require students to make suggestions about the jobs of the different parts they find, or reasons for the structures that they see (e.g. why the heart walls might be thicker in some places than others). As I walk around the room I encourage students to talk with me about what they are observing. Students also have access to a website that shows a series of clickable, large external view photos of a sheep's heart. Clicking on any region of the heart photos highlights that same region in a labelled diagram alongside the photo. This really helps students to locate hard to find structures, such as major blood vessels, atria and valves, on the sheep's heart in front of them. Students are also provided with a digital camera to take photos of different views of the heart and to present these as labelled diagrams in an electronic report of their experience.

This approach is quite different from the highly structured dissection activity that I used to use. And as a result, students seem much more able to connect the textbook diagrams with the real, functioning heart, so I feel more confident that they can genuinely understand more about its structure and function.

6.4: QUESTIONS WE WANT ANSWERED

This PaP-eR is written from a student's perspective and explores issues of prior knowledge, interest, and relevance and a teacher's ability to recognize and respond to these in terms of understanding how they influence learning in particular content (by tapping into students' need to know). The PaP-eR also highlights an important outcome of the teacher's approach, being that students are likely to be more active and responsible learners as they have more ownership over the issues central to the content. The teacher's understanding of the relevance of this content to students' prior knowledge is the catalyst for approaching the teaching in the manner described in this PaP-eR.

What is it about the circulatory system?

It's not very often that I come into a class and get asked what I think about a topic – especially when it happens before we have even started doing the work! Well, when we started doing the circulatory system that's exactly what happened.

Having just changed schools I was surprised at the different way my new science teacher approached teaching us science compared to what I was used to at my old school. I thought it was going to be really boring because when I changed schools I ended up doing the circulatory system all over again, but this time we didn't take the usual approach.

Anyway, let me tell you a little bit about how my new teacher (Ms.Stanislov) taught us. That might make it easier to see what happened and what was different to my old school. So here it is.

We came into class and I was immediately surprised by what was going on (though none of the other kids in my new class seemed to think it was unusual). In my old school the teacher would've started to tell us what we were going to do, what we were supposed to learn and stuff like that but Ms.Stanislov just had a heading on the board saying Circulatory System. She pointed to it and then told us to talk to the person next to us about whatever things popped into our heads when we read the words, circulatory system. We chatted for what seemed like a few minutes so I was really surprised when Ms.Stanislov stopped us by saying 20 minutes was enough time. I couldn't believe how much we had to say to each other.

Anyhow, in my pair, Chrissa and I had a really good talk because her dad had recently had heart by-pass surgery so she knew lots about the circulatory system because she had seen what had happened with her dad and the doctors had explained heaps to her. I couldn't help but think how different all that information is when it has got to do with someone you know. It makes it somehow more relevant. I reckon Chrissa could've written a test on the topic that even Ms.Stanislov would struggle to pass!

So after talking in pairs, Ms.Stanislov asked us about the major ideas that had come up. While we talked she was making some headings on big sheets of paper. When we finished she said that there was probably so much there that it would take us all year to do the work that we were interested in! Then she walked around the room and stuck up the big sheets of paper with the headings on them. I can't remember exactly but I think the headings were something like blood, organ structure, organ functions and, problems related to circulation. She had two sets of these – I think just so there weren't too many people around one sheet - and then she told us that we could go to any of the posters and write up questions we had that we wanted answered. But, she said that we had to talk about our questions with other people at the same poster first so that the questions were 'good questions'.

This good questions thing is something she seems to push with us all the time. She has been teaching us about our own learning and so has been making us think carefully about what we ask so that they are 'linking questions' or 'thinking questions' and stuff like that. I really notice how this approach to questioning (ours and hers) is different from my old school. We used to be able to work out pretty easily what the teacher wanted us to say in my old school, but in this class, I really think Ms.Stanislov wants us to think about what we know and to ask really good questions. In fact, she actually said one time that she was not quite so interested in 'closed questions' because we can get answers to those easily enough through Google. She seems really keen on the What if? type of questions and I found this a little strange at first but in the Circulatory System, it was really easy because I had lots of my own questions and ideas. This topic just seemed to make science that much more interesting than at my old school where we would've been doing boring text book work or listening to the teacher telling us everything.

I really think that what Ms.Stanislov was doing with us was giving us the chance to develop our ideas and our questions because she knew we were interested in the topic and we already knew quite a bit about it. You see things about the circulatory system all the time on TV; shows like ER and things like that and so we do have lots of information about it. In my old school, we raised money last year in the Walkathon for the hospital's dialysis unit and because of that we learnt a lot of information about kidney disease and blood filtering because some guy from the hospital came and explained what a dialysis machine was. We even had some kids who needed dialysis come and tell us about what life was like for them, so I had a lot of ideas from that too. I bet if we did that at this school that Ms.Stanislov would've hooked into that too – at my old school the teacher didn't include it in our science classes, it was like that was something at assembly, not something about science.

Anyway, I rather liked the way we learnt about the circulatory system this time. The questions we came up with were ones that I think were much more fun to learn about than doing the normal 'teacher talks we listen and copy down notes - boring!' routine that I was used to in my old school. This time I really felt like I learnt something because I wanted to know about it.

So the questions we came up with are listed below and I think Ms.Stanislov did a good job with us because we learnt about the circulatory system and yet it didn't feel like we were doing school work. I think she got us to do more work than normal but we just seemed to want to do it. Funny about that, in the past I would only have done what I had to do, I don't ever remember doing things in school because I wanted to!

During the topic Ms.Stanislov kept on returning to our list of questions and saying, 'Have we answered this question now?' or she would help us make links across questions and that sort of thing. In the end I reckon I learnt more about the circulatory system than I realized and I learnt it in a way that I understood the ideas. I know I did, because I was able to teach my mum and dad stuff they didn't know. So I suppose changing schools wasn't such a bad thing after all, hey?

Questions we want answered

1. What causes heart attacks?
2. How does the oxygen that is pumped around the body by the heart know where it's needed?
3. Why are there blood types?
4. What are the other parts of the circulatory system besides the heart?
5. Does a blood vessel end?
6. How much water is there in the blood?
7. How long does it take for the blood to be pumped around the body?
8. What is blood pressure and how does it work?
9. How does the production of blood cells decrease with age?
10. How is your blood affected when blood is taken out (transfusions)?
11. What are varicose veins and why do old people get them?
12. How does the heart function?
13. Can the heart get too much energy and burst?
14. How do you get blood clots?
15. How much of the blood is white blood cells and how much are red, and why do we need them?
16. Are white blood cells actually white?
17. How much blood is there in an average body?
18. How much blood can be lost safely?
19. How fast can your heart normally beat? Can you control it yourself?
20. Why does a child's heart beat easier than an adult's?
21. What are blood types and why do they exist?
22. Can blood change colour?
23. How does the body reject a transplant? Why?
24. How do they keep you alive during a heart operation?

6.5: ROADWAYS

Many teaching resources about the human circulatory system draw upon a transport analogy where blood vessels are compared with roadways leading to a central location, the heart. In this PaP-eR, a teacher asks her students to create and explain a set of workable symbols for this analogy, which she calls the 'Roadways Analogy'. The purpose of this task is to extend her students' understanding of the components of the circulatory system and their specialised functions, and to highlight both the benefits and limitations of analogies for learning science content. The PaP-eR is organised to represent both the teacher's thinking about the task (left hand column), and the task in action in the classroom (right hand column). The PaP-eR begins with the teacher's description of the analogy task.

The human blood circulatory system is often represented to students as analogous to an urban road transport system. In order to develop their understanding of how such an analogy works, I ask my students, in pairs, to select and describe appropriate symbols for the various components and related organs of the circulatory system as a road transport system. I present the task in two parts. First, student pairs must decide how they will represent different types of blood vessels as elements of a road transport system. Then, I ask students to incorporate into the analogy various components of the blood circulatory system, for example, red and white blood cells. Students' choice of a symbol must be consistent with the function of the blood component it represents. The symbols must be 'sensibly' connected and the links for those connections need to be clear. On one level, I find that this task assists students to consider the adequacy of their own understanding of the various components as they attempt to create a series of workable symbols. On a more challenging level, the task encourages students to consider the adequacy, and therefore the inevitable limitations, of an analogy for representing scientific ideas.

The teacher's thinking:	The task in action:
First, the context of the analogy must be familiar to the students. In this case, students need to know about road transport systems so that later they can make appropriate links between the blood system and the road system. I show a short segment of a video in which the blood circulatory system is compared with an urban road system; then we brainstorm some ideas about this together as a class.	<u>Video segment</u>: The Blood as a Transport System <u>Brainstorm activity</u> Write on whiteboard: • What are the different parts of a road transport system? • What sorts of vehicles would you find in a road transport system? List responses under questions.
I hand out Part 1 of the task for students to complete in pairs. Most have little difficulty with this once they understand what the task requires, and students usually find it satisfying and fun selecting and describing an appropriate symbol.	<u>Excerpt from student handout:</u> *A Roadways Analogy – Part 1* In this activity, you and a partner will be making a poster sized 'map' of the human blood transport system. Your map will need to show the different parts of the blood transport system as parts of a road transport system (just as we have been talking about in class). In Part 1 of this task, you will need to decide how to represent each of the following as different parts of your road transport system map: (1) arteries (2) veins (3) capillaries (4) venules (5) arterioles (6) the heart. For each part of the blood system ask yourself: • What is the function of this? • If the blood system were a road transport system, what would this part be if it were part of the road transport system? Your map must include a key that identifies each component.
At this point, I stand back and let students get on with the task. This encourages students to be more self-reliant and gives me an opportunity to move around the room to listen carefully to what different pairs are saying.	Aaron: 'The first one is arteries.' Brent: 'What do we have to do?' Aaron: 'Think of something from the road transport system that is like arteries. You know, like Ms B. said, think of what kind of road is like an artery.' Brent: 'A freeway or something?' Aaron: 'Yeah. Okay, draw a freeway.'
Once I see that most students have finished the task (usually after about 20 minutes), I ask the class to stop and I call for volunteers to explain some of the choices they made and why. This gives students a chance to hear that there is no one "best" symbol for each component (i.e. several sensible possibilities exist for each). It also gives	

The teacher's thinking:	The task in action:
me a chance to encourage students such as Aaron and Brent (who just used the first symbols that came into their heads) to reason more through their thinking. I continue the discussion until I feel that, as much as possible, students can confidently select and think aloud their explanations for symbols for the analogy developed so far. As a result, students usually feel confident with their efforts and see the analogy as workable.	
Now it's time to introduce Part 2 of the task. Students are given a new list of more challenging terms from the blood system, and are asked to do the same task, i.e. choose workable new symbols for these terms that are consistent with the Roadways analogy.	*Excerpt from student handout:* *A Roadways Analogy – Part 2* Now, you will be adding more information to your map. Choose appropriate symbols for each of the following components of the blood system and related systems, to include on your map: (1) body cells (2) red blood cells (3) lungs (4) small intestine (5) carbon dioxide (6) sugars (7) white blood cells (8) platelets (9) oxygen. Make sure you include each of these in your map key. ***You will also need to include a written explanation of why you chose each of the symbols you have used in your map.***
This is where the real value of the task can be seen as students are challenged to really think through how this analogy works (or doesn't work). There is a big variety in students' responses – some have no idea, others try different possibilities of symbols. For some, I can see the process is frustrating but I bide my time and let them have a go at it – or, if I think it will help, sometimes I gently move students along with a question or suggestion. For example, 'What would a symbol that works for this component be like?' and 'Does that exist in a road system?'	Dina: 'Okay, so the red blood cells pick up the oxygen from the lungs and take it around the body. So we can have the red blood cell cars picking up oxygen in the lungs.' Carey: 'And drop off carbon dioxide back there again.' Dina: 'From the cars?' Carey: 'Does carbon dioxide travel around on red blood cells like oxygen does?' Dina: 'I don't know. I think so. Look it up in your book.'
I find that managing my role as a listener can be really tricky. Knowing when to join in and when to 'back off' from a group is difficult. While I need to be physically close enough to student pairs to hear what they are saying, I don't want to	

The teacher's thinking:	The task in action:
encourage students to look to me for ideas and direction just because I am there, and nor do I want to inhibit their talking because of my 'teacher presence'. It is a tricky dilemma to balance. Listening to conversations like this one by Effie and Gina gives me insight into their understandings of the blood circulatory system.	Effie: 'Sugars get dropped off at the cells from the blood. If cells are houses, then sugars could be like people going into each cell "house". Then what happens?' Gina: 'Hang on! If sugars are used up and turned into energy inside a cell, then people can't be the symbol for sugars because people don't get used up!' Effie: 'Oh yeah. Try something else.' Gina: 'We have to choose something where it doesn't matter if it gets used up because you can always get more.' Effie: 'Oh, alright, like food or something. Supermarket shopping.' Gina: 'Then how does the food get to the cell house? You can't just have food travelling along the road by itself, and it can't travel on a red blood cell.'
Gina's last two comments reveal her awareness that sugars are carried along in solution in the blood unlike oxygen which attaches to, and is transported by, red blood cells. Some students, though, do not share this insight – some, for example, have sugars being carried along by "cars". I gently probe them with questions like 'Tell me why you have used cars to transport sugar' and 'Is there a difference between the way oxygen is carried in the blood and sugar?' Sometimes this causes students to rethink their symbols but for some I have to do some "teaching", explaining that the sugars are "in" the blood.	Effie: 'This isn't going to work. Something has to carry the food.' Gina: 'Maybe this whole symbol thing would work better if it was a waterway, rather than a roadway, 'cos you could have stuff carried in the water.' Effie: 'Maybe. Or maybe it's just not possible to make it work, because it's not the same as the real thing?'
To me, the task is really successful when it pushes students' understanding to the point where, like Effie, they begin to see that the analogy breaks down, that it has limited usefulness. For this to be a helpful experience (rather than a 'turn-off') I see my role as encouraging students to work through what they know, and to ultimately recognise that the analogy will not adequately accommodate what they need it to explain. That is, they need to understand that the analogy is useful, but only up to a point, and that this is okay. Part of my teacher role is to help my students recognise when this occurs, and encourage them to see this as a good indicator of their growing understanding of the circulatory system.	

I aim to get students to see that the satisfaction in doing this task comes not from a nicely finished road map where all the symbols can be neatly selected and organised, but rather from the process of being challenged to manipulate their knowledge of the circulatory system in new ways, and of learning something about the helpfulness and limitation of analogy. However, I recognise that a task such as this operates on different levels for different students: for some, it is sufficient that the task serves as a check of their understanding of the basic structure and function of the blood circulatory system while for others, the task fulfils the additional purpose of promoting their awareness of the role of analogy in science.

6.6: WALKING THE HEART

Most students learn the names of the main components of the heart as a vocabulary exercise, a list of terms to memorise. As a consequence, students are usually able to recall these terms on demand, but they may have little sense of the connections between different parts of the heart, or how to use what they know about the heart as a basis for asking questions about how the heart functions. This PaP-eR has two parts. In the first part, the teacher introduces a role play in which students learn to walk the pathway of blood through the heart and lungs to develop a physical memory of the pathway of blood flow. In the second part of the PaP-eR, the teacher builds on the students' confidence in knowing about the heart to encourage them to go further in their thinking, by posing, and asking students to pose, questions about the functioning heart.

PART 1: ROLE PLAY – 'WALK THIS WAY'

As students enter the room they see that the tables and chairs have been pushed back and a large square has been marked on the floor in masking tape.[13] The square is divided into four parts. I tell the students that this box and its squares represent the heart and its chambers. I ask the students to form groups of three or four, and to sit together with their group. Then I give each group a short written description of the pathway of the blood through the heart to the lungs and back through the heart again.

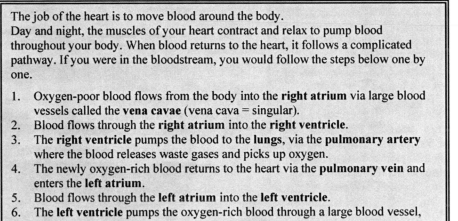

The job of the heart is to move blood around the body.
Day and night, the muscles of your heart contract and relax to pump blood throughout your body. When blood returns to the heart, it follows a complicated pathway. If you were in the bloodstream, you would follow the steps below one by one.

1. Oxygen-poor blood flows from the body into the **right atrium** via large blood vessels called the **vena cavae** (vena cava = singular).
2. Blood flows through the **right atrium** into the **right ventricle**.
3. The **right ventricle** pumps the blood to the **lungs**, via the **pulmonary artery** where the blood releases waste gases and picks up oxygen.
4. The newly oxygen-rich blood returns to the heart via the **pulmonary vein** and enters the **left atrium**.
5. Blood flows through the **left atrium** into the **left ventricle**.
6. The **left ventricle** pumps the oxygen-rich blood through a large blood vessel, the **aorta**, to all parts of the body.

I ask the students to decide, in their groups, which part of the heart each box represents, and to discuss the pathway of blood around the heart. Since many of them are already familiar with some of these ideas from earlier studies, students can usually do this fairly quickly and with little difficulty.

Next, I provide each group with a labelled card (for example, right atrium). Each group must decide which part of the diagram their card matches, and then one member of the group sticks the card to the floor in the appropriate place. Some structures (e.g. aorta, lungs) are not already marked on the floor, so groups with such labels need to realise this and work out an appropriate place on the floor to represent the structure using masking tape, and then position the label for each of these new parts. There is usually a lot of discussion and negotiation within and between groups as students decide where to place their cards. When the class is satisfied that all of the groups have correctly placed their parts, we then proceed to walk the pathway of the blood through the heart. Before we begin to walk I ask all the students to silently look at the floor diagram we have created and to imagine the pathway of the blood as it moves around the

---

[13] Sometimes we go outside and I use chalk to mark out the boundaries of the square.

heart. I find that having this quiet time helps to give more students an opportunity to think through what they know before we start the doing.

Then I ask for a volunteer to walk the path of the blood. As the student walks, I ask him/her to tell the rest of the class which structures s/he is passing through. Then the rest of the group joins in and together the whole class follows in a line along the pathway of the heart-lung blood circulation. I stand on a chair, keeping an eye on proceedings and every few moments I call out 'Stop!' and name a few students who must state which structure they are currently passing through, where they have come from and where they are heading to. For example:

Me: 'Josh, where are you now?'

Josh: 'In the lungs'

Me: 'How did you get there?'

Josh: 'Through the pulmonary artery'

Me: 'Where are you off to next?'

Josh: 'The pulmonary vein'

Me: 'On your way to…?'

Josh: 'The left atrium'

Me: 'OK, thanks!'

I find that an activity such as this helps to consolidate students' learning of the blood pathway, through creating a physical memory by walking. Students usually find this a fun, relatively easy task to complete.

What I have found interesting in using a task like this is that in the informal set-up, students seem to feel quite relaxed and tend to talk more about their thinking about the heart and other circulatory system related issues. For instance, on a couple of occasions, students have told me that the right and left sides of the heart as they are laid out on the floor are "around the wrong way". The mirror image problem then is something we can discuss as a class. I ask one student to lie on the floor next to the heart and ask, 'Which is the left side of the heart? Which is the right side?' Students can then see that representations of the heart are organised as though they are looking at someone else's heart, rather than their own. This seems to help with their difficulty. Another regularly recurring problem that tends to arise during the walking activity is that students don't know where to go after they have left the aorta, before they return to the vena cava. Again, their uncertainty provides an opportunity to discuss how the heart is linked to the circulatory system and why, rather than being just a disconnected 'thing on its own'[14].

When students are feeling confident that they know the pathway well, I can challenge their thinking about the structure and function of the heart with the next part of this activity.

PART 2: PROBLEMS OF THE HEART. 'WHAT WOULD HAPPEN IF … ?'

A core issue in learning Biology involves developing learners' understanding of the important relationship between structure and function. In the second part of this PaP-eR, the teacher draws on this important principle of Biology as she helps her students learn about the structure/function relationship of the mammalian heart. Drawing on students' newly developed confidence of heart structure (from Part 1 above), the teacher now challenges her students to think through and explain the possible outcomes of particular changes to either the structure, or functioning of the heart.

Students return to their groups, sitting around the floor diagram of the heart. Each group is handed a 'problem of the heart' to discuss, including some information relevant to that problem. The task for each group is to discuss together the problem situation they have been given, then use the floor diagram of the heart to show to the rest of the class what would happen to the flow of blood, and describe the possible effects on the body of that problem.

Typically, the problems I hand out are in the form of, 'What would happen if …?' type questions. For example:

- What would happen if a baby were born with a hole in the wall separating the left and right sides of heart?
- What would happen if the pulmonary vein and the pulmonary artery were reversed (i.e. interchanged)?
- What would happen if the thicknesses of the chambers of the heart were reversed (i.e. right was much more thick and muscular than the left hand side)?

---

[14]The problem of students thinking about the heart as a "thing" on its own, not linked to the rest of the circulatory system, is explored in the Human Circulatory System PaP-eR, 'Not Just a Thing, but a Need for a Function.'

- What would happen if the valve between the atrium and ventricle stopped working?
- What would happen if the aorta had a blockage?

As each group acts out their heart problem, the rest of the class is watching. Then, following each group's presentation, I ask a couple of the observer students to describe to the rest of the class what the presenting group has shown. I find that this provides an opportunity for students to clarify what they have seen, and for the presenting group to get feedback on what they have done from an observer's point of view. This can be helpful to the presenters who may then need to further clarify aspects of their performance, and for the observers, who through this process are developing their understanding of the problem being explored.

At this time, too, students tend to raise other issues, for example, what happens in a heart attack? Do all animals have a heart the same as this? Where does blood come from in the first place? The students are often very interested in diseases of the heart as they have heard about or have family members who have suffered from heart disease.

PART 3: 'IT'S A GREAT ACTIVITY, BUT HOW DOES IT HELP THEM WITH THE REAL THING?'

My experiences of using this activity over several years of teaching about the circulatory system have led me to recognise it is a great tool for learning about the pathway of blood flow through the heart and engaging students in thinking about how structure relates to function in the heart. At the same time, however, I am faced with a dilemma. Using an unrealistic box shape to set up my students' thinking about the heart is quite unhelpful to their learning about the structures of a real heart. I know that when they actually look at a real (sheep's) heart, these students will find it extremely difficult to identify atria, ventricles and major blood vessels by size, shape and location because they look so different in reality. (In fact, I find it quite difficult to identify all of these structures myself.) The structures that we have neatly represented in our floor diagram (and that are reproduced in the same ways in the various texts that students regularly see) are convenient schematic views. They do not translate directly on to the actual structures. The text book simplifications of the heart structures are designed to help make clear the pathway of blood flow, but at the same time they become an obstacle to learning about the real heart organ. However, for me, the whole point at this stage is for my students to be able to get a 'feel for the flow' rather than worry about a realistic shape just yet. I know I can deal with the reality shock next.

6.7: MAPPING STUDENTS' KNOWLEDGE OF THE CIRCULATORY SYSTEM

Teaching about the circulatory system presents particular challenges to science teachers because students are often already quite familiar with this topic through their experiences at school (the circulatory system tends to be regularly revisited within the science curriculum, as well as other curriculum areas e.g. physical education or health), and through students' own life experiences. Familiarity with the topic may lead students to quickly disengage from their learning because they believe that they 'already know it'. The challenge for science teachers therefore, is to implement teaching approaches that enable students to (re)engage with the ideas as well as develop and extend their understanding of the topic. This PaP-eR is presented as an excerpt from a discussion between an experienced and a less experienced teacher about an approach to teaching about the circulatory system that acknowledges and builds on these challenges. The PaP-eR is presented in three parts. Part 1 introduces the reasons why the concept mapping task is used, in Part 2 the teachers examine some examples of concept maps together and Part 3 occurs later in the teaching of the topic as the teachers together examine some of the changes they see in the student concept maps that have occurred over the time of the unit.

PART 1: WHY CONCEPT MAPPING?

In Part 1, Sal, a teacher, identifies a problem in teaching about the circulatory system to her middle school science class. She discusses this problem with Rena, her more experienced colleague, who is also teaching this topic to her class. Together they discuss the problem and explore an approach that Rena has developed to address it.

Sal: … As soon as I mentioned to the class that our next topic would be the circulatory system, the groans started up. 'We've done this already! Why are we doing it again?' And I have to say it was hard for me to give them a convincing answer. Students do seem to have had lots of experiences with this topic over the years. So this is a problem for me. I don't want to teach them things that they already know, but on the other hand I still think there are new things they can learn. I'm not sure what to do. What have you been doing with your class? How do you start this topic?

Rena: Choosing how to begin teaching about the circulatory system often leaves me in a bit of a dilemma, too. Students are familiar with the basic components of the blood system because they've met this topic not only at school but also through their own everyday experiences! This is different from some other science topics we teach, because it means engaging students' interest in something that they may feel they already know quite well. What I often find though, is that while many students can recite off a list of terms and simple definitions about the blood system, not so many of them have actually moved beyond this level to an understanding of how the various components link together to form a functioning system. I guess they assume that because they know the terms that they understand the system.

Sal: Yes, I can see that could be a problem that I will be facing with my students, too.

Rena: So, something I do now when I teach this topic to a new group is to start by finding out about what each student already knows, including the kinds of connections they are making between the bits of knowledge they have. I do this by asking them to draw a concept map. First they brainstorm in pairs a list of words that are related to the circulatory system. Then I ask them to each choose no more than 10 words from their list and individually to create a concept map that shows these words and also shows any links that they see between any of the words. I find this is a helpful activity for me and for them. I get to see the range of terms they are already familiar with and the kinds of links they are making, and they can get a picture from their maps of how they 'see' what they currently know.

Sal: Okay. And I like it that this activity actually acknowledges that students already know something about this topic.

Rena: Yes! It also gives students a chance to express their ideas individually because each student gets to choose their own words and makes links that are sensible to them. I find that this is a useful starting approach because they already know a reasonable amount about the topic. But it's not a way that I would use to start off a topic that is less familiar to students, for example chemical bonding, because most of them don't yet have the knowledge of terms or links about that topic to make concept mapping a useful activity.

Sal: I think I see what you mean. So, do you explain to your students how to do a concept map first?

Rena: I don't worry about this so much at the start. If they have no idea I tell them it is a way of showing how different words relate to each other and I might show a brief example. But I try not to get too detailed about it. Mostly they have some sort of understanding of a concept map and even if it is not exactly the same as the way I think a concept map should be, the most important part of the activity at this stage is that they are making a list of the terms they know and starting to think about in what ways the terms might be linked with each other.

Sal: Hmm, I'm thinking that could be a really nice way of tracking their learning through the unit. You know, give it back to them at the end of the unit and see what they write?

Rena: Yes. I even give it back to them a couple of times during the unit and ask them to write on any new words or new links that they can make. If they use a different coloured pen each time they can get a good visual sense of their progress. I think that students can find it quite satisfying to see that even something that many of them think they know well can be developed further. Of course it helps me to track changes in their thinking, too. Another important thing about this being an ongoing task is that I also want them to develop their understanding of what is a good concept map, so although I'm not too worried about how they do their maps initially, I do want them to learn to do a concept map 'properly'. So to assist this, each time we revisit the concept maps we discuss things like what is a link on a concept map, what would it show, etc? At the end of the unit I ask them to draw a 'final' map that incorporates the changes they have made.

Sal: So what sorts of differences do you see in their initial concept mapping efforts?

Rena: It's differences and similarities that interest me. For example, my science class has just finished their first circulatory system concept map and I can already see that there are a number of terms that all of them use, like heart, blood, white blood cell, red blood cell. That's great because it means that I know they've at least heard about these terms before – it's not new vocab for them, although they may not have well developed understandings of the meaning of the terms. And that's okay because it can be developed. Another thing I noticed from their maps is that some students seem to think that all arteries carry oxygenated blood and all veins carry deoxygenated. Alright, so we'll have to do a little work on that. I also look at the links that they make or those they don't make. Then I think how can I explore these ideas with students in teaching this unit? Over the years I've put together a few activities to target particular connections that I think are important and that I want to develop with my students. If you want, I can show you some.

Sal: That would be great. Can I see some of the maps they've drawn?

Rena: Okay let's look at a few examples together.

PART 2: WHAT DO THE CONCEPT MAPS SHOW?

In Part 2, the two teachers examine several of the students' concept maps in order to learn about these students' knowledge of the components of the human circulatory system and the understandings revealed by the links students between these various components, and consider implications for teaching.

Rena: We have just completed the concept-mapping task in class, so this is my students' first attempt at mapping what they know. When you look at Ross's map you can see that he seems to have a pretty good grasp of a range of terms related to the circulatory system. Something that I now do when I look at students' maps is to make a list of the terms that students use so I can compare this with the terms I want them to know. Sometimes I compile this list myself, other times we do it together as a class and we make a chart of the terms that we know so far.

Sal: Ross seems to have organized his map into sections. Like the top bit is about the pathway of blood from the body, through the heart and back off to the body. The left hand side is related to blood vessel types and the right has information about components of blood. That's interesting. It's as though he has three different 'chunks' of information about the circulatory system. I wonder if he thinks of each 'chunk' as related to the others?

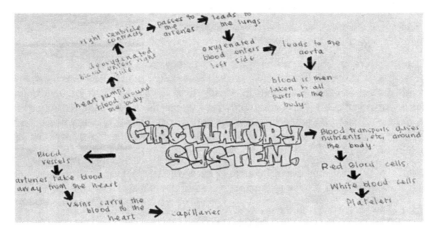

Ross's initial concept map

Rena: Yes, it's almost as though on his map he is showing the physical layout of the body, isn't it? My intention in teaching this unit is to help students learn that a concept map is not a 'picture' that is supposed to look like the thing we are studying, but it's a diagram that shows the relationship between the concepts. I think that can be quite a difficult idea for them to learn.

Sal: I know it's difficult for me! So I imagine it would be quite difficult for these students.

Rena: When I look at Ross's map I also wonder about how he sees the relationship between capillaries and veins or arteries? Capillaries are there but it is not clear what their connection is to the other vessels. It looks a similar situation with the components of blood, too. I wonder how he sees the relationship between red cells, white cells and nutrients? Experience tells me that a few kids will struggle to know what is the role of different blood components, what nutrients are, and how they are carried, and perhaps that is the case for Ross. On the whole though, he seems to have a good overview of the different parts of this system. Here's another example. This one's from Tina.

Rena: Tina seems to have a reasonable grasp of the knowledge here and she is making some clear links between different terms, although she has not written on many of her linking lines the nature of those links. She sees the heart as comprised of chambers and that the heart carries blood. Her map seems more focused on the oxygen carrying aspect of the circulatory system and I'm pretty sure this is because she is also studying Phys.Ed. so perhaps that has influenced her approach. But there is a problem here, too. She has shown oxygenated blood being transported to the lungs, so that's not right, and she doesn't seem to be making a connection between the lungs and exhaling – though maybe that's just the way she drew the map.

Sal: She seems to be connecting up the ideas a bit more than Ross and she has a link between arteries, veins and capillaries, but there is no explanation to say what the link is.

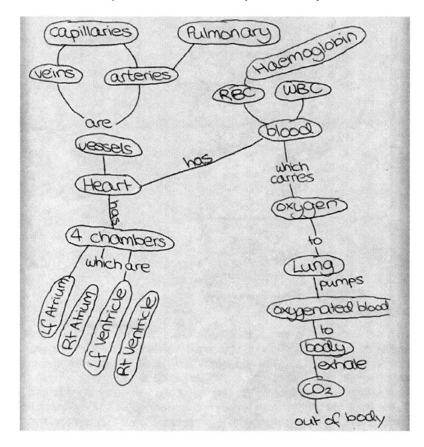

Tina's initial concept map

Rena: That's where the idea of helping students learn about what a concept map is can be really helpful for bringing out those extra elements of students' knowledge. She may have a good sense of the link in her head but not expect to have to write it on the map. It will be interesting to watch how Tina's map changes over the unit. Let's try one more. Take a look at Janine's map.

Sal: Wow! She seems to have a good grasp of the topic already, and the idea of a how concept map works. I can see now how the mapping task really highlights differences between students.

Rena: Yes, I find that doing tasks like this is a really helpful reminder for me that I can't just assume that all of my students know the same things. And it is easy to fall into the trap of thinking that way in teaching a unit if I start off giving them what I think they need to learn, instead of letting the students tell me what they know. Janine has a great network of links that give a sense of the circulatory system as a functioning whole. One thing about Janine's map, though, is that she has too many links for a good concept map. I'd like to see her reduce the number of links, by selecting say 8-10 terms at most and really thinking hard about the nature of the links between those terms. I'll be aiming to do that with the other students too – help them keep the number of terms manageable and really work at the links.

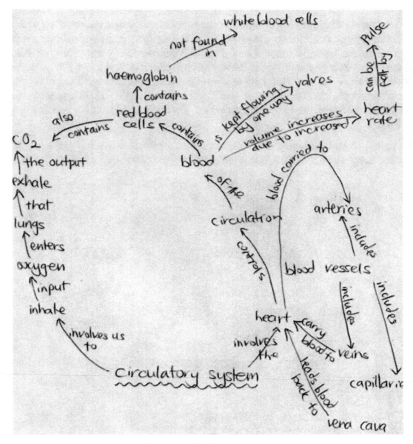

Janine's initial concept map

Sal: So what happens next with this class?

Rena: Next class? Because they only had time to draw their maps today I need to give them a chance to think a little more about what they have drawn. So tomorrow what I will do is mix students up around the room and get them to explain to each other about their concept maps. I find that in this way it can help students become more aware of what they know, because maybe they knew more than they wrote and when they say it to each other these ideas can come out. I'll ask them to focus on the idea of the linking lines a little more, to say what it is that links one word with another, too. Then if they want to, they will have a chance to modify their maps using a different coloured pen. At this stage I try to reassure them that one exciting part about this unit is that they can watch their own knowledge develop, seeing new colours and new lines on the map. It is important to reassure them that they must not feel that they have to know it all at the beginning.

Sal: Do you think I could come along and watch?

Rena: Sure! In fact it would be really helpful for me because I struggle to get around to listen to all of their explanations. I like them to have a go at explaining to me as well as each other so as to push them a little more for clarification or other ideas that they might have.

Sal: It will give me a chance to see this task in action too, so that I can work out how I might use it with my class.

PART 3: REVISITING THE CONCEPT MAPS

Part 3 takes up the conversation later in the unit as Sal and Rena explore an example of one student's revised work. The two teachers consider changes in the nature of links made by the student, organization of the concept map, and how this helps reveal the student's understanding about the circulatory system and about understanding the procedure of concept mapping.

Sal: … How are your class going with their concept maps? Have they completed their final ones yet?

Rena: Yes. In fact, when I look at what they have done I feel really pleased that a number of them have shown significant progress in their learning about the circulatory system. Remember Tina's map? Look at what she has just handed in.

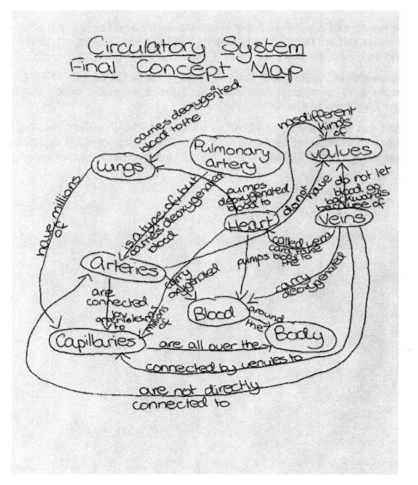

Tina's final concept map

Sal: There's a lot on this map! Especially the linking lines, there's so much more information on them now!

Rena: I think she has done a great job. She's got fewer terms on her map and mostly she has been able to pick out key ideas and describe the relationships between them. Before she didn't really explain how veins, arteries and capillaries were linked and she has been much more explicit about those links here. She has also been able to incorporate new terms we have learnt like venules and arterioles correctly into her map.

Sal: I like that she has included capillaries being found in the heart as well as all over the body. This shows she is really thinking about the structure of the heart as well as its function.

Rena: She has also picked up on the idea that valves are not just found in the heart. That's great. Also, I really tried to stress with them the idea of deoxygenated blood as not being completely deoxygenated, and when I quizzed her about that on her map she really had that idea.

Sal: Hmm, I can see that a great deal of information about students' learning can be revealed through a concept-mapping task such as this. I can't wait to see what the students from my class produce for their final maps.

6.8: COMMENTING ON THE CORE

This PaP-eR is designed to illustrate the range of views and ideas that teachers have when thinking about the CoRe as the big picture for a unit of work.

Central to the structure of this PaP-eR is that in considering the teaching of a unit of work, there are a number of issues that are foremost in a teacher's mind that are signposts of the development of students' understanding of the topic.

In this particular PaP-eR, highlighting some of these issues in the context of the CoRe itself is intended to make more concrete the observable links between experience and the development of a science teacher's pedagogical content knowledge.

It is anticipated, that in developing the PaP-eR as a form of 'jottings' on the CoRe, that it will bring to life one aspect of considering the teaching of a unit of work in ways that experienced teachers might do in preparing their 'global unit plan' or explicit indications of important learning outcomes.

I don't make much of the idea that it's closed because my students don't know what an open system is. They tend to implicitly assume it's closed.

Some students find this confusing. I tell them it's like the figure 8 and goes through the heart and back twice but to different parts of the heart to separate oxyaenated and deoxygenated blood.

I wouldn't expect Year 9 and 10 students to get a good grip of this.

I stop at 'the cell has a membrane which is like an outside barrier' (and leave it at that until Year 11)

I talk about force of contraction making blood flow, not the relationship with blood pressure (unless a student asks about their granny's blood pressure). Again I operate on a need to know basis in terms of the depth of treatment of ideas.

When explaining absorption in the stomach, for example, I just say food is absorbed. Students don't question this – it's a term they probably think they know and aren't aware that there is a deeper meaning – and I don't offer it to them because they have no need to know at this stage.

This is something I always want to know when I first teach a topic.

It's important for students to experience the difficulty of _not_ finding things as they seem in textbooks (e.g., looking at a cell under a microscope).

Students in both my Year 8 and 11 classes often show they _do_ relate body systems. They tend to ask questions like "So when we've exercised and our hearts are beating faster, is that why we breathe harder. They want to get things clarified so they can understand what is happening.

At Year 11, I give them the analogy of a fuel tanker – it carries fuel but doesn't use this for energy: instead it uses its own supply.

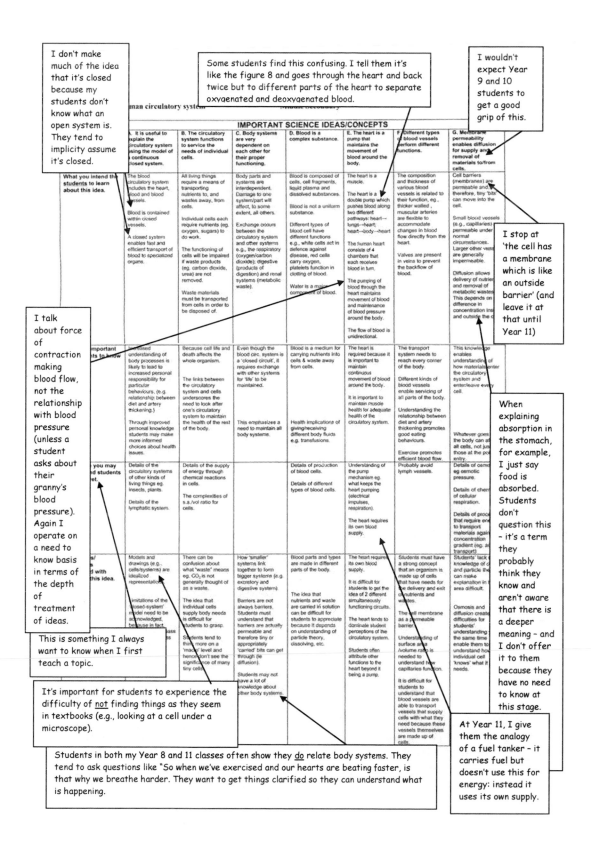

Human circulatory system — Middle Secondary

IMPORTANT SCIENCE IDEAS/CONCEPTS

	A. It is useful to explain the circulatory system using the model of a continuous closed system.	B. The circulatory system functions to service the needs of individual cells.	C. Body systems are very dependent on each other for their proper functioning.	D. Blood is a complex substance.	E. The heart is a pump that maintains the movement of blood around the body.	F. Different types of blood vessels perform different functions.	G. Membrane permeability enables diffusion for supply and removal of materials to/from cells.
What you intend the students to learn about this idea.	The blood circulatory system includes the heart, blood and blood vessels. Blood is contained within closed vessels. A closed system enables fast and efficient transport of blood to specialized organs.	All living things require a means of transporting nutrients to, and wastes away, from each cell. Individual cells each require nutrients (eg. oxygen, sugars) to do work. The functioning of cells will be impaired if waste products (eg. carbon dioxide, urea) are not removed. Waste materials must be transported from cells in order to be disposed of.	Body parts and systems are interdependent. Damage to one system/part will affect, to each other extent, all others. Exchange occurs between the circulatory system and other systems e.g., the respiratory (oxygen/carbon dioxide); digestive (products of digestion) and renal systems (metabolic waste).	Blood is composed of cells, cell fragments, liquid plasma and dissolved substances. Blood is not a uniform substance. Different types of blood cell have different functions e.g., white cells act in defence against disease, red cells carry oxygen, platelets function in clotting of blood. Water is a major component of blood.	The heart is a muscle. The heart is a double pump which pushes blood along two different pathways: heart→lungs→heart; heart→body→heart. The human heart consists of 4 chambers that each receives blood in turn. The pumping of blood through the heart maintains movement of blood and maintenance of blood pressure around the body. The flow of blood is unidirectional.	The composition and thickness of various blood vessels is related to their function, eg., thicker walled, muscular arteries are flexible to accommodate changes in blood flow directly from the heart. Valves are present in veins to prevent the backflow of blood.	Cell barriers (membranes) are permeable and therefore, tiny 'bits' can move into the cell. Small blood vessels (e.g., capillaries) permeable under normal circumstances. Larger other vessels are generally impermeable. Diffusion allows delivery of nutrients and removal of metabolic wastes. This depends on difference in concentration ins... and outside the c...
[Why is it] important [for studen]ts to know [this idea.]	...creased understanding of body processes is likely to lead to increased personal responsibility for particular behaviours. (e.g. relationship between diet and artery thickening.) Through improved personal knowledge students may make more informed choices about health issues.	Because cell life and death affects the whole organism. The links between the circulatory system and cells underscores the need to look after one's circulatory system to maintain the health of the rest of the body.	Even though the blood circ. system is a 'closed circuit', it requires exchange with other systems for 'life' to be maintained. This emphasises a need to maintain all body systems.	Blood is a medium for carrying nutrients into cells & waste away from cells. Health implications of giving/receiving different body fluids e.g. transfusions.	The heart is required because it is important to maintain continuous movement of blood around the body. It is important to maintain muscle health for adequate health of the circulatory system.	The transport system needs to reach every corner of the body. Different kinds of blood vessels enable servicing of all parts of the body. Understanding the relationship between diet and artery thickening promotes good eating behaviours. Exercise promotes efficient blood flow.	This knowledge enables understanding of how materials enter the circulatory system and enter/leave every cell. Whatever goes into the body can all cells, not just those at the po... entry.
[What else] you may [know that] students [don't need to know] yet.	Details of the circulatory systems of other kinds of living things eg. insects, plants. Details of the lymphatic system.	Details of the supply of energy through chemical reactions in cells. The complexities of s.a./vol ratio for cells.		Details of production of blood cells. Details of different types of blood cells.	Understanding of the pump mechanism eg. what keeps the heart pumping (electrical impulses, respiration). The heart requires its own blood supply.	Probably avoid lymph vessels.	Details of osmosis eg osmotic pressure. Details of chem... of cellular respiration. Details of proc... that require ene... to transport materials again... concentration gradient (eg. a... transport)
[Teaching procedures/issues connecte]d with [teaching] this idea.	Models and drawings (e.g. ...culatory systems) are idealized representations. ...imitations of the ...losed-system' model need to be acknowledged, because in fact...	There can be confusion about what 'waste' means eg. CO2 is not generally thought of as a waste. The idea that individual cells supply body needs is difficult to grasp. Students tend to think more on a 'macro' level and hence don't see the significance of many tiny cells.	How 'smaller' systems link together to form bigger systems (e.g. excretory and digestive system). Barriers are not always barriers. Students must understand that barriers are actually permeable and therefore tiny or appropriately 'carried' bits can get through (ie diffusion). Students may not have a lot of knowledge about other body systems.	Blood parts and types are made in different parts of the body. The idea that nutrients and waste are carried in solution can be difficult for students to appreciate because it depends on understanding of particle theory, dissolving, etc.	The heart requires its own blood supply. It is difficult for students to get the idea of 2 different simultaneously functioning circuits. The heart tends to dominate student perceptions of the circulatory system. Students often attribute other functions to the heart beyond it being a pump.	Students must have knowledge of cells that have needs for the delivery and exit of nutrients and wastes. The cell membrane as a permeable barrier. Understanding of surface area /volume ratio is needed to understand how capillaries function. It is difficult for students to understand that blood vessels are able to transport vessels that supply cells with what they need because these vessels themselves are made up of cells.	Students' lack of knowledge of and particle theory can make explanation in ... area difficult. Osmosis and diffusion create difficulties for students' understanding the same time enable them to understand how individual cell 'knows' what it needs.

115

Students tend to acquire the idea of a closed system gradually as they learn about all the parts.

Some students expect to see a ♥ and are surprised when they are presented with a lump of meat.

During the dissection, I tend to check with each group that they have observed this.

Students in my Year 7 class find this "mind blowing".

I think my students do have this idea because I use it to explain burping and farting to Year 8 (who love talking about this kind of thing!)

The secondary students I encounter are not fond of role plays.

Students are often surprised by the small amount of vibration of the heart – the squeeze and contraction happens much faster than they expected.

I probably wouldn't do this with Year 8s because I would want to make too chemical an explanation.

Concept maps are useful for finding out what students do and don't know.

When dissecting a sheep's heart, students ask questions like, "How big is the atrium really?" which tells me they know what they see is not the whole thing.

When they watch a video of open-heart surgery, students often say/ask things like: "Oh gee the heart's going fast!" and "Why is it wobbling like that Miss?"

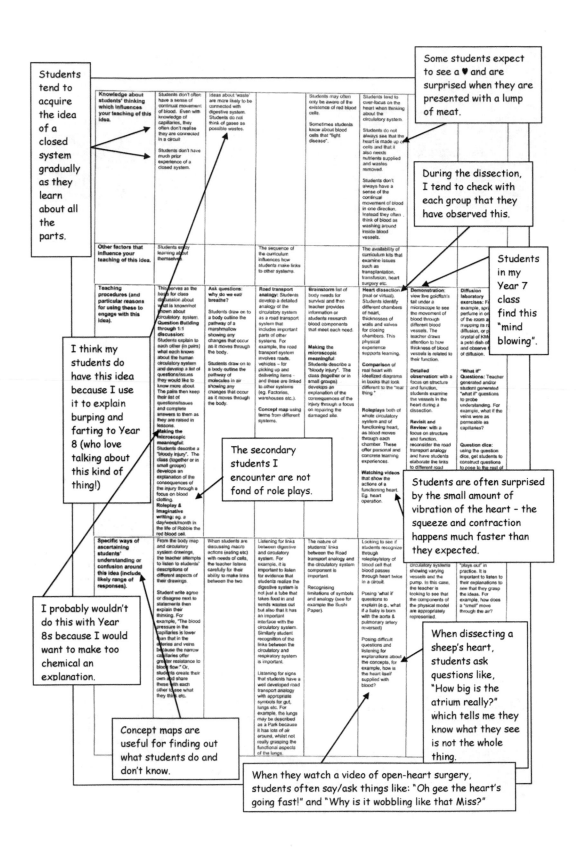

FORCE

This chapter outlines a representation of Pedagogical Content Knowledge (PCK) for the topic Force. Just as in the case of Chapter Five (Chemical Reactions) for this topic we again offer two CoRes as opposed to the single CoRe approach of the topics in Chapters 4, 6 and 8. However, in Chapter Five, the two CoRes represented different teachers' framing of the content, whereas in this chapter, the two CoRes were generated by the same teachers and represent different aspects of teaching about Force, viz. teaching about stationary objects, and about moving objects. Hence, the format for this chapter is a little different to that of the other topics as it includes a first CoRe (Part One: Stationary objects) followed by a second CoRe (Part Two: Moving Objects).

The two parts of the CoRe assume, then, a sequence of teaching that focuses on developing understanding of the forces involved, firstly, in situations where objects are stationary and, secondly, when objects are moving. Inevitably, however, it is not practical to, or even desirable, to follow this division strictly when teaching: indeed, in the first part of the CoRe, situations involving moving objects are used early on to explore students' ideas about force. The presentation in this manner is simply to make the breakdown of the ideas easier to follow and understand.

REMINDERS ABOUT SHAPING FACTORS THAT INFLUENCE CoRe(s) AND PaP-eRs

As is the case with each of the concrete examples of PCK that comprise Chapters 4 – 9, we briefly offer some of the important points that shape our understanding of representing PCK. Repeating this information at the start of each of the chapters (Resource Folios) is designed to remind the reader about the nature of this form of representation of PCK and for that information to be "on hand" for each individual topic portrayed.

Therefore, some of the important points to be kept in mind when considering that which follows in this Resource Folio are that:

- It is very difficult to offer a single example of PCK that is a neat concrete package, able to be analysed and dissected or used as a blueprint for practice by others. Therefore, our approach to capturing and portraying PCK hinges on the understanding that the teaching and the content must be represented in ways that both maintains the complexity of their relationships, but at the same time offers some way of seeing through the complexity in order to gain insight into it.
- Our approach is based on what we have termed a CoRe (Content Representation) and PaP-eRs (Pedagogical and Professional-experience Repertoire). The CoRe outlines some of the aspects of PCK "most attached to that content" but it is not the only representation. It is a necessary, but incomplete, generalization that helps to make the complexity accessible and manageable; it is neither complete nor absolute. Attached to the CoRe are the PaP-eRs, with links to the aspects of this field that they "bring to life". A PaP-eR is of a content area and must allow the reader to look inside a teaching/learning situation in which the content shapes the pedagogy.
- PaP-eRs bring the CoRe to life and shed new light on the complex nature of PCK. They help create ways to better understand and value the specialist knowledge, skills and ability of teachers, thus making that which is so often tacit, explicit for others.

PART ONE: STATIONARY OBJECTS

This Core is designed for students in Middle Secondary School, i.e. Year 10.			**IMPORTANT SCIENCE**
	A: A force is a push or pull.	**B:** Objects distort when forces are put on them. That causes them to exert a force on the object that distorted them.	**C:** Objects that are stationary always have an equal balance of forces acting on them.
What you intend the <u>students</u> to learn about this idea.	A force is a push or a pull **only**. A force on an object is **external** to the object.	Reaction forces (usually) occur because an object distorts (as a result of a force acting on it). Rigid things don't need as much distortion to exert the same (reaction) force as non-rigid things. Reaction forces are real (vs. convenient and imaginary).	If an object is at rest then it must have balanced forces acting on it, i.e. the net force is zero.
Why it is important for students to know this.	Teacher must establish this first or risk students making alternative constructions of everything else, i.e. it establishes a common language necessary for communication of ideas. It helps students to identify what force is: 1) if you can't say what it is that is pushing/pulling, it probably isn't a force; 2) if what is pushing/pulling is not external to the object, it isn't a force on that object.	The distortion explanation is important as otherwise reaction forces seem to merely be an artificial convention.	This is important for understanding one aspect of Newton's first law (i.e. an object at rest will remain at rest unless acted upon by a net force).
What else <u>you</u> know about this idea (that you do not intend students to know yet).	In scientific terms, a force produces accelerated motion. However, that would be a poor way to start teaching about force. At this level, drawings of forces involving arrows to represent direction and magnitude of force assume objects are point masses. From the outset, the teacher follows this convention for his/her own arrow drawings, but does not usually make explicit to students the assumption about point mass. These ideas are gradually made explicit.	The idea of distortion is enough: there isn't a need to draw out the notion of action-reaction pairs (i.e. Newton's third law) because this isn't helpful for developing the idea of distortion.	Early on avoid field forces. A key idea when fleshing out the forces on an object is that when object A exerts an (action) force, there is a (reaction) force back in the opposite direction on object A. It is important not to spend time trying prove that the action and reaction forces are equal in size. If the teacher uses the term 'net force', then it needs to be made explicit that this is the sum of the actual, real forces i.e. the teacher should avoid using the physicists' convention that reduces all discussion to a consideration of just net force, because this clouds students' understanding.

IDEAS/CONCEPTS		
D: **Frictional forces are caused by distortion of two surfaces sliding over each other.**	**E:** **Reaction forces occur in pairs. Each force in a pair acts on a different object.**	**F:** **Field reaction forces are forces between objects that are not touching. Field reaction forces are not due to distortion of an object.**
Frictional interactions result in real forces and are due to tiny bumps on surfaces.	Reaction forces occur in pairs. Each force in a pair acts on a different object.	Field reaction forces (gravitational, magnetic, electric) are the exceptions to the idea that forces cause distortion.
There is a need to establish frictional interactions as leading to sideways forces on surfaces, in order to explain the motion ofobjects later (e.g. objects slowing down, how we walk etc). It is helpful to establish frictional interactions as a "good guy" as well as an impediment. That is, friction can be helpful; friction is not always a "bad thing" (e.g. walking).	This is important for understanding the forces acting in a given situation; for identifying the forces on a given object; and for understanding Newton's third law (i.e. when object B exerts a force on object A, object A exerts an equal force on object B in the opposite direction).	The idea of a field is useful for explaining action at a distance (i.e. how an object can experience a force without anything touching it). The concept of gravity is needed to explain everyday experiences such as falling objects, weight etc.
Direction of forces due to frictional interactions on unpowered wheels.	Action-reaction forces are equal in magnitude.	It is hard to understand what is being distorted for a field force.

PART ONE: STATIONARY OBJECTS

	A: A force is a push or pull.	B: Objects distort when forces are put on them. That causes them to exert a force on the object that distorted them.	C: Objects that are stationary always have an equal balance of forces acting on them.
Difficulties/ limitations connected with teaching this idea.	The idea that a force is a push/pull is NOT tricky, BUT the idea that the force on an object is external to an object IS often problematic for students. These ideas take a long time to develop. Not being clear about the conventions for representing force (especially that the arrow is drawn with the tail at the point of application of the force, and that we assume point mass) can lead to students misinterpreting diagrams and cause the development of alternative conceptions.	It is hard to believe that rigid objects distort.	
Knowledge about students' thinking which influences your teaching of this idea.	Sometimes it is the terminology that causes a problem rather than the concept itself. Finding ways of drawing the distinction matters. Students tend to think all moving things must have something pushing or pulling them, e.g. a ball moving through the air keeps moving because the initial "throw force" is somehow still attached to it and keeps it moving. Often when students talk about the force within an object, what they really mean is 'kinetic energy' or 'momentum'.	Most students don't hold a notion of distortion despite having lots of experience of distortion, e.g. trampolines, springs. Where distortion is quite obvious, students will accept there is a force. The idea that a table pushes up on objects sitting on it is one that some students find very hard to believe and they may even have learned to say that the table is pushing up, but if probed, will likely say, 'Not really,' i.e. conceptual change is evolutionary, not revolutionary.	Students quickly decide for themselves that if something is at rest it must have balanced forces acting on it; much of the early discussion assumes this and only later (when discussing Newton's first law) is this made explicit.

D: Frictional forces are caused by distortion of two surfaces sliding over each other.	E: Reaction forces occur in pairs. Each force in a pair acts on a different object.	F: Field reaction forces are forces between objects that are not touching. Field reaction forces are not due to distortion of an object.
In everyday (and often scientific use) the word 'friction' is used as equivalent to 'force'. This is confusing for students because it does not make explicit the agent of the (frictional) force. e.g. it is hard to tell what is causing the force if one refers to the 'friction on the shoe'; the 'frictional force of the floor on the shoe' is a better expression because the agent is made clear. 'Friction' is best used to refer to a type of interaction, not a force.	Confusion often arises when students forget that the forces in an action-reaction pair act on different objects; instead, students mistakenly think they act on the same object and balance each other, resulting in a net force of zero (i.e. Newton's third law paradox).	The idea that falling objects get faster and faster because gravity increases as they fall is a commonly held alternative conception. 'Gravitational interactions' might be a better way of talking about the 'force of gravity' because 'force of gravity' may imply that gravity is a 'thing'.
Students often believe frictional interactions lead to a 'wearing away'. Therefore they often see frictional interactions as bad rather than useful.		Referring to gravitational interactions as 'gravity' may lead some students to believing that gravity is due to air pressure (i.e. a push from above) or the earth spinning.

PART ONE: STATIONARY OBJECTS

	A: A force is a push or pull.	B: Objects distort when forces are put on them. That causes them to exert a force on the object that distorted them.	C: Objects that are stationary always have an equal balance of forces acting on them.
Other factors that influence your teaching of this idea.	Interpretive discussion facilitated by the teacher is particularly valuable in this area as students' prior knowledge and experiences mean they are often better placed to challenge and convince one another. Students can be reluctant to commit their ideas to paper so the teacher needs to work on building their confidence about this.	It can be too easy to simply teach the ideas in the unit as facts. However this does not help develop students' understanding. Students have a diverse range of ideas which they are willing to defend: this creates a "need to know". The unit can be/should be highly oral with lots of consideration and discussion about situations involving force and not many notes. It is important that the teacher withholds judgement about "wrong" answers while students discuss and clarify their ideas. The cause of reaction forces, viz. that they result from distortion, is not usually explained in textbooks.	Students have lots of real world experiences that can be built on. It is easy for this unit to be taught in a quantitative manner but this does not necessarily help develop students' understanding.
Teaching procedures (and particular reasons for using these to engage with this idea)	**Defining the boundaries:** Draw out alternative uses of the word 'force'. Example of sign: 'No animals on freeway' is useful for distinguishing between scientific and everyday meanings. **Establishing a common form of communication:** Get students to use arrows to indicate direction of force and gradually introduce the idea that the longer the arrow the bigger the force. Establish later: (1) idea of a point mass; and, (2) the convention for locating the arrow with the tail at the point of action of a force. [continued over]	**Making the concrete abstract:** Start with flexible objects where distortion is more obvious and then introduce more rigid objects. **Magic chair:** Teacher asks, "How does a chair know how much to push up for different size students?" Other similar situations to discuss are: (1) The bending of the table top when students stand on a table (where the bending of the table top is obvious) [continued over]	**Developing understanding:** Place an object on a ruler supported at each end by bricks. Ask, 'What happens at the instant when we let go of the object?' Students usually agree that the object distorts the ruler as the object is pulled down by 'gravity'. Then ask, 'How does the object 'decide' when to stop?' Students usually decide 'when the force down and the force up are equal'.

D: Frictional forces are caused by distortion of two surfaces sliding over each other.	E: Reaction forces occur in pairs. Each force in a pair acts on a different object.	F: Field reaction forces are forces between objects that are not touching. Field reaction forces are not due to distortion of an object.
The teacher needs to withhold introducing the scientific explanation for friction for a prolonged period of time; this encourages students to fully engage with their ideas and promotes deeper understanding of the issues involved.		These ideas are best explored fairly late in the unit after contact forces have been considered.
Challenging Views: (1) Have a student push on a wall. Ask, 'What are the forces on the student?' The class will agree that the wall is pushing on the student but won't offer other forces. Ask, 'Why isn't the student moving?' to get students thinking about the "missing force". To get students to start thinking about 'friction', it may be necessary to place something slippery (e.g. soapy water) on the floor so student "slips" when pushing. (2) Create examples of deliberately increasing as well as decreasing friction. **Role play:** Have two columns of students stand with hands on hips so elbows of adjacent students overlap. Have one column step forward. The brushing of elbows demonstrates frictional interaction. [continued over]	**Identifying forces:** Think about a cup sitting on a table with table legs standing on the earth. With the class, work out the forces on the cup, on the table top, on top of each table leg, and on the earth. Distinguish between pairs of balanced forces and pairs of reaction forces. There appears to be a "missing force" on the earth as the only obvious force on the ground is downwards; this helps make plausible the idea that there must be an upwards force ON the earth due to the gravitational interaction between earth and table and earth and cup (since forces on the earth are presumably balanced). [continued over]	**Addressing misconceptions:** Ask, 'Would the gravitational forces on us be different if we moved to a tall building/the moon/Jupiter/on a spinning object etc.?' - hang a weight on a spring in a bell jar and then evacuate; - show photos of astronauts on the moon dropping weights, and walking (i.e. no air and not spinning). Discuss views from above probe. Ask, 'How can they walk?'

PART ONE: STATIONARY OBJECTS

	A: A force is a push or pull.	B: Objects distort when forces are put on them. That causes them to exert a force on the object that distorted them.	C: Objects that are stationary always have an equal balance of forces acting on them.
Teaching procedures (and particular reasons for using these to engage with this idea). **[continued]**	**Concept substitution:** The misconception that moving objects must have a force within is close to the concept of momentum. Some students with this misconception will accept the suggestion that what they are thinking of is called 'momentum' and is not a force.	(2) A table top is observed when a book is lying on it. This is compared with: – the (observable) bending of a metre ruler (supported at each end by bricks) when the book is placed on it. Students can "feel" the upwards force if they put their finger on the ruler and remove the book. – the lesser (observable) bending when the bricks supporting the aforesaid metre ruler are placed closer together (with the book again lying on the ruler). (3) An object is suspended by a(n apparently unstretched) string held by hand. The string is then replaced by a spring which is obviously distorted when the object is attached. **'My friend the builder' stories:** e.g. When a beam for a roof is erected, it initially doesn't fit because the builder has to allow for distortion when the roof is added.	

D: Frictional forces are caused by distortion of two surfaces sliding over each other.	E: Reaction forces occur in pairs. Each force in a pair acts on a different object.	F: Field reaction forces are forces between objects that are not touching. Field reaction forces are not due to distortion of an object.
Key questions: Always return to 'what is being distorted and in which direction?'	THEN divide the reaction forces into those arising from gravitational interactions and those from distortion.	

PART ONE: STATIONARY OBJECTS

	A: A force is a push or pull.	B: Objects distort when forces are put on them. That causes them to exert a force on the object that distorted them.	C: Objects that are stationary always have an equal balance of forces acting on them.
Specific ways of ascertaining students' understanding or confusion around this idea (include likely range of responses).	**Listening for appropriate use of words:** The absence of inappropriate use of 'force' indicates students have grasped the idea that in science we use 'force' to mean a 'push' or 'pull'. **Probe of prior views:** Give students worksheets asking them to draw forces in various situations, e.g. on a girl on stationary swing. **Predict-Observe-Explain (POE):** Ask students to draw forces on each situation: (1) book pushed along a table; (2) trolley pushed along a table; (3) trolley pushed and allowed to come to rest. The above brings out students' misconceptions that force is needed for motion and also that moving objects must have a force within/attached that makes them move.	**Application of ideas:** Give students worksheets containing situations of forces in everyday contexts and ask students to (1) think about what is bending or stretching, and (2) draw the forces acting. **Explain POEs scientifically:** Return to POEs discussed earlier and ask students to explain them using appropriate scientific terms. Check that the use of terms such as 'force' are being used correctly. **Silent experiment:** Later in the unit the teacher conducts a silent experiment while students watch. Attach 1kg weight to string, measure length, record; add 1kg and repeat; etc. up to 4kg; reverse back to 1kg; repeat adding 1kg at a time & recording length until string breaks. Students can discuss the experiment with each other after they have observed the experiment. They then write up the experiment explaining: 'What is this experiment for?' 'Why are we doing this?'	**Return to prior views:** At some later point in the unit, return to the worksheet used to probe students views. Students reflect on, 'What are my answers now?'; 'What did I need to do to change my mind?' **Challenging understanding:** Late in the unit, attach a 100g weight to a horizontal spring balance connected at its other end to a retort stand. Allow the weight to hang. Note the reading on the spring balance is 100g. Replace the retort stand with another 100g weight dangling on the other side of the spring balance. Ask students to predict what the reading on the spring balance will be. Many will not predict that it will still be 100g. Ask students to explain why.

D: Frictional forces are caused by distortion of two surfaces sliding over each other.	E: Reaction forces occur in pairs. Each force in a pair acts on a different object.	F: Field reaction forces are forces between objects that are not touching. Field reaction forces are not due to distortion of an object.
Probing understanding: (1) Ask students what will happen when you slide a block of wood and a block of soap of approximately the same size across a table. Which stops first and why? In each case, what is the direction of the frictional force? What will happen if you do the same thing but this time with two blocks of wood placed on top of each other, and why? (2) Watch someone walk slowly. Ask, 'Which way do the forces arising from frictional interaction act?' (Year 12 students often get this wrong.)	**Warning of prior learning tendencies:** Towards the end of the unit, have 2 students (~equal mass) on skateboards. Ask the class to predict whether or not each will move back an equal distance when – they push each other – one pushes the other, who does not push. Many students will predict that in the second case, one student will move further: hence, students should be warned that they may tend to return to their prior misconceptions and should think carefully before committing themselves to a response.	**Multiple Choice Tasks:** Set multiple choice tasks with distracters that fit with students' prior views.

PART TWO: MOVING OBJECTS

	IMPORTANT SCIENCE		
	A: **When objects accelerate, they change speed and/or change direction of travel.**	**B:** **Newton's 1st law**	
What you intend the <u>students</u> to learn about this idea.	Constant speed motion differs from accelerated motion. Objects travelling at constant speed may change direction. During accelerated motion, an object's speed changes and/or its direction changes.	If something has a net force acting on it, it will either be speeding up or slowing down (or reversing). The net force on an object is the sum of the (real) forces actually acting on the object.	If an object is moving at constant speed, it must have balanced forces acting on it.
Why it is important for students to know this.	These ideas are vital for understanding ideas about Newton's 1st law.	Helps students understand science as providing powerful tools/ideas for explaining phenomena	
What else you might know about this idea (that you don't intend students to know yet).	Only tackle straight line motion. Either avoid two and three dimensional changes in direction unless it comes up OR alert students that only one dimensional motion will be discussed.		
Difficulties/ limitations connected with teaching this idea.	Acceleration is quite a tricky concept. When given the acceleration of an object, many people find it hard to explain what that means in terms of the changes in speed and/or direction of an object.	This law seems counter-intuitive to many people for everyday experiences often reinforce alternative conceptions such as the idea that a moving object **must** have a force acting on it.	
Knowledge about students' thinking which influences your teaching of this idea.	While students may be aware of the idea of acceleration, they don't tend to think of motion in terms of whether or not it is accelerated.	Students have many alternative explanations which are fruitful – i.e., they work! Students are reluctant to abandon their ideas. Students often have trouble distinguishing between the real, actual forces on an object and the 'net' force on the object. Thus, it is important to avoid the physicists' convention of reducing everything to the net force because that is all that matters in calculations.	
Other factors that influence your teaching of this idea.		It's important to distinguish the real, actual forces which are acting on an object, as opposed to the 'net' force.	

IDEAS/CONCEPTS		
C: **Air resists the moment of objects.**	**D:** **Changes in speed are continuous.**	**E:** **Newton's 2nd law.**
The force of air resistance on an object increases with the object's velocity.	An object's speed can't instantaneously "jump" from, say, 60 km/h to 100 km/h. i.e. the object's speed must pass through all the speeds in between 60 km/h to 100 km/h. Changes in speed take time.	More mass needs more net force for same acceleration. The net force on an object is proportional to the object's acceleration.
	This is important for understanding Newton's 2nd law.	
		The meaning behind Newton's second law is often lost when the focus is quantitative. Early on the treatment should qualitative, and should emphasise the difference between the real, actual forces and the 'net' force.
		Students easily forget that the F in F = ma refers to 'net' force only.

PART TWO: MOVING OBJECTS

	A: When objects accelerate, they change speed and/or change direction of travel.	B: Newton's 1st law
Teaching procedures (and particular reasons for using these to engage with this idea).		The unit involves lots of **student discussion** about different situations involving moving objects, the purpose being to identify the forces acting. There is no fixed sequence for this, but there must be discussion about a number of everyday experiences from which assertions about science ideas can be drawn. **Provide, then analyse, personal experiences:** (1) Have a puck on an air table: ask students to find out what they have to do with a ruler to get the puck moving and to keep it moving at steady speed, and explain why. (2) Students pull a laboratory trolley slowly with a spring balance: ask, what happens if they pull the trolley so the spring balance reading stays the same, and why?; what happens if they pull the trolley so it keeps the same speed, and why? **Applying science ideas:** (1) Attach a weight to a spring and observe oscillations: try to unpack what is happening with acceleration and deceleration. Get students to grab the weight at various times and 'feel' the forces pulling up &down. (2) Class discussion of situations that students raise that they want explained. **Predict–Observe–Explain (POE):** To explore balanced and unbalanced forces in situations involving friction, it can be useful to use a bicycle wheel mounted as a pulley, with a bucket of sand hanging from either side: 1) With one bucket (A) higher than other (B), but with both stationary, ask students which weighs more. 2) Pull A down so now level with B. Ask students to predict what will happen when you let go of A. 3) Return to (1) and add a small weight to B, and ask for student predictions about behaviour – will either side move, how far, etc? 4) The same as (3) but with a much heavier weight (so it will cause movement). Ask students whether B's speed is same at two widely separated points in its path. 5) Explore the effects of adding and subtracting large and small weights while the buckets are moving. The above reveal and challenge a range of student misconceptions.
Specific ways of ascertaining students' understanding or confusion around this idea.	Understanding is demonstrated when students are able to appropriately use these ideas to explain new situations.	

C: Air resists the movement of objects.	D: Changes in speed are continuous.	E: Newton's 2nd law.
		Predict–Observe–Explain (POE): To help establish Newton's second law: (1) Have 2 students of very different masses. Ask class to predict the effect of the students pushing on each other. After they have observed what happens, explain. (The explanation will involve revisiting the idea in 'CoRe Part 1' that the 2 students exert forces on each other which are equal.) **Warning about returning to prior views:** Ask students to explain situations involving accelerated and non-accelerated motion. Ask, 'Are you using your old explanations or the scientific ones?' **Applying science ideas:** What do airbags and seatbelts do in car accidents?

Understanding is demonstrated when students are able to appropriately use these ideas to explain new situations.

INTRODUCTION TO PaP-eRs ON FORCE

In this section of the chapter, the PaP-eRs on Force linked to the preceding CoRe are offered. The PaP-eRs in this resource folio have been divided into two sections. In Section One, the sequence of the PaP-eRs represents an intended order of reading because: (1) they roughly indicate a teaching sequence about force; and, (2) they build on issues about teaching force raised in earlier PaP-eRs within the section.

In Section Two, the PaP-eRs are more independent of each other and the order of reading is not so important.

TABLE OF CONTENTS OF PaP-eRs ON FORCE

SECTION ONE

The PaP-eRs in this section include:

PaP-eR 7.1A: The big ideas
PaP-eR 7.1B: Newton's third law-a key to understanding force
PaP-eR 7.1C: Developing ideas of force and reaction force
PaP-eR 7.1D: Being specific about force
PaP-eR 7.1E: Developing students' ideas about friction

SECTION TWO

The PaP-eRs in this section include:

PaP-eR 7.2: Familiar forces
PaP-eR7.3: Issues to be resolved with Year 10
PaP-eR 7.4: Features of force
PaP-eR 7.5: Does gravity need air?
PaP-eR 7.6: What students think

READING THESE PaP-eRs

In a similar way to that which Chapter 5 is organised, the PaP-eRs in this chapter are offered in two separate sections as noted above. The PaP-eRs link to the two parts of the CoRe in a variety of ways and should be delved into, cross-linked, and referenced in ways that the reader feels appropriate in coming to better grasp the essence of PCK as portrayed through this work.

As in all of the PaP-eRs in each of Chapters 4 – 9, it is immediately evident that they illustrate a variety of formats, each designed to capture and portray particular and distinctive aspects of PCK. With each portrayal offered we encourage readers to seek to identify with the given situation and to reflect on their own approach to such work. By so doing, we hope that these PaP-eRs help to create new ways of framing existing understandings of the pedagogy, content and context, that impact the teaching of Force and that science teachers are able to draw new meaning from it.

SECTION ONE

7.1A: THE BIG IDEAS

In this part of the PaP-eR, an experienced teacher reflects on how he decides 'what are the big ideas' when teaching about force. His thinking about this has evolved as a consequence of his experiences of teaching students about force, of conversations with academics about teaching and learning in science and of reading about research in this area. Importantly, the big ideas that shape his teaching about force – **pedagogical** big ideas – are not necessarily science big ideas.

My initial experiences of teaching about force reinforced for me a point highlighted by the research literature on students' understanding of science, i.e. that there are things about force that many students simply don't "get". This caused me to rethink my approach to teaching about force. Typically, the teaching of force focuses on the scientific idea of force as encapsulated in Newton's first and second laws of motion – that is, force is something that, when unopposed, causes accelerated motion. While physicists often regard this idea about force as unproblematic, and unambiguously define what a force is, many students find this big idea of science to be unhelpful in identifying and understanding the forces acting in a given situation. As I began to realise this, I started to think, 'How can I frame the teaching of big science ideas about force in ways that are meaningful to students?'

As a consequence, my teaching approach now focuses on the ideas and beliefs that students have that need to be challenged, or don't have but need to develop, before they can make significant progress in their understanding of force. For example, many students do not believe that reaction forces – such as the force that a table exerts upwards on a book – are "real forces". This is because they don't hold notions of distortion that are important in understanding the origins of (non-field) reaction forces, even though they have lots of experiences of distortion (e.g. trampolines, springs, slingshots). That is, they don't have the conception of surfaces being distorted when forces are exerted on them, and of distorted surfaces exerting forces back on the object causing the distortion. To address this, I spend a lot of time developing the idea that an object distorts when a force is exerted on it, and that this means that it exerts a force back on the thing that caused it to distort. Importantly, I find that this seems to make the idea of reaction forces more intelligible for students. Thus, although not usually found in science text books, distortion and its links with force constitutes one of the big ideas in my teaching about force, because it helps overcome problems with student understanding that I've become aware of during my practice.

7.1B: NEWTON'S THIRD LAW: A KEY TO UNDERSTANDING FORCE

Newton's third law[15] is often under-emphasised in junior science classes, and sometimes even omitted. Some teachers of senior physics are also dismissive of it, seeing it as amounting to a statement of the Law of Conservation of Momentum, but a somewhat less sophisticated form. In this PaP-eR, a teacher explains why he regards some of the ideas in Newton's third law as central to developing students' understanding of force.

Faced with the task of teaching about force, it's easy to think that it makes sense to teach Newton's first[16], second[17], and third laws of motion in that order. Over the years, I've come to question that perceived wisdom. The first two laws focus on the idea of net force and accelerated motion. Early in my teaching, I tended to assume that net force as a concept was relatively straightforward and focused instead on helping students to understand ideas about acceleration. I've come to realise though that the concept of the net force on an object is far more problematic than I had imagined and that this is linked to students' difficulty in identifying all the actual real forces on the object that add to produce the net force. This is particularly so for those forces that we commonly call 'reaction forces' arising from the object's interaction with another object. This led me to think that students need to know something about Newton's third law before they can sensibly use Newton's first and second laws.

I'll give some examples to explain what I mean. Suppose we take a book lying at rest on a table. From a physics point of view, there are two real forces that are considered as comprising the net force (which is zero): the gravitational force of Earth on the book downwards and the force of the table on the book

---

[15] Newton's third law states that when object A exerts a force on object B, object B exerts a force on object A which is equal in size, but in the opposite direction.

[16] Newton's first law states that an object at rest will remain at rest and a moving object will continue to move in a straight line at constant speed unless acted upon by a net force.

[17] Newton's second law states that the net force on an object is the product of its mass and acceleration.

upwards[18]. Many students do not naturally "see" that the table exerts a force upwards on the book, and, even when told, do not really believe that such a force exists. They ask, 'How does the table know that it has to exert a force?' For such students, there is only one real force (that of the Earth on the book) and, as well, the reason why the book does not move is because the table is "in the way".

A second example is that of a ball bouncing against a wall. To explain why the ball changes direction as it hits the wall involves the idea that the wall exerts a force on the ball: the wall exerts a force on the ball that is equal and opposite in direction to the force that the ball exerts on the wall as it hits it. Again students find it hard to believe that somehow the wall 'knows' to exert a force on the ball.

A third example is the everyday experience of walking. When walking, a person's foot exerts a force downwards and backwards on the ground as it contacts the ground. The ground, in turn, exerts an equal sized force on the foot which is upwards and forwards; the forwards component being responsible for the person's forward motion. It is very hard to convince students that the ground really exerts a force on us and that this enables us to walk.

All of these examples involve what we call 'reaction forces'. Their occurrence can be explained in terms of Newton's third law (e.g. the table exerts a force on the book which is equal and opposite to the force the book exerts on the table; the wall exerts a force on the ball that is equal and opposite to the force the ball exerts on the wall; the ground exerts a force on the person that is equal and opposite to the force the person exerts on the ground). One way of dealing with these kinds of examples is to delay their discussion until Newton's third law has been introduced, but they crop up all the time in class discussion and I've found that students soon lose interest if I keep saying that we'll talk about them later. The main trouble, though, is that even when they are familiar with the third law, many students really struggle with it, finding it hard to imagine (1) that the table/wall/ground can exert a force and (2) that the table/wall/ground "knows" how much force to exert.

So the approach I take now is to tackle a key feature of Newton's third law before we look at the first and second laws. The bit that I focus on is the idea that any interaction between two objects that are in contact with each other results in a force on each object. (That these two forces are always equal in size is not important at this stage and is something we deal with much later.) We begin with the notion of force as a push or a pull and then develop these ideas:

When object A pushes or pulls on object B, it compresses or stretches, i.e. distorts, the surface of object B.

When object B is compressed or stretched (i.e. distorted) by object A, object B exerts a force back on the thing that is distorting it (i.e. object A).

The more object B is compressed or stretched, (i.e. distorted), the greater is the force that it exerts on the thing that is distorting it, i.e. object A.

We consider a range of situations involving objects in contact with each other, including some where the distortion is obvious and some where it is not, and this usually generates lots of student discussion about these ideas[19]. Gradually, the notion of distortion makes 'reaction forces' becomes much more plausible to students, who find it easier to believe that the table/wall/ground in the above examples exerts a force. I find the time spent discussing and developing these ideas is well spent, for it helps students to better identify all the actual forces on an object; hence, they also are better able to work out the net force on the object. As a teacher, this enables me to promote more meaningful linkages by students of the ideas of net force and accelerated motion which are present in Newton's first and second laws, this being the opposite of what appears to be a logical sequence in teaching.

7.1C: DEVELOPING IDEAS OF FORCE AND REACTION FORCES

In this part of the PaP-eR, a teacher describes aspects of her approach to introducing the idea of force to students. At the same time she introduces the idea of 'reaction forces' as arising when one object exerts a force on another: many students struggle with this idea, so she uses a lengthy teaching sequence to try to make this plausible and understandable. This sequence involves students' consideration of the forces involved in the situations shown in the accompanying photographs, and their observation of the deflection of a beam of light reflected from a mirror lying on a laboratory bench when several students step onto the bench.

From the outset, I tell students that a force is a push or a pull. We have lots of discussions where I ask them to identify the forces in a given situation. I stress that if students can't identify what it is that is

---

[18] Actually, there is a third force – the 'buoyancy' force of the air – but we generally ignore this in middle secondary school because it is very small in comparison to the other two forces, and the concept is difficult. Its inclusion adds a layer of complexity to the discussion that is unhelpful in developing the central ideas that the table must be pushing up on the book, since the net force on the book is zero.

[19] This teaching approach is elaborated in the following PaP-eR in 7.1C.

pushing or pulling, then what they are thinking of is probably not a force. I also stress that there is no need to use 'fancy' words like 'momentum' and 'energy' when describing forces – I don't labour the point that these are different concepts but just emphasise that forces should be able to be described in terms of pushes or pulls.

Very quickly we move into the area of 'reaction forces' – although I don't use this term at this stage. I begin by asking the students to draw some arrows to show what they think are the forces on a book resting on a table (see Picture 1). When (and only then) they have all committed themselves to a response, I ask students to tell me, and the rest of the class, what they think.

Students often feel reluctant to reveal what they think for fear of being ridiculed by their peers and/or the teacher. I work hard at trying to promote an atmosphere in which students feel it is safe to say what they think, so by the time we get to this discussion about the forces on a book lying resting on a table, students are at least reasonably able to say what they really think.

I run the discussion by asking one or two students to tell the rest of the class what they think are the forces on the book, and then ask for reactions to this from the other students. So much of the discussion involves the students explaining and arguing about their ideas, with my role being that of facilitator. Often, though, there are moments when I need to jump in and make comments or introduce new demonstrations to help move students' thinking along.

Here are some typical things that students say and do (see shaded areas), my usual response (underneath the shaded areas), and my thinking about this (shown in the right hand column).

Students' & teacher's usual response	Teacher's thinking
Some students will have drawn arrows like this ↓↓↓↓ above or below the book and labelled them 'gravity'.	
Me: Let's have some agreement. Let's draw a single force acting through the centre – it's the same as having all those little arrows.	It's important early on that we establish a common form of representation of forces to avoid possible confusion. Gradually I'll introduce the scientific convention for representing forces – a directed line located at the point of action of the force and labelled in the form of 'force of A on B'. For the moment I accept the label of 'gravity', but later I'll encourage students to use the more specific 'force of Earth on book'.
Some students might have some arrows to represent "air pressure".	
Me: Can we just assume that we can ignore air pressure at this stage? But we will come back to this later.	Air pressure complicates the discussion at this stage, and its net effect is very small compared to other forces on the book. I want to introduce the idea of the "normal" reaction force of the table on the book as a consequence of the table being distorted by the book pushing down on it.
Usually a student will have an arrow drawn ↑ under the book.	
Me: So you think the desk is actually pushing up?	It's very important to ask these questions because many students believe the table is not really exerting a force on the table – that it is just "stopping" or "resisting" the book from falling are typical views.
Tom: No, it's just stopping the book from falling through the desk.	
Me: So the desk is not exerting a force upwards?	

Students' & teacher's usual response		Teacher's thinking
Ann: No, a force is a push or pull. The table is not pushing or pulling. It is just resisting – you know, stopping it.		Although Ann's comment that the table is not pushing is wrong, I'm pleased with the linkages to the idea that a force is a push or a pull that she is trying to make. `
Me (when it seems like no new ideas are going to be introduced into the discussion): OK, so you all agree that gravity is really pulling down and is a real force but the table is not really pushing up so there is not a real force from the table.		It's important to sum up the discussion to date so that all are aware of the issues trying to be resolved.
Me: Let's consider another example and come back to this later. Draw the forces on the book if I place the book on the palm of my hand. (My elbow is resting on the table; see Picture 2.)		This next demonstration and discussion help act as a bridge to the notion that the table might be exerting an upwards force on the book.
Brad: I don't think this is any different to the book on the table. The hand's resisting just like the table.		
Cathy: Since your elbow is on desk, the hand is just resisting.		
Me: What if my elbow is not resting on the table? (See Picture 3.)		There tends to be a lot of argument and discussion between students as they try to clarify the issue of what forces are on the book for themselves. I only ask questions like this one and the next one if the students themselves do not introduce these ideas.
Mary: If your elbow is not on desk, then your hand is pushing up because of your muscles.		It's tempting to jump on an answer like Mary's which seems to be correct, but I know that many students will not yet be convinced that the hand is pushing up.
Me: How would you know if I was pushing up?		
Pete: Your hand would be moving up.		Pete's belief is very common and it is important that it is challenged with a counter example. This helps to move students towards the idea of "net" force which we will explicitly talk about later.
Me: If that's the case how do you know that gravity is pulling down? Shouldn't it make the book move down?		

Students' & teacher's usual response		Teacher's thinking
Me: This might help clarify for those who aren't sure whether my hand is pushing up. (I put two books on my hand. See Picture 4.) Me: Is my hand applying force just to the bottom book?		
Yes. (This tends to come as a chorus from the class, suggesting their consensus.)		I can tell from the expressions on students' faces that they now consider my hand is pushing up on the bottom book.
Me: Is it bigger than before?		
Yes. (Again, there is consensus.)		
Me: Let's think about this a bit more. Now we agree that my hand is pushing on the bottom book, and it pushes harder when there are two books being held in my hand. Can you tell me what are the forces on the top book?		While most students might now consider that my hand is exerting a force on the book, at least some will *not* therefore conclude that the table must exert a force on the book lying on it, thinking perhaps that an inanimate object cannot push. I try to bring this issue to the fore by asking them to describe the forces on the top book when I again hold two books in my hand.
Ellie: Gravity.		
Mark: The bottom book pushes up on the top book.		
Me: Is the bottom book really pushing up?		Again, rather than accept Mark's response, which is actually correct from the scientific perspective, I ask this question because I know that many students will still not believe that an inanimate object can exert a force.
Fred: No, the hand is pushing up on the top book.		This response (that it is the hand that is pushing) suggests that my suspicions are correct (although underlying this answer is also perhaps the notion that objects can exert forces on things they are not in contact with).

I'll continue with other demonstrations involving a spring attached to a retort stand: first a pen is hung from the spring and then a book (instead of the pen) (see Pictures 5 & 6). In both cases I'll ask for the forces on the pen/book. 'Gravity' is always offered. Some students will revert to former types of explanation saying there is a 'resistance' from the spring on the pen/book and others respond that the energy of the spring stops the pen/book from falling: with both types of answers I'll remind students that they should be able to use "push" or "pull" to describe a force. However, more students than was the case with the book on the table will now tend to consider there is an upwards force on the pen/book, in this case from the spring. I'll ask these to defend their answer to the rest of the class. Usually someone will say, 'The spring exerts a force because it has been stretched a tiny amount.' This comment is crucial because it helps make understandable the idea that the spring, an inanimate object, can exert a force. While some students who had not previously considered that the table might be able to exert a force on the book lying on it might now be prepared to reconsider their beliefs, I know that many will still not think that this is possible. Two more demonstrations will help resolve this. Firstly, students observe a book lying on a metre ruler supported at each end by bricks (see Picture 7). They eventually agree that because the book is heavy, the ruler bends until its upwards force on the book balances the book's weight. Secondly, the deflection of a laser beam shining onto a mirror lying on a bench when several students stand on the bench is noted (see Picture 8). The ensuing discussion moves towards agreement that the students are compressing the table by a tiny amount.

When this sequence of demonstrations and class discussion is complete, the students will be ready for some closure on the issue of the force of the table on the book: that the table pushes back on the book because the book compresses the table an infinitesimally small amount. I'll generalise this to include the example of the pen/book on the spring: whenever things are distorted they exert a force back on the thing that is doing the distorting. Students seem to understand and accept this idea but I know that later, given a new situation such as a person standing on the ground, many will revert to their previous ideas if challenged and asked whether the ground is REALLY exerting a force on the person ...

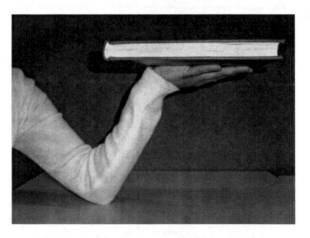

Picture 1: Book lying on a table

Picture 2: Book on hand with elbow resting on table

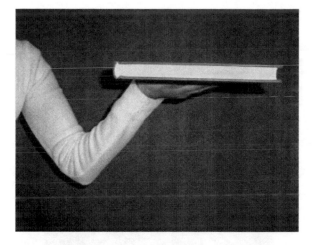

Picture 3: Book on hand (with elbow unsupported)

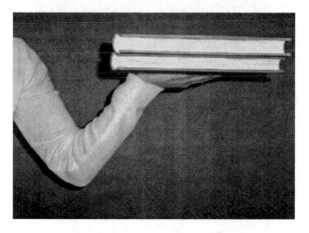

Picture 4: Two books on hand (with elbow unsupported)

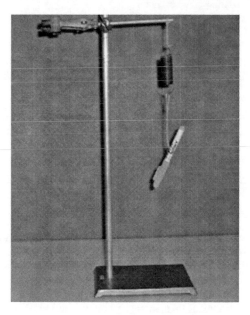

Picture 5: Pen hanging from spring attached to retort stand

Picture 6: Book hanging from spring attached to retort stand

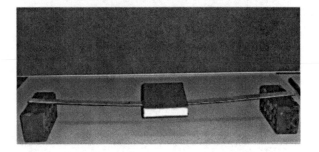

Picture 7: Book resting on a metre ruler supported at each end by a brick

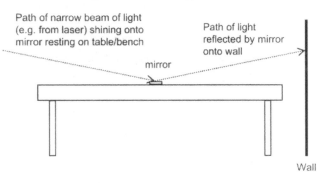

Picture 8: The setup of equipment before the student steps onto the table or bench[20][21]

7.1D: BEING SPECIFIC ABOUT FORCE

When discussing a particular force, students, teachers, and textbooks are often vague about the cause (or agent) and the object (or receiver) of the force, and also the location of the force. In this PaP-eR, a teacher explains how, through reflecting on the various ways she and her students drew force diagrams, she came to recognise the importance of using the scientific convention for representing force, i.e. the size and direction of a force is represented by the length and direction of an arrow which is drawn with the tail located at the point of action of the force, and labelled in the form 'Force of A on B'.

---

[20] While it may be convenient to use a laser, it is not necessary as long as the light beam is narrow.

[21] The spot of light on the wall moves when a student steps onto the table/bench.

I was looking at some students' drawings of the forces acting on a book lying on a table. The different ways students had represented the gravitational force of the earth on the book started me thinking: what do their diagrams mean?

Here is a selection of the parts of their drawings that show the gravitational force of the earth on the book:

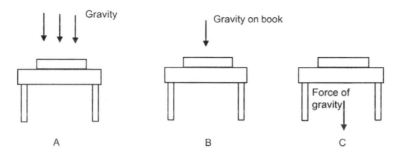

The problem for me was that none of their diagrams showed the "force of gravity on the book" actually "on" the book. The first two (A and B) – with arrows drawn downwards but located above the books – made me wonder if at least some of these students were actually thinking about 'air pressure' rather than gravity. (I know that it is common for some students to think that gravity and air pressure are related, and that gravity decreases when air pressure decreases.)

As I thought further about these diagrams, I began to consider other possible understandings that the students might have had when drawing them. For example, assuming that the students who drew diagrams A and B weren't confusing gravity with air pressure, I wondered if their placement of the arrows above the book meant they thought that "gravity" is something above the book that pushes down on it.

As I thought about this further, I wondered whether all three of the diagrams A – C were telling me that the students concerned thought of gravity as a "thing" permeating space in much the same sense as the "force fields" of science fiction, not recognising that scientists use the word "gravity" to describe the nature of the particular type of interaction between two or more objects arising from their masses. In the case of the book on the table, I questioned whether these students had the scientific view that the "force of gravity" was in fact "the force of planet Earth on the book".

As I struggled to work out what these diagrams were telling me about students' understanding, I began to reconsider the kinds of pictorial representations of ideas related to force and motion that I used in my teaching. I realised that I often drew arrows that had varied meanings, and that I had always assumed that the students understood their intended meaning.

Take, for example, the next drawing. Sometimes I intended the arrow to imply movement (e.g. 'Jack is moving'), or direction (e.g. 'the direction that Jack is moving in').

Other types of diagrams I often drew were like the next ones (see D & E below) to show something pushing or pulling.

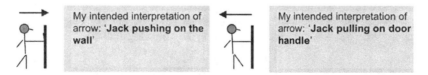

At other times I would use arrows to represent the actual forces arising from these pushes or pulls, as in the next set of drawings (F & G below).

As I reflected on this, I realised that I often drew arrows without being clear about which of the possible meanings I was using. My diagrams were often unlabelled (i.e. without the words shown in bold in diagrams D – G), leaving them open to misinterpretation. I had to admit that frequently I drew diagrams like the ones above of Jack pushing or pulling (i.e. D & E), but not the corresponding ones beneath (i.e. F & G) which followed the scientific convention of showing the label, location and direction of the force. Yet this second task of identifying the location, direction and name of a force is not straightforward for students, something brought home to me during a lesson when I asked students to draw the forces arising (1) when Jack pushed on the wall, and (2) pulled on the door handle, as above. The incorrect responses in H & I were argued by a number of students:

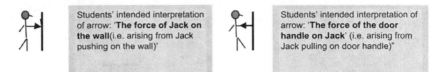

The response in diagram H does not follow the scientific convention for locating the tail of the arrow representing a force at the point of action of the force, but instead confuses the arrow with the pushing action that caused the force. It is possible that the students who gave this response were thinking about the origin of the force (viz. Jack's hand) rather than the point where the force acts (viz. the door). (In fact, from a scientist's perspective, diagram H shows a force acting to the right on Jack's shoulder.) The response in diagram I shows the "reaction force" on Jack's hand that would arise if Jack was pushing on the door handle rather than pulling. Students who gave this response may have been confusing the feeling of the door "giving" as it opens with the (incorrect) idea that it must therefore push on the person opening it.

Thinking about these multiple possible interpretations, I began to see that there was little wonder that students were often unsure, or just wrong, about what forces acted, and where, when the very diagrams I was using to explain ideas were themselves frequently unclear. This was not helped by the fact that sometimes my diagrams followed the scientific convention (e.g. diagrams F and G) and sometimes they did not (e.g. diagrams D and E), and that I did not make this explicit to students. I comforted myself with the thought that lots of textbooks also tend to be vague and inconsistent like this, but nevertheless vowed to take care to be more specific in my teaching from now on!

These days I am careful to consistently use the scientific notation in my teaching and to insist that students use it too, i.e. an arrow is drawn to represent the direction of a force, with its length representing the size of the force (in other words, the longer the arrow, the bigger the force) and the tail of the arrow drawn at the point where the force acts. Importantly, the arrow is labelled in the form 'force of A on B'. This helps students to better understand what I'm teaching. It also helps them to better identify the forces acting in a given situation. We now spend a lot of time just identifying forces and representing them using the scientific notation, for I've come to realise that using the scientific notation is a non-trivial task and is actually of value pedagogically! Consistent use of the scientific notation by both myself and my students removes much of the ambiguity surrounding what diagrams involving forces mean. It enables me to be more confident interpreting what students mean and thus to monitor and, if necessary, challenge their learning.

However, while my students seem to better be able to use the scientific convention for representing force, I find the task of representing forces, such as the gravitational force of Earth on a book lying on a table, is still challenging for them. The idea that the gravitational force of Earth on each "bit" of the book can be represented by a single equivalent force though the book's centre of mass adds another layer of complexity for students to grapple with. Nevertheless, because we now spend much more time in class considering and discussing these issues, I find that, given the task of representing the forces acting on a book lying on a table, fewer students represent the gravitational force of Earth on the book like the diagrams A – C and more respond in a way that suggests a better understanding as in the following drawing.

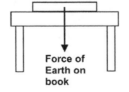

Force of
Earth on
book

7.1E: DEVELOPING STUDENTS' IDEAS ABOUT FRICTION

Students are often aware that friction involves surfaces rubbing against each other. However, they do not associate friction with forces. In addition, students often think of friction in a negative sense, e.g. as something that wears away surfaces. In this PaP-eR, a teacher describes how he helps to develop student understanding of friction using the following ideas: (1) surfaces can be thought of as having lots of little "bumps"; (2) that when two surfaces slide over each other, these bumps are pushed and distorted sideways; and, (3) that the distorted bumps on one surface exert forces back on the other surface that caused the distortion. The teacher's approach also provides students with a powerful way of predicting the direction of forces arising from frictional interactions, and enables them to see positive and important aspects of friction in daily life.

In my unit on 'Force', I begin by introducing the scientific notion of force as involving a "push" or a "pull". I then develop ideas about (non-field) forces arising from objects being distorted by considering a range of situations involving stationary objects (e.g. a book on a table, a book hanging from a string). There is always a lot of student discussion about the forces involved, and at some point a student will usually argue that stationary objects, if they are to remain stationary, must have balanced forces acting on them. This is a fairly intuitive notion, but one that I make explicit – it is, of course, an important part of Newton's first law of motion (although I don't refer to this law until later in the unit when we have discussed ideas of accelerated motion).

When I feel satisfied that most students grasp the ideas that a (contact) force on an object causes distortion of that object, and that this distortion leads to a force being exerted on the object causing the distortion, *and* that the forces on stationary objects must be balanced, I introduce a situation involving a stationary object where there seems to be a "missing force". I hope that students will ultimately see that friction accounts for this "missing force". I ask a student (whom I'll call "Sarah") to lean with her hand against a wall. Then I put this question to the class: 'What are the forces on Sarah?'

The discussion usually begins with a student talking about the force that Sarah's hand is exerting on the wall. Sarah's hand is not exerting a force on Sarah, but I withhold making a comment about this for two reasons. Firstly, I want to get all students' ideas out in the open so that the class has the opportunity to consider and debate them. Secondly, I know that encouraging the students to think about the effect of Sarah leaning on the wall, viz. distortion of the wall, usually results in a class discussion about the consequences of this distortion, viz. that the wall pushes back in Sarah. At this point, I sum up the discussion to date with a drawing on the board as follows:

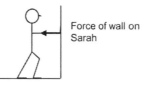

I ask Sarah to push as hard as she can on the wall. Then I pose the question (if a student doesn't): 'If the wall is pushing on Sarah, why doesn't Sarah move?' This usually promotes a lot of discussion. At some stage, a student will say something like, 'If Sarah didn't have any grip on the floor, she wouldn't be able to lean and push.' I want students to think about what is happening that enables this grip between Sarah and the ground, so I ask, 'What would happen if I poured very soapy water on the ground under Sarah's shoes?'

Students generally agree that Sarah's feet will start sliding in the direction away from the wall; some students will say this is because there is less "grip" between Sarah's shoes and the floor, while others will say this is because there is less "friction". I suggest that both groups of students seem to be referring to the same thing, i.e. that "friction" and "grip" have similar meanings. I don't dwell on this, and the students seem happy enough with this. However, despite their use of these terms, I know that few students, if any, will associate "friction/grip" with the ideas about force that we have developed. To help them start making these links, I ask, 'Why is there a grip, or friction, between Sarah's shoes and the floor when there is no soapy water under Sarah's shoes, and why does the soapy water reduce the grip or friction?'

The discussion then moves towards a consideration of the soles of Sarah's shoes: are they flat? do they have some "tread"? do they have some "ripples"? The class generally agrees that if Sarah is not to slip when standing on soapy water, she needs some 'bumps' on the soles of her shoe. (It helps the discussion if Sarah is wearing shoes that have a lot of tread!) If need be, I ask, 'What happens to those bumps while Sarah is leaning against the wall and not moving?' This leads to the class to considering how the bumps on Sarah's shoes are being pushed and distorted by the floor, and that the direction of this push is towards the wall.

KEY

——— The "floor bumps"

— · — · The "shoe bumps"

Direction of push on
"shoe bumps"

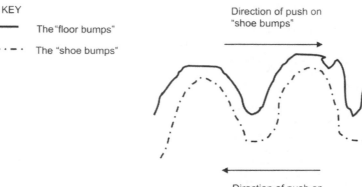

Direction of push on
"floor bumps"

Eventually I bring the discussion to closure, making the point that all surfaces, even very smooth ones, can be thought of as having tiny bumps, so that when two surfaces (such as a sole of Sarah's shoe and the floor) rub over each other, the bumps on each surface push and distort sideways the bumps on the other surface. In the case of Sarah leaning against the wall as shown above, her "shoe bumps" push and distort the "floor bumps" away from the wall and these distorted floor bumps push the shoe bumps back towards the wall. A diagram on the board helps.[22]

This is a tricky idea, and not readily found in textbooks; indeed, friction is not well understood by scientists, but the model I present is one that students find plausible and helpful. Importantly, it helps students to understand that "friction" between two surfaces involves each surface exerting a sideways force on the other.

Next I return to the picture I drew earlier on the board and remind the students of our original dilemma, viz. if the wall exerts a force on Sarah when she pushes on the wall, why doesn't Sarah move? I point out that, on the basis of the foregoing discussion about friction, we should add extra forces to the diagram, and I draw these in like this:

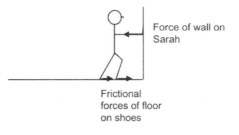

Force of wall on
Sarah

Frictional
forces of floor
on shoes

I then invite the class to reconsider the question, 'Why doesn't Sarah move?' The students quickly decide that this is because the frictional forces on Sarah's shoes from the floor balance the force of the wall on her. (Because my focus is on helping to make the idea of frictional forces plausible to students, I don't worry about the relative sizes of the forces on Sarah's shoes at this stage.)

How do I know that the above model for friction, and the discussion preceding it, helps students understanding of friction? In my experience, even physics students often struggle to identify the direction of the frictional forces that enable someone to walk, having learned that friction "opposes" motion. Following the activity above, I ask my students to think about a person who has just taken a step, with both feet on the ground but one foot in front of the other; and I set them the task of predicting the direction of the frictional force on the person's back foot. The ensuing student discussion resolves this question much more quickly than the earlier discussion about Sarah leaning with a hand on the wall. This time the class predicts that that the force on the person's back foot arising from the frictional interactions between the person's foot and the ground is in the forwards direction. The speed with which the class correctly agrees on this answer is a strong indicator of the power of the understanding that has developed during the discussion of Sarah leaning against the wall.

---

[22] This can also be demonstrated with a role play. Two columns of students face the front of the room. The distance between the columns is a bit less than an arm's length. Each student has his/her hands on his/her hips. The columns represent two surfaces in contact, and the elbows represent the bumps on the surfaces. As one column moves forwards, there is a brushing of elbows between the two columns. This is analogous to the frictional interaction when surfaces slide over each other, in which the bumps on each surface push and distort the bumps on the other.

SECTION TWO

This second section of PaP-eRs, although organised numerically, can of course be read in any order as they are designed as stand-alone items in their own right.

7.2: FAMILIAR FORCES

In this PaP-eR a teacher describes an activity in which she provides an opportunity for students to make explicit their initial understandings about what constitutes a force. The purpose of the activity is to distinguish between literal and metaphorical uses of the word 'force', and to clarify that science is concerned only with the literal meaning of force as a physical action; that is, a push or a pull. The activity also serves as foundation for learning about forces as originating from an external agent.

I think it is important for students from their earliest experiences of learning about forces to establish clearly the idea that in science, a force is a push or a pull. This in itself is not a tricky idea; however, it is essential for students to distinguish between their everyday uses of the term force (e.g. I was "forced" to come to school!) and that which they will encounter in science.

> **Class task: Form pairs and take turns to discuss for a few minutes your experiences of forces while coming to school. Think about how you got to school from the time you got up to the time you arrived. Use the word 'force' in your pair discussion as many times as you can.**

For this task, I ask for volunteers to give one example from their discussion about their experiences of forces on the way to school. I write each example on the board and underline the word 'force' in that example.

Here's an example of what my year 10 class came up with:

1. 'My mum forced me to get out of bed this morning.'
2. 'I was forced to have a cold shower because my brother used up all the hot water.'
3. 'I had to force open my eyelids when the alarm went off.'
4. 'The force of gravity kept me from flying around the room.'
5. 'I forced the toast into the toaster.'
6. 'The cat was forced outside when we left for school.'
7. 'I was forced to wait at the train station because the train was late.'

Then, I ask students to think about the meaning of the word 'force' in each of the sentences. Can they think of a word or words to replace 'force' in each sentence that will still make the same idea? Can they see anything that is similar or different about the meaning of the word, 'force' in the way that it is used? This is what they said:

making someone (or something) do something; having to do something (sentences 1, 2, 6,7)

a physical action (3, 5)

an invisible pull (4)

From these ideas, I explain to students that the word 'force' is used with a wide variety of meanings in everyday conversation. However, in this unit and in science generally, we will be concerned only with the literal meaning of force, as a physical push or pull.

To help my students think some more about this idea, and practise using it, I ask them to think again about getting to school. This time, I ask them to focus on all the physical actions that they experienced, and the effects of these actions, and then to try to describe these actions by acting them out for their partner. They seem to really enjoy this activity, as they noisily act out their force experiences!

I then call for one volunteer to show the class what she has just shown to her partner. Last time I taught this unit, Karolina was happy to have a go, so I invited her to stand up on the front table and act out her experiences as she related them to the class.

I forced open the front door to leave the house, and forced one foot in front of the other towards the front gate. I forced open the gate and it swung open and forced my body through the opening and onto the street. I forced my bag up onto my back and it made me feel weighed down, it was so heavy. I forced my feet to run towards the bus and they lifted and moved along the street ...

From time to time as Karolina talked and made the different actions, I stopped her to ask the students, 'What are the forces here that Karolina is describing? What other words could you use instead of force?' The class was fantastic at picking up the ideas – they were quickly able to substitute words like 'twist, lift, push, pull, turn ...' to describe Karolina's actions. With my encouragement they also began to recognise that each time there was a physical action (e.g. 'I twisted the door handle') there was also an effect ('the door handle twisted'). This is an important point (although it often seems trivial to students at the time) that serves as a foundation for later learning about the characteristics of forces as involving an agent, receiver and effect.

As students gain confidence describing the effects of the various forces, I may challenge their thinking further by asking, 'Can you see the force that is acting in this situation?' I expect students to struggle with this question because of the 'everyday' perception that you can actually see the push or pull, whereas in science it is only the effects of the force that can be seen, not the force itself. I'm concerned just to raise the issue at this stage, and only if the group seems ready to go a little further. I know this is complex idea and one that we will be returning to regularly throughout the unit.

I find the effectiveness of this activity lies in its apparent simplicity. Students usually find it a fun and non-threatening introduction to the topic of forces, and they look forward to the unit ahead. Students' ideas about forces can be brought out and explored by linking to an everyday activity that they are all familiar with, viz. getting to school. At the same time, the activity sets up a strong foundation for learning about forces – students start to become aware of the forces around them and to think about the origin and effect of these forces. Moreover, the activity creates a strong episode in students' memories that I can link to in later lessons when more complex ideas about forces are developed ('Remember when Karolina got up on the desk ...?').

7.3: ISSUES TO BE RESOLVED WITH YEAR 10

This Pap-eR illustrates one teacher's approach to beginning a unit about force with his Year 10 class. Prior to their formal learning about this topic, the students complete a "survey" designed to elicit the ideas about forces that they already have developed through everyday experiences. The teacher then presents the range of survey responses to the class for discussion. This survey/discussion approach is designed to give students a chance to begin to articulate their views about forces and to generate a "need to know" about the topic of forces that will serve as the impetus for the activities of the unit. For the teacher it is also a helpful way of gaining insight into the students' thinking about forces.

Each year, before we officially begin learning about force, I ask my Year 10 students to complete a survey that explores some of their ideas about this topic. The survey consists of 10 multiple-choice questions that relate to a range of everyday situations involving forces. Although it is short, the survey raises many of the ideas that we will deal with in the entire unit. The survey serves several important purposes as a starting activity for this unit. First, it gives students a chance to express their thinking about a topic that they are already familiar with, at least in an "everyday" sense. Students have all had experiences of things moving, and many of them can also offer explanations of why things move, so this activity gives them a chance to articulate their thinking and in so doing, begin to recognize that they already have some ideas about this topic. (This is surprising to some students who assume that until we've done it in class that they know little, if anything, about the topic.) Second, for me as their teacher, I want to know the range of ideas held by the class so that I can modify the curriculum accordingly, building on prior knowledge and challenging misconceptions. I know that students often have deeply held views about forces based on their daily experiences that can be difficult to shift, so knowing individual students' ideas early in the unit enables me to identify which aspects I need to spend more time on, and with which students.

I give out the survey in class, ask students to fill it in and hand it back to me. I emphasize that this is not a "formal" assessment task, it is simply a way of checking out the different ideas we have as a class. I want to know what they really think – even if they are unsure (or think their ideas are a bit silly!). I also tell them that throughout the unit they will have a chance to review what they wrote to see if/how their ideas change, and to check progress in their thinking. Following the class, I collate students' initial responses. Then, in the next lesson, I present the class tally for each question to "start the ball rolling" regarding issues about force that this class needs to resolve.

Taking a look in my classroom, the scene would be (typically) something like this:

Me: Let's look now at the class responses for Question 2. This was the question about the ball moving along a flat table.

Q. 2. A ball is rolling along a flat table. It slows down and stops at **X**. Which of the following statements could explain this? (Choose one)

		Class Tally
a.	The ball ran out of force	12
b.	The ball just stopped naturally	0
c.	Friction caused the ball to stop	3
d.	Gravity caused the ball to stop	4

Tim: Well, it seems like we all agree on something. There's no one who thinks that the ball just stopped naturally.

Andy: Most people think that the ball ran out of force. I do, anyway! So are we right, Mr. B?

Me: There are some people in the class who don't agree with you, Andy. They think something else caused the ball to stop moving. So, I'm going to answer your question by asking you (and the rest of the class) this: What do we need to know to know, which alternative is correct?

Grace: I don't know what you mean.

Heath: I think I get it. Can I try? Umm, we need to know what causes a ball rolling along a table to slow down and stop?

Me: Uh huh.

Jen: Does something moving stop moving when it runs out of force, or is it something else, like outside the ball that causes it to stop?

Me: Thanks, Jen.

Ed: I've got a question. What does friction or gravity do to movement? Does it slow movement down?

Me: Alright, these are great questions. Let's take a moment while I write them on the board. Does anyone have another question that you would like to add to this list?

Grace: I've got another one. Are there other things that stop something from moving? You know, things that weren't in the survey question?

Me: Okay Grace! Sounds like you are getting on to this! So, let me ask everyone now, would it be fair to say that what you seem to be asking is, 'Why do things stop moving?'

Since it is students' discussion of issues that drive the unit, a crucial role for me in reporting back the survey results is to help students move from simply looking at the range of responses and asking, 'Which is correct?' to articulating questions about forces that we can address. In this way, I find that students' sense of ownership over their learning is greatly enhanced – something that I found hard to generate in my previous ways of teaching this topic because the students just didn't seem that interested. In fact, I find that students' willingness to defend their often strongly held views about force is a great driver of our discussions. It is also important to regularly return to our list of issues throughout the unit to check what we have resolved. This proves very satisfying for most students as they can have a tangible record of the progress of their learning. The survey approach is not useful for all science topics, though. Over the years I have come to see that the value of the survey approach depends very much on students' existing preconceived ideas about the topic. Force is one that is well suited to just such an exploration.

FORCE - SURVEY A

1. Which of these words give the best idea of force?
    (you can choose more than one)

    (a) push   (b) pressure   (c) pull
    (d) energy   (e) momentum   (f) motion

2. A ball is rolling along a flat table. It slows down and stops at X. Which
    of these could explain this? (choose one)

    (a) The ball ran out of force
    (b) The ball just stopped naturally
    (c) Friction caused the ball to stop
    (d) Gravity caused the ball to stop

3. A skate board rider is moving down a gently sloping path. The person is going
    at the same speed all the time. She is not getting faster or slower.

    Which of these sentences about the total force on the rider is correct?

    (a) There is no total force on the rider because her speed is steady
    (b) There must be a total force on the rider because she is moving

4. A boy holds a ball steady in the palm of his hand. He drops his hand away
    from the ball very quickly. Just after he lets it go, but before it has
    really started to drop down, would there be a force on the ball?

    (a) No, it's not moving yet
    (b) Yes, there is gravity

5. A person in leaning against a brick wall.

    Is the person putting a force on the wall?

    (a) No

    (b) Yes

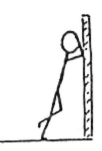

6. A car is parked on a hill. It is not moving.

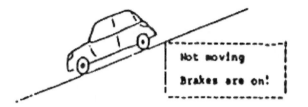

    Not moving

    Brakes are on!

    Which of the following is correct?

    (a) There are many forces on the car but the total force is zero

    (b) There are many forces on the car and the total force is downwards

    (c) There are no forces on the car at all

7. A football has been kicked toward the goalpost.

    As it moves through the goalpost what are the forces on it?
    (you can choose more than one)

    (a) The force of gravity

    (b) The force of friction

    (c) The force of the kick

3

8 – 10. A person throws a tennis ball straight up into the air just a small way. . . .

The questions are about the total force on the ball.

8. If the ball is on the way up, then the force on the ball is shown by which arrow?

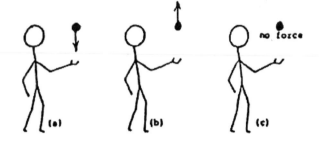

9. If the ball is just at the top of its flight, then the force on the ball is shown by which arrow?

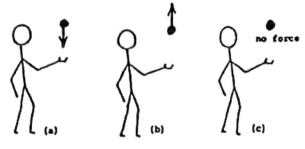

10. If the ball is on the way down, then the force on the ball is shown by which arrow

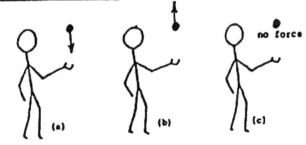

Source:
Osborne, R.J., et al. (Eds) (1980-81).*Working papers 14 – 28, Learning in Science Project.*Hamilton, NZ: SERU, University of Waikato

7.4: FEATURES OF FORCE

In this PaPeR, a teacher learns about her students' understanding of force interactions via a written task that requires students to identify and explain examples of force from everyday life. Through reading and thinking about one student's response to the task, the teacher is able to gain insights into both the nature of this student's understanding about force and how the task can provide insights into students' thinking in ways that "standard" science task responses do not often allow.

I have found that providing opportunities for non-traditional forms of writing in science, such as imaginative writing, can be helpful for encouraging students not only to recall what they have learnt but also to explain and link their ideas together in ways that regular bookwork tasks do not usually provide. Recently, I asked my Year 10 students to complete an assignment in which they wrote about the forces they encountered in a real or imaginary situation. I wanted to know how my students were progressing with the ideas that they had encountered so far in our forces unit study. I wanted to see whether students were able to correctly apply the scientific idea of force as involving a physical action in a range of different everyday situations and whether they were able to recognise particular features of force and write about them using their own words.

> Write about your experiences in a real or imaginary activity in which you encounter different examples of force. Include a range of situations and describe how you deal with them. You may write in any appropriate form: for example, a letter, a newspaper article, a diary entry, story, poem, or essay. Your writing should be about 500 words in length.

Fiona, one of my "better" students, handed in this story. My thinking about her work is shown in the callout boxes.

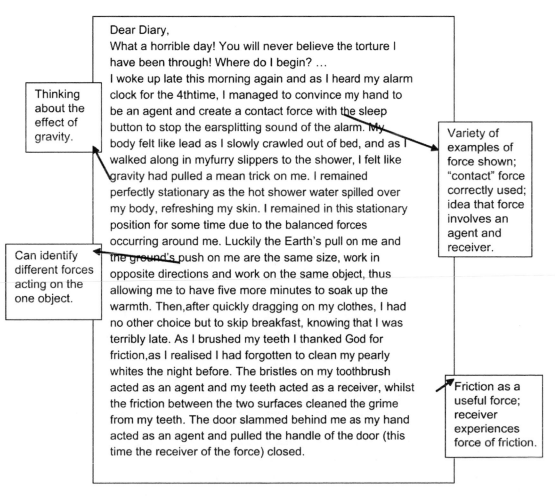

Thinking about the effect of gravity.

Can identify different forces acting on the one object.

Dear Diary,
What a horrible day! You will never believe the torture I have been through! Where do I begin? …
I woke up late this morning again and as I heard my alarm clock for the 4thtime, I managed to convince my hand to be an agent and create a contact force with the sleep button to stop the earsplitting sound of the alarm. My body felt like lead as I slowly crawled out of bed, and as I walked along in myfurry slippers to the shower, I felt like gravity had pulled a mean trick on me. I remained perfectly stationary as the hot shower water spilled over my body, refreshing my skin. I remained in this stationary position for some time due to the balanced forces occurring around me. Luckily the Earth's pull on me and the ground's push on me are the same size, work in opposite directions and work on the same object, thus allowing me to have five more minutes to soak up the warmth. Then,after quickly dragging on my clothes, I had no other choice but to skip breakfast, knowing that I was terribly late. As I brushed my teeth I thanked God for friction,as I realised I had forgotten to clean my pearly whites the night before. The bristles on my toothbrush acted as an agent and my teeth acted as a receiver, whilst the friction between the two surfaces cleaned the grime from my teeth. The door slammed behind me as my hand acted as an agent and pulled the handle of the door (this time the receiver of the force) closed.

Variety of examples of force shown; "contact" force correctly used; idea that force involves an agent and receiver.

Friction as a useful force; receiver experiences force of friction.

Shows awareness of friction as involving an interaction between two surfaces.

Shows awareness of effects of friction; also needs to be aware that friction helps bus to move quite a tricky idea though.

Sprinting towards the bus stop I watched the bus move at constant speed as friction was created before my eyes between the tyres and the road allowing the bus to grip the ground. Motioning my hands frantically in front of the bus and urging the bus driver to stop I managed to wave him down and climb aboard the bus. The bus seat was a support force as I was the receiver of the force from the seat which was the agent. Luckily the force of the earth and the force from the ground were both the same size and working in opposite directions as the bus once again began to move at constant speed. As I ran through the school arch way carrying my late slip in one hand and my books in the other, I made my way to the science room for my science lesson. I was extremely tired from my busy morning and as I held my head up with my hand, my hand was the receiver of a reaction force where my head was the agent.

So as I half heartedly listened to the teacher Mrs. Jolly explain that somehow we all experience a thing called gravity or weight because apparently weight is a force which can be measured in Newtons according to how much our matter is attracted to Earth, I suddenly became interested! I thought this weight system seems pretty cool. Unfortunately then the bell rang and I leapt out of my chair only to find myself on the ground, the result of unbalanced forces that worked against me. Gravity had pulled me to the ground and a large graze appeared on my knee. The rest of the day was equally bad; I failed a Maths test, forgot my PE uniform and found out my house burnt down!!

Has been able to identify the upwards force from the seat on her.

Seems to be thinking about force on hand from head and force on head from hand as an action/ reaction pair.

Able to apply idea of force to situations with which she is familiar. Students often find it difficult to identify the agent of a force.

Seems to recognise that net force is zero for bus to travel at constant speed. There are other forces at work here too that I would not expect her to fully explain (e.g. air resistance, forwards frictional force on driving wheels, backwards frictional force on non-driving wheels).

Awareness of unbalanced forces and their effects.

Bus as receiver of downwards force of the Earth and upwards force of the ground is implied though would have been better if she had stated this.

Reading through Fiona's story, I am reminded that of course not every student produces work of this quality, but neither would I expect that they could! While Fiona has most successfully taken up the challenge to really explore her thinking about forces here, a wide range of students can benefit from a task such as this where the purpose is to encourage students to articulate what they know. Through this less structured kind of writing task, I can more readily get insights into a range of students' thinking about forces. These insights do not come so easily from other more structured kinds of tasks, such as question/answer worksheets in which students' responses are more closely guided. I come to understand more about students' concepts of force through the examples they choose to write about, and the explanations they provide.

7.5: DOES GRAVITY NEED AIR?

Students' ideas about the relationship between gravity and air are often very different from those accepted by scientists. This PaP-eR explores one teacher's awareness of the misconceptions of his Year 10 students about these concepts and how he endeavoured to make plausible for them the notion that gravity can exist in the absence of air.

As part of their work in a unit about Force, I ask students to keep a "thinking page" where they write questions or ideas that they have about forces that come up from their work in class, or other related experiences. I find that learning about this topic typically raises lots of questions for students as they begin to link their school science learning with their experiences outside class. By regularly collecting their "thinking page" I can monitor students' questions and concerns and more closely shape the curriculum around their particular needs. For instance last week, Sam, one of the quieter students in the class wrote this question on his 'Forces thinking page'.

Mr. Dyson, does gravity need air to work?

This question struck me as one that students often struggle with. Sam's question also prompted me to think about other confusions about gravity and air that are commonly held by students. These include:

- where there is no gravity, there is no air (e.g. there is no gravity in space);
- gravity only exists on earth; and,
- as objects fall toward the earth (or moon), they get faster and faster because gravity increases.

In helping students learn about forces, it is important that they understand that gravity is not related to air and more broadly, how the concept of gravity allows explanation of everyday experiences such as falling objects, weight, etc.

After reading Sam's question, I decided that, in the next lesson, I would use an approach to challenge students' thinking about the relationship between air and gravity. Here's what I did. First, to encourage students to think through their ideas about air resistance, I held a flat sheet of paper at shoulder height and asked them to predict how long they thought it would take for the paper to reach the floor after I let it go. (I have found that asking students to predict the outcome of a demonstration considerably helps to increase their engagement with the ideas. In this case, their prediction also sets the scene for what happens next.) After a brief discussion of their predictions, I dropped the paper and compared their predictions with how long it took for the paper to hit the ground. I then asked the students to offer their ideas about how I might increase the rate of fall, using the same piece of paper and dropping it from the same height? They quickly predicted that crumpling the paper into a tight ball would achieve this result. We tried this a few times as different students wanted to test their paper crumpling abilities! In this way, I set the scene for talking with the class about how changing the shape of the paper changed the paper's rate of fall. Through our discussion I wanted students to recognise the following things:

- air affects the way things fall;
- air gets in the way as things fall;
- air provides some resistance to things falling because of collisions between the air particles and the surface of the thing that is falling; and,
- increased surface area means increased resistance (more collisions) as things fall through the air.

In my previous approach to teaching these ideas about gravity and air, I would have simply "told" the students about the relevant science. However, more recently I have come to see that there is more to shifting students' thinking than simply telling them what to think. For meaningful learning to occur, students need to have experiences where they can begin to articulate new ideas for themselves. This will support later learning when more complex ideas about forces are developed later in the unit (for instance, "freefalling" and terminal velocity).

Following our class discussion, when I felt convinced that most students were comfortable with these four ideas (i - iv above), I introduced a second demonstration. This time, I placed a coin and feather together into a glass tube and inverted the tube. Then, using a vacuum pump, I evacuated the air from the tube and repeated the demonstration. Before inverting the tube each time, I asked the students to predict any difference in the rate of fall between the two objects. (This usually presents no problem for students when the air is present and the tube inverted. However, they are often fascinated to see that, when the air is removed from the tube, the two objects fall at the same rate.) The purpose of this demonstration is to help students to recognise that: (i) things fall when air is not present; (ii) the rate of fall is the same for all objects when air is not present; and, (iii) air causes things to fall at different rates.

Elaborating these ideas one step further, I showed a short video clip of the Apollo 11 moon mission in which one of the astronauts releases a heavy object (a 1.32 kg hammer) and a light object (a 0.03 kg feather) simultaneously from approximately the same height and allows them to fall to the moon's surface. (The objects fall together and strike the surface simultaneously.) After viewing the video clip I asked students to explain what they have seen and to link it to the ideas they have encountered about air and falling. From these class activities, I want to feel confident that they have grasped the ideas that objects fall at the same rate on earth in the absence of air, objects fall at the same rate on the moon and the rate of fall on the moon is less than the rate of fall on the earth. Listening to students explain their thinking to me and to each other is an important means for me to monitor their understanding of these concepts. (This also includes listening for the common confusions I mentioned earlier.)

However, even after the demonstrations, video and discussion, there is still an unresolved problem which some students will pick up on. So far, we've really only dealt with the effects of air resistance. Although I have been able to provide students with convincing evidence of the effects of the presence or absence of air on falling objects, I have not yet dealt with what gravity is or how gravity works. And unlike air resistance, such ideas are not readily understood through practical demonstration or teacher explanation. In fact, the nature of gravity is something that scientists also find difficult. Gravity is not currently well understood by the scientific community, although it is a useful construct that enables scientists to predict some of its effects in different situations. So I offer the following explanation of gravity to the students: Every object in the universe seems to attract every other object with a force that is related to the size of their masses. We call this force gravity (although scientists aren't quite sure what gravity is). Because gravity is only a very weak force, we only notice it if at least one of the objects has a huge mass (such as the earth). I tell students that I cannot give them tangible evidence of what gravity is, in the same way that I was able to demonstrate the effects of air resistance. In the past this has led to an interesting diversity of student responses about what kind of knowledge science can offer and the different ways in which science knowledge is constructed and developed (e.g. some students are convinced that science offers conclusive answers to all questions; others are satisfied that science does not offer "answers to everything"). I emphasize to students that although there are some things that scientists don't understand well, these ideas are still useful to explain why certain things happen. Gravity is an example of such a phenomenon. I think is it important for students to begin to grapple not only with knowledge of science concepts, but also with ideas about the nature of scientific knowledge. Knowing about how science (and scientists) work is something we are then able to revisit in different units of work.

Following the day's demonstrations and activities, I again picked up Sam's 'Thinking Page' and this time found the following note:

Today, Mr. Dyson showed us that air affects how things fall, but he wasn't very helpful on how gravity actually works.

7.6: WHAT STUDENTS THINK

PART A: UNPACKING STUDENTS' THINKING

In the first part of this PaP-eR, a teacher, Ms. Brown, draws on her experience of teaching about force as she comments on the understandings that are revealed by students' responses to an exercise asking them to identify the forces acting on a golf ball after it has been hit by a golf club.

Early in her unit on Force, Ms. Brown gave her students this question.

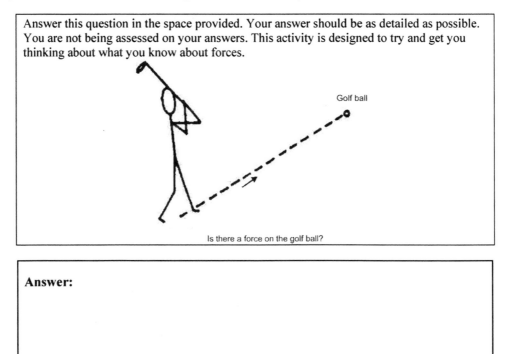

Later as Ms. Brown perused her students' responses, she commented on the answers from three students, Robyn, Sam and Ashley, shown below. Her comments are shown in "call-out" boxes.

The idea that the force that started the golf ball moving – the "propelling" force – is still "attached" to the golfball and keeps it moving is a common misconception and is difficult to successfully challenge!

I presume Robyn is referring to the force of air resistance which is in the opposite direction to the golf ball's velocity. Students often struggle to accurately explain their ideas in words.

Robyn:

There is a force on the golf ball from the golf club when the player hit it. There will be a force in front of the ball as well that eventually will get stronger and the ball will slow down and roll along the ground until it comes to a complete stop.

Robyn hasn't mentioned the downwards gravitational force of the earth on the golf ball which is a constant force throughout the ball's flight. It would be interesting to see whether Robyn would show this force in a force diagram.

Sam:

There is the force of the golf club hitting the ball up into the air which is stronger than the gravity pulling it down towards the ground. Once that force runs out, the air resistance slows the ball down and gravity pulls the ball to the ground again.

This idea that the "propelling force" decreases or "runs out" is not as common as the "propelling force" misconception *per se* but it is very resistant to challenge.

Both Sam and Ashley seem to consider that the gravitational force of Earth comes into play once the force of air has slowed the ball down, i.e. they don't appear to understand that there is a constant gravitational force on the ball from the earth throughout the ball's flight.

Notmany students are able to clearly distinguish in this way between the force/s which started the motion and the force/s after the motion: and those who can may not be able to do this in all contexts.

Ashley:

The ball starts to move because the golf club pushes it. Once the club has no contact with the ball, the forces on the ball are gravity and air. Air resistance slows the ball down allowing gravity to pull the ball to the ground. Eventually the ball hits the ground.

PART B: CHALLENGING STUDENTS' THINKING

Recognising the value for learning of explaining one's ideas about force and listening to those of others, the teacher uses a particular teaching procedure involving discussion to challenge and develop students' understanding.

Following the above exercise, Ms. Brown planned several class periods in which the students explored ideas about the change in velocity of falling objects including: (1) the notion that different objects fall with the same acceleration in a vacuum; (2) in air, where objects have the same shape and surface area but different masses, the one with the larger mass will fall faster due to the effects of air resistance; and (3) the force of air resistance on a falling object increases as the object's velocity increases.

Ms Brown then chose to use a discussion activity called a CUP (Conceptual Understanding Procedure)[23] to further promote her students' understanding of the forces on a ball in flight. She felt that many students were likely to be still confused in their thinking, partly because they were influenced by everyday explanations of motion that were often counter to scientific ideas: in cases like this, she often found giving students the opportunity to discuss their ideas with each other helped clarify their thinking.

The format of a CUP involves three stages:

- students working alone for a few minutes on a semi-quantitative exercise requiring a diagrammatic response;

- students sit in small groups of three or four and try to reach a consensus response to the exercise; and,

- an interpretive discussion where each small group explains and defends their responses to the whole class, the purpose being for the whole class to reach consensus on the correct answer to the exercise.

Ms. Brown designed a CUP which was a modified form of the exercise on the golf ball that the students had done earlier but this time involving the ball tossed in the air. She hoped this would draw out students' ideas about the way the golf ball's velocity changed as it moved upwards in the air and later as it fell, and the reasons for these changes.

Having introduced the CUP and given the students time to think alone about their responses, Ms. Brown moved around the while the students discussed and argued their ideas in their small groups. Snippets of discussion encouraged her to think that at least some students seemed to have a reasonable understanding of the physics ideas in the exercise:

But of course gravity is still acting – do you think it's suddenly cut off just because the ball's moving upwards?

The ball slows down as it moves upwards and speeds up as it falls.

The reason why the ball falls towards the earth is because of the force of gravity but the air pushes back on the ball so it doesn't accelerate as fast as it would in a vacuum.

Ms. Brown knew that, coming from peers rather than from her (i.e. the teacher), these remarks were more likely to be effective in challenging any misconceptions that a student might have. She'd found in the past that students often found explanations from their peers easier to understand than those from their teacher.[24] Ms. Brown also felt that explaining one's ideas to others also often helped the student doing the explaining to reach a clearer understanding. The CUP process itself helped her as the teacher to monitor the progress in her students' understanding, and thus she noted with satisfaction this remark from Robyn, who had considered that the force from the golf club stayed with the golf club in the earlier exercise:

Oh, I get it now! The ball started to move because the girl threw it upwards but that force is gone now. The only forces on the ball are air resistance and gravity and these both slow it down while it's moving upwards.

This comment confirmed Ms. Brown's belief that, while developing students' understanding of force was not straightforward, discussion had an important part to play in the process.

---

[23] See http://www.education.monash.edu.au/centres/sciencemte/conceptualunderstandingprocedure.html

[24] Ms Brown used to worry that the class would reach a consensus that was "wrong" from a science perspective whereas her experience using CUPs was that usually the class reached an answer that was in fact "correct". Indeed she had found that even if the class consensus was not in accordance with the scientific view, students would now have a genuine interest in resolving the question, an issue that further teaching could address.

Jane throws a golf ball straight up in the air and catches it as it falls.
Think about the ball at each of these points:
- ➤ A and B on the way up
- ➤ C the highest point it reaches
- ➤ D and E on the way down

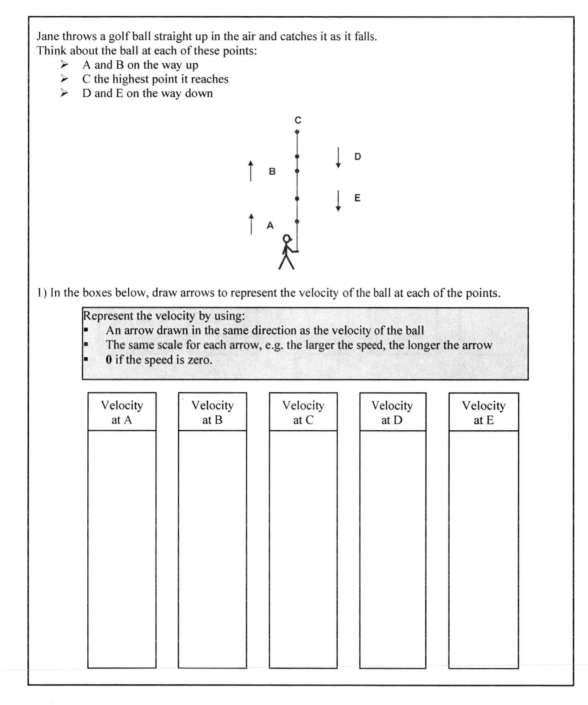

1) In the boxes below, draw arrows to represent the velocity of the ball at each of the points.

Represent the velocity by using:
- An arrow drawn in the same direction as the velocity of the ball
- The same scale for each arrow, e.g. the larger the speed, the longer the arrow
- **0** if the speed is zero.

Velocity at A	Velocity at B	Velocity at C	Velocity at D	Velocity at E

2) In the boxes below, draw arrows to represent the different forces acting on the ball at each point. Use different colours for different types of forces.

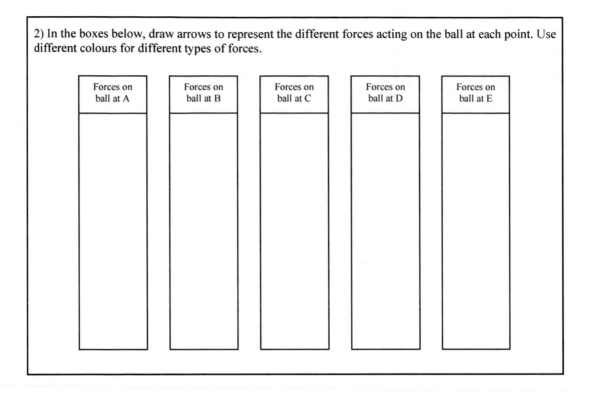

Forces on ball at A	Forces on ball at B	Forces on ball at C	Forces on ball at D	Forces on ball at E

ELECTRIC CIRCUITS

This chapter outlines a representation of Pedagogical Content Knowledge (PCK) for the topic Electric circuits.

REMINDERS ABOUT SHAPING FACTORS THAT INFLUENCE CoRe(s) AND PaP-eRs

As is the case with each of the concrete examples of PCK that comprise Chapters 4 – 9, we briefly offer some of the important points that shape our understanding of representing PCK. Repeating this information at the start of each of the chapters (Resource Folios) is designed to remind the reader about the nature of this form of representation of PCK and for that information to be "on hand" for each individual topic portrayed.

Therefore, some of the important points to be kept in mind when considering that which follows in this Resource Folio are that:

- It is very difficult to offer a single example of PCK that is a neat concrete package, able to be analysed and dissected or used as a blueprint for practice by others. Therefore, our approach to capturing and portraying PCK hinges on the understanding that the teaching and the content must be represented in ways that both maintains the complexity of their relationships but at the same time offers some way of seeing through the complexity in order to gain insight into it.
- Our approach is based on what we have termed a CoRe (Content Representation) and PaP-eRs (Pedagogical and Professional-experience Repertoire). The CoRe outlines some of the aspects of PCK "most attached to that content" but it is not the only representation. It is a necessary but incomplete generalization that helps to make the complexity accessible and manageable; it is neither complete nor absolute. Attached to the CoRe are the PaP-eRs, with links to the aspects of this field that they "bring to life". A PaP-eR is of a content area and must allow the reader to look inside a teaching/learning situation in which the content shapes the pedagogy.
- PaP-eRs bring the CoRe to life and shed new light on the complex nature of PCK. They help create ways to better understand and value the specialist knowledge, skills and ability of teachers thus making that which is so often tacit, explicit for others.

	IMPORTANT SCIENCE			
This Core is designed for students in Middle Secondary School, i.e. Year 10.	**A:** To obtain an electric current, there needs to be a continuous loop from one terminal of a battery to the other.	**B:** An electric current is a flow of net charge in one direction. The materials that make up the circuit provide the charged particles that flow when there is an electric current.	**C:** A battery provides the energy for an electric current.	**D:** When there is a current in a circuit, energy flows from the battery to the user.
What you intend the <u>students</u> to learn about this idea.	A circuit contains the following: • source of energy (e.g. battery) • something that needs this energy to work, i.e., an energy 'user' (e.g. light globe) • wires that connect the two ends of a user to the two terminals of the battery.	All substances contain charged particles. In some substances these charged particles can be moved relatively easily in the one direction to create a current. These moveable charged particles are negatively charged in metals (i.e. electrons) but in other cases (e.g. salt solutions) may be both positive and negative ions. A flow of negatively charged particles in one direction is equivalent to a flow of positively charged particles in the opposite direction. When measuring current, the charge on the charged particles is important. The size of the current at a given point in the circuit is the net charge moving in a given direction past that point in one second. [continued over]	The action of the battery is analogous to lifting an object in a gravitational field and so giving it gravitational potential energy. Regardless of the current, the battery always provides the same amount of potential energy per unit of charge flowing through the battery. The number of 'volts' written on the side of a battery tells us how much energy it provides to the circuit as one coulomb of charge passes through the battery. $1\ V = 1\ J/C$	An electric current involves not only a flow of charge around a circuit but also a transfer of energy from battery to user (e.g. a light globe). In the user this energy appears in forms such as heat and light that are useful in our everyday lives. The energy transfer from battery to user/s is not quite 100% because a tiny amount of energy is lost in the connecting wires in the form of heat. As charge flows around a circuit, potential energy is lost. The potential energy lost when one coulomb of charge flows between two points in a circuit is called the potential difference (P.D.) between those two points. The potential difference between two points in a circuit connecting wire is very, very small. [continued over]

IDEAS/CONCEPTS			
E: **A battery creates an electric field within the materials that make up the circuit. This field is the cause of current when the circuit is closed.**	**F:** **An electric circuit is a system in which changes in one part can affect other parts.**	**G:** **A voltmeter measures how much energy is lost when one unit of charge moves from one point in a circuit to another.**	**H:** **The brightness of a globe depends on the rate at which energy is being transferred to the light globe.**
A battery causes an electric field within each circuit component and a potential difference across its ends. The electric field in each user/ connecting wire simultaneously pushes all the moveable charged particles in the user/wire. As these charged particles are pushed, they experience a kind of "friction" as they collide with other "fixed" charged particles in the user/wire. This results in heating of the user/wire. The energy for this heating comes from the potential energy the circuit loses as charged particles are pushed through the user/wire by the electric field. If there is a potential difference between two points in a circuit, we can infer there must be an electric field between them. [continued over]	For a given battery, the size of an electric current depends on the number and types of users in the circuit (i.e. the total resistance to the movement of charge). When there is one user in the circuit, the potential energy per coulomb lost across the user (i.e. the potential difference) equals the potential energy per coulomb provided by the battery. If another user is added in series, the potential energy per coulomb lost across each user depends also on how hard it is to move the charged particles in the users (i.e. the users' resistances): users with a higher resistance will have a higher potential difference.	When there is a net flow of charge between two points in a circuit, there is a net loss of potential energy from the circuit between those two points. A voltmeter has a very high resistance. It works by allowing a tiny current to pass through it and measuring how much potential energy is lost for every coulomb of charge passing through it. This tells us how much energy is lost per coulomb (i.e. the potential difference) between the two points in the circuit that the voltmeter is connected to.	When there is a current in the filament of light globe, the filament may become very hot because it is made of wire with a high resistance. If the filament wire reaches a high enough temperature, it actually starts to glow. The energy for this heating and light comes from the potential energy lost from the circuit when there is a current within the globe. The hotter the globe filament the greater its brightness, and the faster the time rate of energy transfer to the filament. The time rate at which energy is being transferred to the filament is called the "power of the filament", or in everyday language, the "power of the globe". The power marked on a light globe indicates the power required to give optimal brightness.

	A: To obtain an electric current, there needs to be a continuous loop from one terminal of a battery to the other.	B: An electric current is a flow of net charge in one direction. The materials that make up the circuit provide the charged particles that flow when there is an electric current.	C: A battery provides the energy for an electric current.	D: When there is a current in a circuit, energy flows from the battery to the user.
[continued] **What you intend the students to learn about this idea.**		Charge is measured in coulombs. The current is the same at all points in a series circuit.		Energy is conserved, i.e. the potential energy provided per coulomb of charge by the battery equals the sum of the potential energies lost per coulomb (i.e. all the P.D.s) around the circuit.
Why it is important for students to know this.	This is an essential pre-requisite for understanding scientific models of electric circuits.	The meaning of current in everyday life is often vague, and seen to be synonymous with 'voltage'. Understanding the scientific meaning of electric current is important for making sense of the models that scientists use to explain electric circuits. The twin ideas that charged particles are present in all substances, and may be moveable, are important for understanding why some substances conduct and others do not; and that even so-called insulators can conduct if there is a strong enough source of energy. [continued over]	Understanding the role of the battery in a circuit as a provider of a fixed amount of energy per coulomb is essential for predicting and explaining circuit behaviour.	Electrical circuits play an important role in our everyday lives. It is easy to overlook that their central purpose is to provide energy. This explains why batteries run "flat". From both a scientific and an environmental point of view, it is important to understand that the energy we get from an electric circuit (e.g. the light in a globe) is not "free" but involves depletion of energy in the source.

E: A battery creates an electric field within the materials that make up the circuit. This field is the cause of current when the circuit is closed.	F: An electric circuit is a system in which changes in one part can affect other parts.	G: A voltmeter measures how much energy is lost when one unit of charge moves from one point in a circuit to another.	H: The brightness of a globe depends on the rate at which energy is being transferred to the light globe.
For a given user/wire, the greater the potential difference between the ends of the user/wire, the greater the electric field (and hence the greater the push on charged particles).			
Scientists often use the idea of a 'field' to explain 'action at a distance', i.e. how one object can affect another when the two are not in contact. In particular, the electric field idea helps explain how the battery can affect the moveable charged particles in a circuit simultaneously. The idea of a field also helps explain why energy is lost in a resistor/ light globe when there is current within it. It also helps explain why the energy lost in a resistor/globe changes when another resistor/globe is added in series. [continued over]	These ideas are important for predicting and explaining the energy lost and current in different parts of a circuit.	Electrical meters, like ammeters, and voltmeters need a current to work and actually change the circuit they are measuring. These effects are usually tiny because, relative to the rest of the circuit, the ammeter has a very small resistance while the voltmeter has a high resistance. However, the changes they make to a circuit may be significant if the circuit's resistance is relatively small compared to the ammeter or relatively high compared to the voltmeter.	Students' thinking about electric circuits tends to focus mainly on current. By considering the factors affecting the brightness of a globe, they may become aware of the need to consider the rate of energy transfer, which is important in many everyday applications of electric circuits. Thinking about the brightness of a globe may also help students to understand that energy is "used up" in a circuit, not current (which many tend to believe); and reinforce the idea that electric circuits are important for their ability to provide energy in useful forms.

	A: To obtain an electric current, there needs to be a continuous loop from one terminal of a battery to the other.	B: An electric current is a flow of net charge in one direction. The materials that make up the circuit provide the charged particles that flow when there is an electric current.	C: A battery provides the energy for an electric current.	D: When there is a current in a circuit, energy flows from the battery to the user.
[continued] Why it is important for students to know this.		These ideas are also important in helping to explain why some substances have a higher resistance to electric current than others. Understanding that the charged particles are already in the circuit is an important factor for understanding why current is (virtually) instantaneous when a switch is turned on, and helps dispel a common perception that batteries are a source of charge.		
What else **you** know about this idea (that you do not intend students to know yet).	Charge can jump across a gap if the energy per unit charge provided by the battery is high enough. There can also be a current (albeit varying) in other non-continuous circuits (e.g. those containing capacitors). [continued over]	The flow of charge involves interactions between charged particles in the circuit. The electron drift model. The current in a wire is proportional to the average drift velocity of the moveable charged particles and the concentration of these charged particles, i.e. how many there are in a unit volume. [continued over]	Internal resistance of the battery. The chemical reactions in the battery. Why a battery provides a fixed amount of energy per coulomb, and why this depends on the chemicals it contains. The term 'emf' is best avoided at this stage.	A more sophisticated treatment would consider that energy is transferred from the battery to the user via electromagnetic fields around the circuit. The relationship between energy changes and work. Concept of potential. The energy loss in very long connecting wires (e.g. in overhead transmission wires from a power station) can be significant.

E: A battery creates an electric field within the materials that make up the circuit. This field is the cause of current when the circuit is closed.	F: An electric circuit is a system in which changes in one part can affect other parts.	G: A voltmeter measures how much energy is lost when one unit of charge moves from one point in a circuit to another.	H: The brightness of a globe depends on the rate at which energy is being transferred to the light globe.
Understanding the connection between electric field and potential difference is important if students are to make sense of explanations in text books etc. that imply that potential difference is a cause of electric current.			
The size of the field differs in different circuit components. In a wire of uniform cross section, the size of the electric field equals the potential difference between the ends of the wire divided by the length of the wire. When a switch is closed, it takes a finite, although tiny, amount of time, for the field to "build up" in the circuit. [continued over]	Ohm's law and the relationship $V = IR$.		The resistance of a light globe increases with temperature. The power loss in a light globe is the product of the potential difference across the globe and the current in globe.

	A: To obtain an electric current, there needs to be a continuous loop from one terminal of a battery to the other.	B: An electric current is a flow of net charge in one direction. The materials that make up the circuit provide the charged particles that flow when there is an electric current.	C: A battery provides the energy for an electric current.	D: When there is a current in a circuit, energy flows from the battery to the user.
[continued] **What else you know about this idea (that you do not intend students to know yet).**	The role of resistors in helping control the amount of energy made available to each 'user' in a circuit is not discussed until the more fundamental ideas of charge and energy flow have been established.	Thus, in a given wire, the larger the current, the faster the drift velocity of the charged particles. In a component (e.g. a light globe) the wire is attached to, the charged particles may have a slower drift velocity and, yet, if the concentration of charged particles is higher, still yield a current which is the same. Current is measured in amperes. Conventional current. Alternating current		
Difficulties/ limitations connected with teaching this idea.	We are talking about something that cannot be seen, and are reliant on meters to tell us what is happening in a circuit.	No one model explains all features of an electric circuit. Water circuits are often used as an analogy but students often find these of limited use because their experience of water flow tends to be limited to the domestic water supply which is not a closed loop and includes taps which may or may not be open. Many of the ideas about moving charged particles are difficult to "prove". [continued over]	Energy is a very abstract concept, potential energy even more so. The action of a battery is complex. It is often convenient to treat it as a 'black box' which provides electrical potential energy to the electric circuit. However, it is important to stress that it provides potential energy to the circuit by separating charged particles inside the battery; that the amount of potential energy it provides is related to the nature of the chemicals; and that it provides a fixed amount of energy for every coulomb, no matter what the current. A difficulty with the black box explanation is that students may take it to literally mean that charged particles carry potential energy in the same way, for example, as railway trucks carry coal. This is a problem because students may thus think that current causes potential difference. [continued over]	

E: A battery creates an electric field within the materials that make up the circuit. This field is the cause of current when the circuit is closed.	F: An electric circuit is a system in which changes in one part can affect other parts.	G: A voltmeter measures how much energy is lost when one unit of charge moves from one point in a circuit to another.	H: The brightness of a globe depends on the rate at which energy is being transferred to the light globe.
The inference that, for two given points in a circuit, a greater potential difference leads to a greater push, and hence a greater current, is not always true, e.g. a break in the circuit, a thermistor, diode, a capacitor. Conventions about direction of electric field.			
The idea of a field is very abstract. The field within a wire is affected not only by the battery but by both the fixed and moveable charges within the circuit (i.e. by the wires and other components in the circuit). Physicists often treat 'potential difference' as the "cause" of a current. This is because the idea of potential difference is intimately tied up with the notion of 'field' – the existence of one implies the existence of the other. [continued over]	These ideas are complex to understand. Explaining them involves several demonstrations and models. It is easy to reduce explanations to mathematical manipulations of Ohm's law and V = IR, but this does little to promote student understanding.	It is easy to refer to the reading on a voltmeter as 'voltage'. This is problematic because the term is given different meanings by teachers/ textbook authors (e.g. to mean potential, potential difference, emf) which is confusing for students. It is important to emphasise that the reading on a voltmeter connected across a battery when a circuit is open tells about the energy per coulomb it provides, but across a user connected to a battery is about the energy per coulomb being used.	Use of light globes as current meters in early work in this unit may lead students to think that their power depends only on the current in them, rather than the brightness – so it is important to address this issue at a later stage.

	A: To obtain an electric current, there needs to be a continuous loop from one terminal of a battery to the other.	B: An electric current is a flow of net charge in one direction. The materials that make up the circuit provide the charged particles that flow when there is an electric current.	C: A battery provides the energy for an electric current.	D: When there is a current in a circuit, energy flows from the battery to the user.
[continued] Difficulties/ limitations connected with teaching this idea.		They also depend on students having some understanding of a simple atomic model, e.g. negatively charged electrons orbiting a positive nucleus. Students need to understand the concept of charge. In addition, the language teachers and textbooks use may reinforce a popular misconception amongst students that charge is an object rather than a property of an object; e.g. we may speak of 'a moving charge' when we mean 'a moving charged particle' or a 'charge carrier'.	Understanding the concept of potential difference is made more difficult for students by the use, and frequent inconsistent use, of the terms 'voltage' and 'voltage drop' (i.e. instead of potential difference) in textbooks and other resources.	
Knowledge about students' thinking which influences your teaching of this idea.	Students often think that only one wire needs to be connected between battery and user (the 'unipolar model'). Students often do not recognise that a torch battery has two terminals (i.e. the central terminal and the outer casing). [continued over]	Students think that the battery is the source of 'charges' or charged particles (which they tend to think of as 'electricity'/ 'voltage'/ 'volts'/ 'amps'). Unless encouraged, students don't tend to see links between different science topics that they have studied; [continued over]	Student thinking about electric circuits tends to focus on current rather than energy or energy differences. Everyday language about "charging" batteries tends to reinforce the misconception that they provide charge. It is a good idea to talk about the energy provided by the battery in terms of joules/coulomb instead of volts to help reinforce the notion of the battery as an energy provider. Thus a '1.5 V battery' is referred to as a '1.5 joules/coulomb battery'. Similarly, for potential difference.	

E: A battery creates an electric field within the materials that make up the circuit. This field is the cause of current when the circuit is closed.	F: An electric circuit is a system in which changes in one part can affect other parts.	G: A voltmeter measures how much energy is lost when one unit of charge moves from one point in a circuit to another.	H: The brightness of a globe depends on the rate at which energy is being transferred to the light globe.
Some teachers try to avoid using the idea of 'potential difference' at this level: however, this is problematic when trying to explain the cause of electric currents, and why there are different amounts of energy lost in different circuit components.			
The idea of fields is most easily approached by talking about gravitational fields which students can more easily relate to. Therefore it is helpful if they already have some understanding of gravitational fields and gravitational potential energy (Some pre-teaching of these ideas may be necessary before introducing electric fields.) [continued over]	Students tend to think locally not globally. That is, they often think a change affects only the part of the circuit where the change has been made. Students tend to think that the current in a circuit is constant even when changes are made to parts of the circuit.	Students' prior experience of meters tends to include those that do not influence the system being measured (e.g. rulers, bathroom scales). Thus students tend to think that electrical meters are passive devices and do not affect the circuit they are measuring. [continued over]	Many students believe intuitively that "something" is "used up" in a circuit, and tend to consider this "something" is current. The early introduction of these ideas about the brightness of light globes helps to challenge this, and to raise students' awareness that both energy and current may be linked.

	A: To obtain an electric current, there needs to be a continuous loop from one terminal of a battery to the other.	B: An electric current is a flow of net charge in one direction. The materials that make up the circuit provide the charged particles that flow when there is an electric current.	C: A battery provides the energy for an electric current.	D: When there is a current in a circuit, energy flows from the battery to the user.
[continued] **Knowledge about students' thinking which influences your teaching of this idea.**	Other misconceptions are: • current passes out of both battery terminals to the user (the 'clashing currents model') • current is "used up" as it passes around the circuit (the 'attenuation model').	so they may not connect ideas about electricity with ideas they have studied about ionic substances for example. In particular they have difficulty linking macroscopic ideas like current etc. to microscopic ideas like electrons. The concept of net charge is difficult. A net charge of zero is often taken as implying that there are no charged particles present. Students realize that current involves the flow of charged particles but don't recognize the rate aspect of current. Thus, at this stage, it is better to use coulombs/sec as a unit for current (rather than amps) to help reinforce the notion that current refers to a rate of flow of charge.		
Other factors that influence your teaching of this idea.	'Electricity' is used in everyday life to mean current/voltage/charge/energy and is best not used. [continued over]	Students need to have some notion of atomic structure and this will need revisiting. In particular, they need [continued over]	Many of these ideas are best approached using metaphors/models/analogies. In each case it is important to be clear about the similarities and differences between the metaphor/model/analogy and the phenomenon being considered. [continued over]	

E: A battery creates an electric field within the materials that make up the circuit. This field is the cause of current when the circuit is closed.	F: An electric circuit is a system in which changes in one part can affect other parts.	G: A voltmeter measures how much energy is lost when one unit of charge moves from one point in a circuit to another.	H: The brightness of a globe depends on the rate at which energy is being transferred to the light globe.
The idea of a field is useful when responding to students who, thinking that moving charged particles in a circuit carry energy, ask 'how do they "know" how much energy to give each resistor in the circuit?' Students often think of potential difference as an **effect** of current rather than a **cause**. Linking potential difference to electric field helps to make this causality explicit and understandable.	.	As with the energy per coulomb provided by the battery, it is a good idea to refer to the readings on the voltmeter (i.e. potential difference) in terms of joules/coulomb rather than volts because it is easy for students to forget that $1\ V = 1\ J/C$.	
The relationship between electric field and potential difference is often not made explicit when teaching about electric circuits.	Qualitative approaches, rather than quantitative, help focus student attention on understanding. Thus, formulas are best avoided at this stage.		It is important to focus on qualitative reasoning to help promote understanding.

	A: To obtain an electric current, there needs to be a continuous loop from one terminal of a battery to the other.	B: An electric current is a flow of net charge in one direction. The materials that make up the circuit provide the charged particles that flow when there is an electric current.	C: A battery provides the energy for an electric current.	D: When there is a current in a circuit, energy flows from the battery to the user.
[continued] Other factors that influence your teaching of this idea.	Many students (especially girls) do not have much practical experience with electric circuits (beyond turning on a household switch!). Girls in particular are often reluctant to try connecting up circuits, and to say what they think for fear of being wrong.	to be familiar with the idea of charge, that charge may be positive or negative, and that objects with the same charge repel each other while those oppositely charged attract. This is an opportunity to make some links between a number of different areas in the science curriculum, e.g. atomic structure, chemical reactions, structure of ionic compounds and metals, heat conduction.	It is helpful if students have already encountered the ideas of gravitational potential energy and gravitational field.	
	The current "meters" usually used in introductory courses are torch light globes (also called bulbs). Torch light globes are unreliable current measurers because different globes with the same power markings may have slightly different brightnesses due to the manufacturing process. Thus all globes need to be tested before giving them to students or otherwise risk students drawing wrong conclusions and/or becoming disillusioned by their practical work.			
Teaching procedures (and particular reasons for using these to engage with the ideas).	Give students a battery, torch light globe and some connecting wire. Ask students to connect them up so the globe lights up. (N.B. do not provide a globe holder!) [continued over]	Water Circuit Model: An analogy can be drawn between a simple circuit (i.e. containing a battery and a light globe) and a water circuit containing a pump and a turbine. [continued over]	Gravitational Analogy (is helpful for developing ideas about field, potential difference and constancy of energy provided per unit charge by the battery): An analogy can be drawn between lifting a ball to a certain height (and giving it gravitational potential energy) and the effect of a battery, which separates charged particles and gives them electrical potential energy. The ball (if allowed to move) will fall down to the ground due to the gravitational field and lose gravitational potential energy. [continued over]	

E: A battery creates an electric field within the materials that make up the circuit. This field is the cause of current when the circuit is closed.	F: An electric circuit is a system in which changes in one part can affect other parts.	G: A voltmeter measures how much energy is lost when one unit of charge moves from one point in a circuit to another.	H: The brightness of a globe depends on the rate at which energy is being transferred to the light globe.
Using light globes as a current "meters" can lead students to believe that the brightness of a globe only depends on current – as students' understanding develops, they need to become aware that the brightness of a globe actually depends on its power (which is the product of the potential difference across the globe and the current in it).			
As well as teaching procedures in Big Ideas C & D. **The Jelly Bean Role Play** (is helpful for developing the idea of energy per coulomb: when extended to two resistors, the role play develops students' "need to know" about fields): Student "charged particles" each collect a fixed number of jelly beans (candy) [continued over]	**Predict-Observe-Explain (POE):** In each example below, ask students to predict what will happen to the brightness of a light globe, then demonstrate what happens and ask them to explain their observations: • the battery is replaced with one with a different number of 'volts' marked on it. [continued over]	**Practical Exercises:** Give students the opportunity to measure potential differences and currents in • a circuit with a battery and one light globe • a circuit with two batteries in series and one light globe • a series circuit with two identical batteries and two identical light globes. [continued over]	**Predict-Observe-Explain (POE):** Ask students to predict which will be brighter, a 40 W globe or a 75 W globe when connected to the mains supply. Most will correctly predict 75 W. Then ask them to predict which will be brighter when the two are connected in series. Most will wrongly predict 75 W. [continued over]

	A: To obtain an electric current, there needs to be a continuous loop from one terminal of a battery to the other.	B: An electric current is a flow of net charge in one direction. The materials that make up the circuit provide the charged particles that flow when there is an electric current.	C: A battery provides the energy for an electric current.	D: When there is a current in a circuit, energy flows from the battery to the user.
[continued] Teaching procedures (and particular reasons for using these to engage with the ideas)	The task helps to establish the conditions necessary to obtain an electric current. In particular, students need to be encouraged to trace the current path in the light globe from its central terminal through the filament to the globe's casing (which is the "other" terminal).	Points to note: • the water is already in the pipes and turbine just as the charged particles are already in the wires. • the battery's role is similar to that of the pump. • although we can't see the water moving, we can observe the effects of it moving (e.g. movement of turbine). Similarly we can't see charge moving but we can see the effect of that movement (e.g. globe lights up). The Bicycle Chain Analogy and the Rope Model are useful for discriminating between energy flow and current and for demonstrating constancy of current in a given circuit.	Likewise charge movement (i.e. current) in a circuit is due to an electric field and results in a loss of electrical potential energy from the circuit. It's important to stress that batteries always give equivalently charged particles the same amount of potential energy (which corresponds to always lifting a ball to the same height). (If teachers wish to include the idea that the charged particles do not accelerate, but move with a constant 'drift' velocity, the above analogy can be modified so that the ball is dropped so it rolls down a very long flight of stairs: in such a case, the ball's collisions with the steps results in the ball falling at a roughly constant speed.) **The Bicycle Chain Analogy** (helpful for developing idea of energy flow, for distinguishing the latter from charge flow, and for demonstrating constancy of current in a given circuit): The motion of a bicycle chain at constant speed is analogous to current in a complete circuit. The chain transfers energy from the pedal to the back wheel. The rider of a bicycle provides, via the pedal, the energy for the chain to move. The chain gives this energy to the back wheel. The energy in the back wheel is lost as heat due to frictional interactions between the tyre and the road. [Also includes teaching procedure in Big Idea E]	

E: A battery creates an electric field within the materials that make up the circuit. This field is the cause of current when the circuit is closed.	F: An electric circuit is a system in which changes in one part can affect other parts.	G: A voltmeter measures how much energy is lost when one unit of charge moves from one point in a circuit to another.	H: The brightness of a globe depends on the rate at which energy is being transferred to the light globe.
representing energy, as they pass the 'battery' and 'give up' some of this 'energy' as they reach/ pass through different obstacles or 'resistors'. If each student represents a 'coulomb' of charge and the jelly beans represent 'joules' of energy, the number of 'joules' given up by each student 'coulomb' when they reach a 'resistor' can be linked with the idea of potential difference.	• Another identical light globe is connected in series. • With the second globe still connected, another (similar) battery is inserted so there are now two in the circuit. **The Bicycle Chain Analogy** (is helpful for developing the idea of a system): If the back wheel is replaced with a heavier one, the chain will move more slowly unless the rider pushes harder. **The Rope Model** (helpful for illustrating the effects of changing the battery or the resistance in a circuit; and for demonstrating constancy of current in a given circuit): Students form a circle and loosely hold a continuous loop of thin rope horizontally. One student acts as the 'battery' and pulls the rope so it slides through the hands of the other students, the 'resistors'. The student resistors can feel the change in the heating of their hands arising from frictional interactions when they lightly increase their grip on the rope or when the student battery pulls harder.	**The potential difference should be measured:** • Across each battery (ideally when the circuit is open) and each globe when the circuit is closed • In a series circuit, across two batteries (ideally when the circuit is open) and, if appropriate, across two light globes when the circuit is closed • Between two points on one of the circuit wires when the circuit is closed. Students should explain their measurements in terms of joule per coulomb and coulomb per second.	If used early in this unit, this POE can be used to show that the power marked on a globe indicates the power needed for optimum brightness. Later in the unit, the relative resistances of the two globes can be discussed.

	A: To obtain an electric current, there needs to be a continuous loop from one terminal of a battery to the other.	B: An electric current is a flow of net charge in one direction. The materials that make up the circuit provide the charged particles that flow when there is an electric current.	C: A battery provides the energy for an electric current.	D: When there is a current in a circuit, energy flows from the battery to the user.
Specific ways of ascertaining students' understanding or confusion around this idea (include likely range of responses).	**Predict-Observe-Explain (POE):** Connect a torch globe to a battery so the globe lights up. Ask students to predict if there is acurrent in each wire, and if so, its direction. Then get them to observe the direction in each wire as shown by an ammeter which has the zero in the centre of the scale. Then ask students to explain their observation. The above POE can also be modified to ask students to predict the relative size of the current in each part of the circuit.	**Evaluating the appropriateness of a model:** 1. After considering the Water Circuit Model, ask the students to list the ways in which scientists' view of electric circuits is dissimilar to the water circuit. 2. Ask students how the water "circuits" in their everyday lives differ from the closed one above. **Predict-Observe-Explain (POE):** After they have observed the brightness of one light globe connected to a battery, ask students to predict the relative brightnesses of each globe when two more identical globes are connected in series. Then connect up the circuit and ask them to explain their observations. This helps challenge the notion that charge is provided by a battery and is "used up" as it moves around the circuit.	**Evaluating the appropriateness of an analogy:** 1. After considering the Gravitational Analogy, ask the students in what ways is the analogy dissimilar to an electric circuit. 2. Ask students how the Bicycle Chain Analogy is similar/dissimilar to an electric circuit. 3. In the Jelly Bean Role Play, at some convenient moment ask students to stop moving. Ask what they might need to do to make their role play more accurately represent what happens in a circuit (e.g. they may note that the 'charged particles' are not evenly distributed. 4. Add an extra resistor into the Jelly Beans Role Play circuit. Ask students what they need to do to mimic what happens in a "real" circuit. At this point students may want to know how the current "knows" how much energy needs to be given to each resistor: this is an opportunity for introducing the idea of 'field' and discussing the limitations of the Jelly Bean Model. **Concept Map:** Draw a concept map using the terms 'battery', 'charged particles', 'potential energy', 'user'. [Also applies to Big Idea E]	

E: A battery creates an electric field within the materials that make up the circuit. This field is the cause of current when the circuit is closed.	F: An electric circuit is a system in which changes in one part can affect other parts.	G: A voltmeter measures how much energy is lost when one unit of charge moves from one point in a circuit to another.	H: The brightness of a globe depends on the rate at which energy is being transferred to the light globe.
[Includes teaching procedures for Big Ideas C & D.]	**Design a role play or model:** Give students a circuit and ask them to design a role play or model to explain scientists' view of what happens in a circuit.	**Predict-Observe-Explain (POE):** Connect two identical light globes, A and B, and a switch in series to a battery. Close the switch and measure the potential difference between points X and Y on either side of A. Ask students to predict the potential difference across X and Y when A is removed from its socket with the switch still closed. Most will be surprised to find that it is non-zero, and has doubled. Ask them to explain. (This is tricky – it challenges students' misconception that the resistance of the gap in the socket (which is now the resistance between points X and Y) is zero because the light globe has been removed. Actually the resistance of the socket gap is extremely high ($\rightarrow\infty$) and much, much greater than that of globe B in the circuit. Thus the socket gap gets almost the whole share of the potential energy/coulomb provided by the battery.)	

INTRODUCTION TO PaP-eRs ON ELECTRIC CIRCUITS

In this section of the chapter, the PaP-eRs on Electric circuits linked to the preceding CoRe are offered. The PaP-eRs in this resource folio have been organized in a sequence that represents an intended order of reading; however, they are still able to be read as stand alone PaP-eRs.

TABLE OF CONTENTS OF PaP-eRs ON PARTICLE THEORY

The PaP-eRs in this section include:

8.1: THE JELLY BEAN ROLE PLAY – SOME PROS AND CONS

Many teachers like using the Jelly Bean Role Play as an approach to teaching about electric circuits. In the role play, two students are assigned the roles of "battery" and "light globe". The "battery" is given a bag of jelly beans which represent "energy". The "battery" and the "light globe" stand about 3 or 4 metres apart. About 10 more students act as "moveable charged particles", and are asked to form a complete "circuit" between the "battery" and the "light globe". After a direction for the "current" has been agreed upon, the "moveable charged particles" start to move around the "circuit". As they pass the "battery", the "moveable charged particles" are handed two jellybeans which they then give to the "light globe" as they pass it. The "light globe" eats the jelly beans and then does something (e.g. waves his/her arms) to represent the action of a real light globe producing heat and light. The role play is intended to show that in an electric circuit containing a single battery and light globe, the battery supplies a constant amount of energy per charged particle and that this energy is transferred to the light globe where it appears as heat and light.

Students generally find the role play to be fun – especially if they get to eat the jelly beans! – and, once completed, often feel that at long last they have finally begun to understand electric circuits. In this PaP-eR, an experienced science teacher shares with a beginning science teacher some of the pros and cons of this role play in terms of student learning.

SOME PROS

Mr. Hall, who was halfway through his first year of teaching, was talking to Ms. Smith, an experienced physics teacher, about ways of teaching a unit called Electric Circuits to his Year 10 general science class that he was planning to begin the following week.

'I've heard that kids love the Jelly Bean Role Play that is suggested in the course guidelines. They find it such a change from sitting down all the time and, of course, there are jelly beans to eat into the bargain.'

Ms. Smith smiled. 'Yes, students do enjoy it. And it does help develop their understanding of some science ideas about circuits although I've found that if I'm not careful, it can give them ideas that I have to "unteach" later!'

'Really? Have you got time to talk about how you use the role play? The ideas in electric circuits seem so complex and I was thinking that it looked like a good way of developing students' understanding.'

'Mm,' Ms. Smith responded, 'Well, recognising the ideas are complex is a good start! I think it's important to give the students a couple of periods for playing around with a few simple circuits first because many of them have very little prior experience with circuits, beyond turning on the light switch at home or inserting some batteries into the latest electronic gadget. So I give them an activity designed to help them understand how to make a complete circuit – in other words, how to connect up a battery and a light globe so the light globe lights up. I also give them some activities that explore how to change the brightness of a light globe in a circuit. Like what happens if you've got a circuit containing one light globe and a battery, and you connect an extra battery or you add an extra globe in series. After the class has got the idea that adding a battery makes the globe brighter, whereas adding another globe in series makes it dimmer, they are ready to start thinking about what is happening when there is a current in a circuit. That's when I get them to do the role play. It helps students to understand some of the science ideas about electric circuits. Basically, I want students to understand that in a complete circuit, there is a flow of charged particles and a transfer of energy from the battery to an energy user such as a light globe. Students often confuse current with energy, and the role play helps them to discriminate between the two. It helps develop other ideas as well. For example, when I think students have got the idea that the "charged particles" in the role play each get the same number of jellybeans, which they then give to the "light globe", I go to the board and summarise what is happening.' She scribbles on some paper:

'Energy' supplied by 'battery' per 'charged particle'
= 2 Jellybeans/'Charged particle'
= 2 J/C

'Energy' transferred to 'light globe'/used up per 'charged particle'
= 2 Jellybeans/'Charged particle'
= 2 J/C

'I think I can see where you are going with that," interposed Mr. Hall. "You're wanting to stress that energy is conserved and also get students used to the units of J/C because they are the same ones that scientists use. I guess at some point you'll tell the class that scientists use J to represent the number of joules of energy and C to representing the number of coulombs of charge, and that 1 joule/coulomb is the same as one volt!'

Ms. Smith nodded. 'Yep! And the students do, too – or at least the idea that each charged particle in the role play should get the same number of jellybeans and give these up to the light globe. I test this by asking them to predict what would happen if the "battery" gave each charged particle four jellybeans. Usually they quickly decide that each "charged particle" would give all four jellybeans to the "light globe" although there is some discussion before everyone realises that the "light globe" has to show he/she has been given more energy by, for example, waving his/her arms more rapidly.'

'When I think they have got the idea that energy is conserved, we go back to using a two jelly bean battery in the circuit; I tell the class that if this was a real circuit, the light globe would actually get a tiny bit less than two jelly beans from each charged particle, and ask why. This leads to a consideration of energy 'lost' in the wires and paves the way for some discussion of resistance in later lessons.'

'One of the other things that I do,' Ms. Smith continued, "is to wait for a moment when the "charged particles" are bunched up a bit or unevenly spread as they move around the circuit. Then I call out "stop" and ask the class what the "charged particles" could do to represent the current in a circuit more accurately. Usually they pick up fairly quickly that the "charged particles" need to be uniformly spread as they move around the circuit.'

'That's a nice way of reinforcing the idea that the current is the same everywhere," said Mr. Hall. "It seems to me this role play has lots of potential – no pun intended! – for helping students' understanding of circuits. And is there a reason why the battery provides two jelly beans, not one say?'

'Yes, but it's fairly trivial – it's because some of the modifications to the role play that we explore later involve two light globes in series. If the battery provided one jelly bean per charged particle, the jelly bean would have to be cut in two so half could be given to each light globe. This could provide an added complication that might distract students from thinking about how energy is shared in a circuit with two light globes in series, which is really tricky to understand. So I stick with a two jelly bean battery!'

'Well, that all seems fairly straightforward to me,' observed Mr. Hall.

'Yes, it is in some ways,' replied Ms. Smith, 'but, of course, real circuits are more complex to understand than the role play suggests. And it's important to help students understand this if their learning is to progress.'

'Once the class is familiar with the role play and can see the way it links with the behaviour of a simple circuit, I then spend some time considering aspects of a simple circuit that the role play doesn't explain. One of the things that I want the students to understand is that this role play, like all models, has its limitations, and that understanding the limitations of a model is an important part of understanding both the model and the thing that it is modelling! In other words, to understand both the role play and electric circuits, you have to understand the ways in which the role play is different to an electric circuit. And because of these limitations, which are ones that scientists also face with models they develop, we have to modify our model or seek a better one. I try to develop these ideas by considering what happens when a second light globe is introduced into the simple circuit we have talking about.'

Ms. Smith continued, 'So I ask the students how the role play needs to be modified to model what happens when in a circuit with two light globes in series. This is a really difficult question for many students. Some will want to give both jelly beans to the first light globe. We talk about what that would mean in a real circuit – one globe would glow and the other wouldn't – which is contrary to what they observed during their experimental work when they set up two light globes in series. Eventually someone may correctly suggest that one jelly bean should be given to the first light globe and one to the second. This presents a problem for lots of students – how do real charged particles "know" in advance of arriving at the second light globe that the second light globe is present in the circuit and that they should "give" the first light globe only half of what they had given it when it was the only light globe in the circuit. It's important to acknowledge this difficulty, for it is a problem that even applies to circuits with one light globe – why is all the energy provided by the battery given to the light globe? Before considering this issue, I talk about the ways that scientists have to modify their ideas when their models or explanations do not explain some aspect of phenomena. I close the lesson by telling the students that scientists use the idea of fields to explain what determines how much energy the light globes receive in an electric circuit: I tell them that it's a bit like the changeable speed signs that we now have on our roads – the ones where the speed limit changes according to the time of day or traffic conditions. Just as the speed signs control the speed of traffic at different points on the road, the field controls how much energy the charged particles give to each light globe in the circuit. And just as the speed signs can be changed to suit changes in the traffic conditions or time of day, so too the field can change to accommodate changes in the circuit. I reassure them that I'll be following up these ideas in later lessons to help them better understand the ideas.'

'If you're interested I can talk about what I do in those lessons some other time. But for now, how about we get a cup of coffee and then I'll tell you about what I think are some negative aspects to using the role play.'

SOME CONS

Ms. Smith sipped her coffee. 'One of the difficulties with the role play is that it can reinforce students' tendency to think of charged particles in anthropomorphic terms – in other words, the charged particles are like people and what they do is a function of their own decision-making processes. Even though we use the idea of a field to explain the behaviour of charged particles, this view that charged particles have to decide how much energy to 'give up' tends to linger.'

'And of course, the idea that charged particles carry energy to the light globe is also a bit misleading. Really a more scientific one understands that the energy transfer to the light globe is a consequence of the battery pushing the charged particles through the circuit. It doesn't worry me that students don't have this view yet, but I've found that one consequence of the idea that charged particles carry energy to the light globe is that some students, once they've been introduced to the idea of potential difference, think that current causes potential difference.'

'So there are some drawbacks to using the role play. It's vital that students understand how the role play is both similar and dissimilar to a real circuit and are exposed to a number of other analogies, metaphors and models to explain circuits. And I think it's important to revisit each of these from time to time. It's especially important after some new science ideas have been developed to see what, if any, are the links between the new concepts and each analogy, metaphor and model that has been discussed. For example, after my students have encountered some ideas about power, say, I go back to the role play and get them to think about what aspects, if any, of the role play might link with power. And I get them to do this for other analogies, metaphors and models we have used.'

'Gee,' exclaimed Mr. Hall, 'I've never thought about a role play as problematic before! I've just tended to think a role play is good to do occasionally because it's a bit different and it's easy. You've helped me see things about simplifying content that I hadn't thought of, I suppose it can actually impede understanding. I'll remember that next time I'm worried about acknowledging the complexity of science ideas like electric circuits with my students. I'm starting to realise there'll need to be lots of class discussion in this unit and that the role play could be a springboard for generating some of this discussion. I'll try it and let you know how I go ...'

8.2: LANGUAGE MATTERS

In this PaP-eR, an experienced science teacher talks about words that he avoids when teaching about electric circuits because they are problematic in terms of student learning.

In science, we often give words meanings that are quite specific and different to everyday meanings. So like many science teachers, I've always been careful about the language I use and tried to help my students understanding the specialised way that science uses words. With experience I've also found that the language we use matters in a different way and that certain words are best not used at all because they often end up confusing students. Here are some words I don't use when talking about electric circuits.

ELECTRICITY

In everyday life, the word 'electricity' can be used to mean a form of energy, an electric current, or an area of science, while in science, it is only used to mean the latter. Thus talking about 'the electricity in the circuit' often creates confusion amongst students because 'electricity' means different things to different people, and because it is often incorrectly used from a scientific perspective. Some of the confusions result in students not being not sure whether you are referring to energy or electric current, or thinking that electricity is a 'thing' in the circuit with its own special identity that is quite separate to current and energy. So instead I talk about the current in the circuit and the accompanying transfer of energy from battery to user – in fact, I don't talk about 'electricity' when discussing electric circuits!

CHARGES

Students tend to think that current is always a flow of electrons and forget that it can involve other charged particles as well. They also don't tend to make links between the ideas they are currently learning about and other topics they have studied in science. I want them to remember that all substances contain charged particles, and that what determines whether a substance conducts or not is the availability of charged particles that can be moved relatively easily. So I like to talk about 'moveable charged particles' to help remind them of these ideas.

And I refer to 'charged particles' not 'charges' to reinforce the notion that 'charge' is a property of substances, like mass. I find that using the expression 'charges' when talking about charged particles is unhelpful because students tend to focus on the charge aspect and forget that we are talking about actual things, i.e. particles that have a charge. As a consequence, students often think objects with zero charge must have no 'charges', i.e. contain no charged particles at all. This is especially relevant later on when I want to develop the idea that we measure current in terms of the net flow of charge (i.e. the total amount of charge carried by the moveable charged particles) in one second past a point.

VOLTAGE

Voltage is a very vague term and what it means is not clear – some text books I've come across use 'voltage' in a way that implies it is the same as potential difference, others imply it is potential, and others suggest that it is both potential difference and emf – which are different concepts. These same books may also talk about voltage difference which is also confusing: depending on whether you think voltage is potential difference, potential or emf, then voltage difference must be 'potential difference difference', 'potential difference' or 'emf difference'. So I don't use 'voltage' and instead talk about energy lost (or gained) per unit charge and potential difference.

Sometimes my careful use of words may seem a bit pedantic to students, and of no real import: indeed I myself find it difficult to always be consistent about the words I use and don't use because they are so often used in different ways by others (e.g. textbooks, other students). And nor am I trying to say that teaching electric circuits is merely about using correct language; nevertheless, I find it does help to pay attention to matters of language in dispelling misconceptions and promoting student understanding.

8.3: IT'S LIKE A …

This PaP-eR shows a collection of analogies and models that were included in a unit of work on Electric Circuits prepared by the teachers in a science department. The inclusion of these analogies and models was not intended to be prescriptive but rather as an aid to teachers teaching the unit, especially those teaching it for the first time who were looking for ideas to help promote their students' understanding.

SOME USEFUL ANALOGIES AND MODELS FOR TEACHING ELECTRIC CIRCUITS

Note:

(1) It's important to stress to students that no single analogy or model helps explain all electrical phenomena. Student understanding can be helped by:

- asking them how the analogy/model is similar to an electric circuit and how it is different;
- asking them to develop their own analogies and models; and,

(2) Both these activities also give you, the teacher, some insight into their understanding.

Phenomena/ science ideas/ to be explained	Analogy or model	Details of explanation
Why a light comes on so fast when a switch is turned on.	Bucket brigade.	Imagine a line of people holding buckets standing between a pond and a log of wood. The buckets are full of water from the pond. Suddenly the log catches alight and each person in the line passes on their bucket to the person next to them in the direction of the fire. The person at the end of the line nearest the fire empties his/her bucket on the fire. A bucket doesn't have to move very far or fast and yet the effect – water (whose origin was the pond) added to the fire – is very fast. Similarly, when a light switch is turned on, the moveable charged particles in a circuit don't move very far or fast but energy from the power station/battery appears very quickly at the light.
	Turning on a domestic water tap	If a tap is turned on, we don't have to wait for water to flow all the way from the dam because water is already in the taps. Similarly, the effect of turning on a light switch is almost instantaneous because the moveable charged particles are already in the circuit: as soon as they move, energy from the power station/battery is transferred to the light.
Why the current in one part of a circuit may be affected by changes in another part.	The traffic jam analogy.	Suppose a car is at the tail of a long line of cars moving at 100 km/h on a freeway. The car at the head of the line suddenly slows down to 40 km/h because of roadworks; the car behind also slows down, and the one behind that, and so on. Ultimately, all the cars in the line slow down, even though they have not yet reached the roadworks. Similarly, if the resistance (or potential difference) of part of a (series) circuit changes, the current is affected everywhere, not just in the section where the change occurred.
What resistance is.	Blocked drains.	If water drains from a sink more slowly than usual, we know there is likely to be some obstruction in the drain pipe. The obstruction acts like resistance in a circuit. The obstruction slows the rate of water flow and resistance slows the rate of flow of charged particles.
In a circuit containing more than one user, why the energy from the battery is shared between users/how the current "knows" when it gets to the first user that it must keep some energy to give to the next, and so on.	Pushing three identical heavy boxes in a line.	Suppose you have three identical heavy boxes (A, B and C) arranged side by side with sides touching. If you push box A from behind, then boxes B and C will also be pushed. Once all three are moving at the same speed, the energy from your push will be evenly divided between all three boxes and each will have been given less energy than would be the case if you were using the same size push on a single box.

Phenomena/ science ideas/ to be explained	Analogy or model	Details of explanation
Why the battery gives a constant amount of potential energy per unit charge and why this is independent of the current.	Charge escalator[25]	A real escalator will always lift a one kilogram weight to the same height, and so give it the same amount of gravitational potential energy. Similarly, the battery is like a charge escalator, "lifting" each unit of charge to the same "height" and giving it the same amount of electrical potential energy. Some points to make: ▪ The 'height' of the charged escalator is fixed and so too is the amount of potential energy per unit charge given by the battery. ▪ The amount of energy per unit charge provided by the battery is independent of the current just as the speed of the escalator does not affect the height that charge is lifted.
Energy is transferred from the energy source to the user when there is a current in a circuit; and energy is different to current.	The bicycle chain model.	The bicycle chain forms a continuous "circuit". As the rider turns the pedals, he/she puts energy into the "circuit", just like a battery. As the chain moves, energy is given to the back wheel, just like energy is given to the user in an electric circuit carrying a current. Some points to make: ▪ The chain is continuous and keeps going round and round at a constant rate. In an electric circuit containing one user, the current is also continuous and constant and not "used up". ▪ Energy is transferred from the rider to the back wheel when the chain turns just as energy from the battery is transferred to the user when there is an electric circuit.
What is an electric field, electrical potential difference and potential difference.	The gravitational model.	Assuming students are already familiar with ideas about gravitational fields and gravitational potential energy the following ideas can be elaborated: ▪ Scientists find it convenient to use the idea of a field to help explain how objects can affect each other without touching, i.e. "action at a distance". For example, we know that the space around Earth is affected by Earth's mass in such a way that, objects with a mass that are located in that space, experience a force towards Earth: this space around Earth is considered to be a gravitational field. The Earth's gravitational field provides the means whereby an object in it can be affected by Earth when not in physical contact with Earth. Similarly, the space around a charged particle (Q) is affected by its charge and is called an electric field; this means that other particles carrying a charge experience a force either towards or away from Q when they are located in Q's electric field. The separation of charge within a battery leads to an electric field within the battery and within the external circuit. This field within the circuit provides the means whereby the battery is able to push the moveable charges that are within the circuit.

[25]See page 226 of Knight, R. D. (2004). *Five easy lessons: strategies for successful physics teaching.* San Francisco: Addison Wesley.

Phenomena/ science ideas/ to be explained	Analogy or model	Details of explanation
		▪ Objects falling under the influence of Earth's gravitational field lose gravitational potential energy; when a one kilogram object falls between two points in Earth's gravitational field, the difference in gravitational potential energy is called gravitational potential difference. Similarly, charged particles that are moved by an electric field lose electrical potential energy; when one coulomb of charge is moved between two points in an electric field, the difference in electrical potential energy is called electrical potential difference (or, usually, just potential difference). In both gravitational and electric fields, the potential difference between two points is affected by the size of the field (i.e. how hard the field pushes).

8.4: WHY ONE TEACHER AVOIDS USING V = IR

In this PaP-eR, an experienced teacher reflects on the way his approach has shifted from a quantitative one in which students spend a lot of time applying V = IR to solve problems to one in which the emphasis is on students' understanding and reasoning about the behaviour of electric circuits.

Mr. Barrett was tidying up his filing cabinet when he came across a folder containing exercises on electric circuits that he had given to his Year 10 science classes in his first year of teaching. Included in the folder was a photocopy of a response sheet from one of his students, Tom, on which he, Mr. Barrett, had written some comments.

Mr. Barrett smiled to himself, reflecting on how much his teaching had changed over the years, for he had found that Tom's approach to solving circuit questions was not unusual. Gradually, Mr. Barrett had reduced the number of problems involving $V = IR$ that he gave his classes because the students tended to treat such exercises as a form of applied mathematics, and did not seem to see the necessity of using the ideas about electric circuits that they had discussed in their lessons in order to complete the task. Nor did they seem to develop much understanding about circuits from these activities. Importantly, he had found that they did not seem to see a circuit as a system in which changes in one part can affect other parts or that energy is conserved in a circuit; they also seemed to think the battery was a provider of constant current rather than constant emf. As a consequence, Mr. Barrett had developed the theory that introducing V = IR before these ideas were established was counter productive because students used it as an algorithm without thinking about its relationship to the physics of a circuit, and had modified his teaching approach accordingly. His emphasis was now much more qualitative and his focus was on understanding, rather than on correctly solving problems.

The current in a circuit containing a resistor (X) and a battery with an emf of 1.5 V is 1 A.
(a) What is the resistance of X?

V = 1.5 V   I = 1 A

R = V/I

R = 1.5/1 = 1.5 Ω

(b) Suppose another resistor (Y) with a resistance of 2 Ω is added in series to the above circuit. What will be the potential difference across Y?

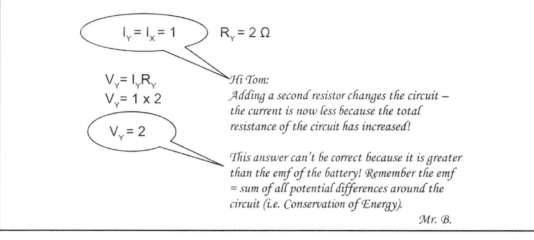

$I_Y = I_X = 1$ $R_Y = 2\ \Omega$

$V_Y = I_Y R_Y$
$V_Y = 1 \times 2$

$V_Y = 2$

Hi Tom:
Adding a second resistor changes the circuit –
the current is now less because the total
resistance of the circuit has increased!

This answer can't be correct because it is greater
than the emf of the battery! Remember the emf
= sum of all potential differences around the
circuit (i.e. Conservation of Energy).

Mr. B.

Re-reading the questions on Tom's answer sheet, Mr. Barrett thought about the kinds of questions he would probably ask now for the same circuit:

The current in a circuit containing a 1.5 Ω resistor (X) and a battery with an emf of 1.5 V is 1A.

(a) (i) What is the potential difference across the resistor X?
    (ii) Explain your answer.

Suppose a 2 Ω resistor (Y) is added in series into the above circuit.

(b) (i) Will the current in resistor Y be 1 A/ less than 1 A/ greater than 1 A? (Circle the correct alternative.)
    (ii) Explain your answer.
(c) (i) Will the potential difference across X be 1.5 V/ less than 1.5 V/ greater than 1.5V? (Circle the correct alternative.)
    (ii) Explain your answer.
(d) (i) Will the potential difference across Y be 1.5 V/ less than 1.5 V/ greater than 1.5V? (Circle the correct alternative.)
    (ii) Explain your answer.
(e) (i) Will the potential difference across Y be the same as/ less than/ greater than the potential difference across A? (Circle the correct alternative.)
    (ii) Explain your answer.

These questions tested student understanding of potential difference, the effect of resistance on the current in a circuit, conservation of energy and how energy is shared when there is more than one resistor in a circuit. Importantly, they did not involve the use of V = IR, which Mr. Barrett now delayed introducing until the later years of secondary school. While the content and wording of the questions he asked varied according to the year level of the class, one thing did not vary: this was the second part of each of the above questions, which asked students to explain their answers. For while students might be tempted just to guess the correct response to a question, Mr. Barrett had found that the requirement for an explanation encouraged them to think much more deeply and promoted a better understanding of the basic science concepts about electric circuits that he wanted them to develop.

8.5: STRINGS AND LIGHT GLOBES

In this PaP-eR, a teacher develops a simple model that provides her Year 9 students with a sensory experience that helps them understand how a light globe works. The teacher then builds from this shared experience to help develop in her students a more scientific understanding of the concepts of current and resistance.

Ms. Travers started the class by asking if she could have some volunteers. Hands shot up. Ms. Travers selected a group of students and asked them to stand in a circle. After giving each student part of a single piece of string to hold horizontally with fingers loosely curled around it, Ms. Travers then tied the two ends to form a complete closed loop.

'O.K, Karen,' she said, speaking to one of the students in the circle, 'I want you to hold the string with both hands more firmly now and your job is to pull the string so that it moves in an anticlockwise direction.'

Karen proceeded to pull the string so it passed through each student's hand in the circle.

'O.K. Jim, now I want you to curl your fingers around the string more.'

'Ouch,' exclaimed Jim, 'that's hot!'

'Sorry about that!' laughed Ms. Travers. She turned to address the class. 'Now what do you think this activity is all about?'

After a moment or two's hesitation, several responses came from the class.

'Electric circuits!'

'The string is the current in a circuit and Karen is the battery!'

'Jim's got a high resistance because his hand gets hot when there is a current.'

'Okay, thanks. You have some good ideas. Would anyone like some more information about what was being done in this activity?' asked Ms. Travers.

'Yes, I do. I'm not sure why Jim's hand got hot,' volunteered David.

'I think I can explain why,' said Jim. 'First, I was holding the string loosely. Then, when I began to hold it more tightly, there was more drag or friction between my hand and the string than there was with the others holding the string because I had a tighter grip and so it was harder for the string to pass through my hand. This means that the string was like the current in a circuit and I was providing a high resistance to the current with my hand.'

Ms. Travers felt there was a possible source of confusion here for students and decided to probe further.

'So, are you saying the current is the string, Jim? What do others think about this?'

Meiling raised her hand. 'I'm a bit confused. Does that mean that the current in the circuit wire is moving, even though the wire itself isn't moving?'

'Does anyone want to respond to Meiling's question?' asked Ms. Travers.

'I'll have a go,' said Jim, 'I think we are saying the same thing. A current is moving charged particles and when there is a current in a wire, electrons in the wire move, not the wire itself – we can tell that the wire doesn't move when we set up a complete circuit. Although the string looks similar to a wire, the movement of the string represents the movement of electrons in the wire, not the wire itself!'

'Thanks, Jim,' Ms. Travers nodded. 'Remember yesterday, at the end of the lesson when Marie asked why a light globe shines when there is a current in it? Can anyone see a way of explaining that now using this model?'

'I can!" answered Marie excitedly. "The light globe filament is a very thin wire. Because the wire is thin it would be hard for the electrons in the current to pass through so there would be a kind of friction between those electrons and the other bits that make up the wire, like there was between the string and Jim's hand. So the filament gets very hot, and we learned when we did the "heat" unit that when metals get very hot they glow.'

Mrs. Travers looked around the class. Marie had done an excellent job of explaining this difficult idea and although she could see nods of agreement from other class members during Marie's explanation, she was not sure how well they had taken this idea on board.

'Okay,' said Ms. Travers, 'here's a task I want all of you to do for homework to help me get a picture of your understanding of the purpose of this activity. Write your ideas about the ways in which the string model is similar to a simple circuit, and the ways in which it is not. You'll need to think carefully about this!'

After the lesson, as she reflected on the use of the string activity with her Year 9 class, Mrs. Travers noted the following in her work planner:

I realise that having a string that looks like a wire can result in some students thinking that the string represents the wire and that a current is the wire moving. Even though this issue has been raised and resolved in class today, it's important that I revisit and explore it when we discuss the homework at the start of the next lesson. I may need to build on Marie's explanation to ensure that class realises that the current is not the wire but is in the wire!

Plan for next lesson:

Discuss homework and build a class list of ways in which the string model is like an electric circuit and ways it is not.

Talk about one of the problems with the string model being that it doesn't make much use of the science ideas we have developed so far – scientists like explanations that build on ideas they have already developed. So while the string model helps us understand what happens in a globe filament, a more scientific model would use ideas about moveable electrons in metals etc.

Re-visit Marie's explanation. Elaborate on the motion of the current electrons in a wire and develop a model of energy transfer resulting from the current electrons "bumping" into the other particles that make up the wire and making them vibrate more (and linking this increase in vibration to an increase in temperature, and ultimately light being produced if the temperature is high enough). Important to emphasise that while this is a more "sciencey" model than the string model, it is still a model and has its own limitations.

A writing activity: Imagine you are one of the electrons in a current in a light globe filament. Write a story about your experiences as you move inside the filament. (Some things to think about: What would you see as you looked around you? What would happen to you as you moved through the filament? What would you feel?)

8.6: HELPING STUDENTS TO DISCRIMINATE BETWEEN CHARGE AND CURRENT

Students often confuse charge and energy, possibly because in everyday life we speak of charging batteries when, in scientific terms, we mean re-energise. In this PaP-eR, a teacher helps her students to understand that current involves a flow of particles that have a charge, and that charge is not the same as current.

To help her students understand some science ideas about a simple electric circuit, Ms. Gauchi had used a model in which trucks are loaded with coal at a coal depot, deliver the coal to a factory, and return to the depot to be reloaded: the coal depot is intended to be analogous to a battery, the trucks to moveable charged particles, the coal to energy and the factory to a resistor or light globe.

The following day she gave the students an activity which involved explaining, in terms of the truck model, why the light globes in a circuit containing two identical torch light globes in series and a battery shine with equal brightness, but less brightly than a single globe connected to a similar battery. The task was a challenging one, and Ms. Gauchi was interested to see how her students would account for the circuit's behaviour in terms of the truck model: would they realise that the model would have to be modified to include two factories with each truck delivering half its load to each factory? Wandering around the classroom, she listened to the comments that students were making as they worked in their groups. In one group, John and Matt were explaining the truck model of a simple circuit to a group member who had been absent for a few days:

John: 'Well current is the actual flow of electrons. The trucks are like the current that carries the charge which is the energy on each truck.'

Matt: 'The current is roughly the amount of trucks travelling down the highway, which are like the wires in a real circuit, and the charge is the amount of energy they carry.'

As the group continued to talk, Ms. Gauchi realised that although the students seemed to understand that current and energy were different, there was nevertheless some confusion about this issue. While their comments suggested that they saw current as involving a flow of electrons, the students did not seem to realise that electrons cannot lose their charge, and that charge is different to energy. Ms. Gauchi pondered the ways in which she might help them to understand this.

The next lesson, she organized a role play outside in which students acted as trucks moving around a closed loop that had been drawn on the ground. Each student truck carried a piece of paper labelled "negative charge". As each student truck passed a point in the loop labelled "depot (battery)", they were handed a piece of paper labelled "coal (energy)" which they delivered to another point labelled "factory (light globe)" before returning to the depot.

Afterwards, the students returned to the classroom. Ms. Gauchi wrote the terms 'current', 'charge', 'electrons', 'energy', 'light globe' on the board and asked the students to discuss with their usual groups the ways in which these terms were linked and to draw a group concept map.

That night, as she perused the various groups' concepts maps, she noted with interest the concept map from John and Matt's group which suggested that they no longer considered that charge was the same as energy.

Ms. Gauchi made a mental note to remember that an understanding that current was not energy did not imply an understanding that charge was not energy, and to emphasise that while energy is 'used up' when there is a current, the flowing electrons carry charge which is not used up.

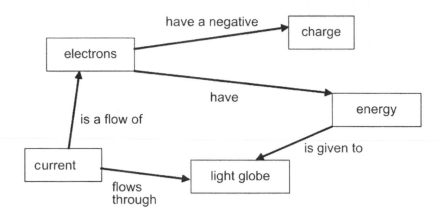

CHAPTER NINE

GENETICS

This chapter outlines a representation of Pedagogical Content Knowledge (PCK) for the topic of Genetics. As was the case of Chapter Five (Chemical Reactions) and Chapter Seven (Force), for this topic we again offer two CoRes as opposed to a single CoRe. However, in Chapter Five, the two CoRes represented different teachers' framing of the content whereas in this chapter, similar to that of Chapter Seven, the two CoRes were generated by the same teachers and represent different aspects of teaching this topic, viz. teaching about genetics at a micro and macro level. Hence, the format for this chapter is similar to that of Force as it includes a first CoRe (Part One: Micro) followed by a second CoRe (Part Two: Macro).

The two parts of the CoRe assume a sequence of teaching that focuses on developing student understanding of Genetics, firstly, in situations where the scope of the ideas are at the micro level and, secondly, where the scope of the ideas are specifically focused on the macro level. However, it is not practical, or even desirable, to follow this division strictly when teaching. In fact, in the first part of the CoRe, situations involving thinking about Genetics at the micro level are used early on to explore students' ideas but they naturally link to moving out to the bigger picture that is the macro level.

The presentation of the two CoRes in this manner is designed to make the breakdown of the ideas easier to follow and understand in terms of the essential elements of Big Ideas and the influence of these on responses to the prompts in the left hand column of the CoRe.

REMINDERS ABOUT SHAPING FACTORS THAT INFLUENCE CoRes AND PaP-eRs

As is the case with each of the concrete examples of PCK that comprise Chapters 4–9, we briefly offer some of the important points that shape our understanding of representing PCK. Reiterating this information at the start of each chapter (Resource Folios) is intended to remind the reader about the nature of this form of representation of PCK and for that information to be at hand for each individual topic portrayed.

Therefore, some of the important points to be kept in mind when considering what follows in this Resource Folio are:

- It is very difficult to offer a single example of PCK that is a neat concrete package, able to be analysed and dissected or used as a blueprint for practice by others. Therefore, our approach to capturing and portraying PCK hinges on the understanding that the teaching and the content must be represented in ways that both maintain the complexity of their relationships but at the same time offer some way of seeing through the complexity in order to gain insight into it.
- Our approach is based on what we have termed CoRe (Content Representation) and PaP-eRs (Pedagogical and Professional-experience Repertoire). The CoRe outlines some of the aspects of PCK "most attached to that content" but it is not the only representation. It is a necessary, but incomplete, generalization that helps to make the complexity accessible and manageable; it is neither complete nor absolute. Attached to the CoRe are the PaP-eRs, with links to the aspects of this field that they "bring to life". A PaP-eR is of a content area and must allow the reader to look inside a teaching/learning situation in which the content shapes the pedagogy.
- PaP-eRs bring the CoRe to life and shed new light on the complex nature of PCK. They help create ways to better understand and value the specialist knowledge, skills, and ability of teachers thus making that which is so often tacit, explicit for others.

	IMPORTANT SCIENCE	
This CoRe is designed for students in Middle–Upper secondary school (i.e. Year 10).	**A:** **The cells of all organisms contain information in the form of DNA that primarily determines the characteristics of that organism**	**B:** **Genes are inherited**
What you intend the <u>students</u> to learn about this idea.	The bodies of living things (beyond unicellular organisms) are made of cells and cell products. DNA is a complex chemical found in the nucleus of every cell in complex organisms. DNA is a store of coded information.	A gene is a "unit" of information (a "piece" of DNA) that codes for the production of a particular characteristic (e.g. blood group). Genes direct various cell functions. Groups of genes are organized as chromosomes. Each species has a particular number of chromosomes.
Why it is important for students to know this.	Basis of knowledge required to understand heredity. Students need to know that this applies to all organisms including plants, bacteria and fungi. Individual characteristics are the result of interaction between genes and the environment.	To understand the significance of genes as the blueprint for how an organism develops and functions.
What else <u>you</u> know about this idea (that you do not intend students to know yet).	Fine details of DNA structure; some other cellular organelles have DNA; viruses don't have DNA.	Each gene encodes for a particular protein (however, it is increasingly difficult to maintain the idea that genes determine a unique protein sequence). Chromosomes are only visible during cell division.

IDEAS/CONCEPTS		
C: A copy of the genetic information inside a cell is made during the process of cell division	**D:** Different genes are 'switched on and off' in a cell	**E:** Genes can be manipulated
DNA replicates exactly (unless there is a mutation). There are two types of cell division: (1) reduction division for producing sex cells (half number of chromosomes); (2) replication division for producing body cells (full set of chromosomes). Reduction division occurs in the sex organs of plants and animals. Replication division occurs throughout an organism's body. Prokaryotic cells divide by a process called binary fission.	Alleles are different combinations of proteins that control the expression of a gene, and which result in traits that can be dominant or recessive. Different genes are "switched on" in a cell according to the cell's location (e.g. liver genes in a liver cell; pigment production in a flower cell). Different genes act together. Individual characteristics are often the result of interaction between different genes.	Genes can be "exchanged" within (and between) an organism. The process of gene recombination is a naturally occurring way in which genes can be exchanged. With technology we can make deliberate choices about which genes can be exchanged. Cloning (process for duplicating DNA)does not necessarily result in whole new organism.
Need to know how genetic information is passed on. Need to be able to explain how DNA replication can have 2 different end points: (1) reduction (for production of sex cells); (2) replication (for growth, replacement and repair).	Need to recognize that even though most cells contain all genetic information, only certain information is required in any one cell at any particular time. Most genes in most cells are not needed so almost all are "switched off" (or never "switched on") in a given cell and may be switched on and off at different times.	Need to have a grasp of these ideas in order to make informed choices as citizens. Students need to understand the difference between therapeutic vs. reproductive cloning (i.e. cloning cells vs. cloning whole organism) to understand current issues reported in the media.
Fine details of DNA replication, details of processes of division (meiosis and mitosis).	The actual processes of gene regulation, such as transcription factors and breakdown of mRNA, etc.	Notion of recombinant gametes and linked genes to produce greater variation.

	A: The cells of all organisms contain information in the form of DNA that primarily determines the characteristics of that organism	B: Genes are inherited
Difficulties/ limitations connected with teaching this idea.		What actually constitutes a gene is a very complex question that is still unclear to biologists.
Knowledge about students' thinking which influences your teaching of this idea.	Some students think chromosomes are found in the blood. Many students think that only genes influence what/who you are. They also think that one gene controls one characteristic (e.g. eye color). Most students have heard of DNA but don't really know what it is so need to start off at macro level.	Students struggle with the differences between gene/ chromosome/ DNA.
Other factors that influence your teaching of this idea.	Students have pre-conceived ideas about biology and don't expect it to be difficult. They think they just have to know information and don't realise they need to be able to apply it. Genetics is very complex.	
Teaching procedures (and particular reasons for using these to engage with this idea).	Think, Pair, Share – Draw a picture of where you would find DNA, genes, chromosomes in a person, plant, mushroom, bacteria. Probe of students' thinking. Drawing activity – Draw yourself and one parent. Indicate on your drawing any characteristics that you believe you inherit from that parent. Gives students opportunity to think about interaction between genetics and environment. Practical activity – Do some simple DNA extraction procedures to look at DNA of various organisms (e.g. banana, wheat germ). Gives students some sense of macro appearance of DNA.	**Metaphor activity** – Gene as unit of currency. Ask students to develop their own analogy that can be used to illustrate the concept of a gene. Develop the analogy to illustrate genes being switched on and off in a cell. **Model making/Drawing** – Use materials to create physical models. Students draw their understanding of the relationship between DNA, genes, cells & chromosomes. **Genetic Engineering** – Students are asked to genetically engineer organisms from a list of instructions. Students have to choose parents with appropriate alleles to get desired characteristics – often a check if students understand the ideas of dominant and recessive.

C: A copy of the genetic information inside a cell is made during the process of cell division	D: Different genes are 'switched on and off' in a cell	E: Genes can be manipulated.
Similarities between terms; large number of new terms.	An understanding of inheritance and of genotype/phenotype is necessary for students to make appropriate predictions in pedigree analysis.	This is a large area that can make it difficult to decide on the level of depth covered and the types of issues.
A source of confusion is differences in the number of daughter cells in mitosis and meiosis and chromosome number in each. Students may be confused by many new and similar terms (e.g. chromosome, chromatid, chromatin).		Many students are interested in gene technologies. Students have limited knowledge of cloning, and tend to think about it in terms of whole organisms Students tend to think all cloning is "bad". Many students struggle with complex processes of transcription/translation/ protein synthesis.
Unlabelled diagrams – Students get a copy of two unlabelled simple diagrams of mitosis and meiosis and try to explain what they see happening to chromosomes ateach stage. Emphasis on process and possible reasons not learning labels. **Model making** – mitosis and meiosis (using pipe cleaners) to strengthen the learning experience by manipulating a 3D model. **Role Play** – pairs of similar height students (represent idea of chromosomes of same size) – link arms. Pairs carry cards with alleles on them (e.g. ABO blood type) to show that alleles are carried on chromosomes. **Interactive animations/videos** – mitosis/meiosis. Students can see how chromosomes change at different stages and why gametes have ½ chromosome number, and why halving is important.	**Case study** – Students analyse data from case studies to build an explanation for genes being switched on and off at different times in an organism (e.g. haemoglobin production). **Popular culture** – Use examples from popular culture (e.g. Harry Potter) to explore the inheritance patterns of particular alleles within a family/population. **Pedigree Analysis** – Students analyse pedigrees to infer genotype of individuals and to make predictions about possible outcomes of crosses.	**Sci-fi and fantasy movies** (e.g. GATTACA) to explore issues and possibilities related to genetic engineering. Use of **software/websites** to illustrate process of therapeutic cloning e.g. 'Click and Clone': Website – can clone a mouse by "clicking" and find out what procedures are involved in cloning. Helps students to understand differences between therapeutic and reproductive cloning, also adds to whole class engagement and discussion and can lead to development of more questions from students.

	A: The cells of all organisms contain information in the form of DNA that primarily determines the characteristics of that organism	B: Genes are inherited
Specific ways of ascertaining students' understanding or confusion around this idea (include likely range of responses).	Student confusion is often revealed in attempts to draw where DNA is found in different types of organisms (e.g. that DNA is found in blood/brain/sex organs, only in humans, or that there is no DNA present in plants, fungi or bacteria.).	Student confusion is often revealed in their written work when they use the wrong words (e.g. gene instead of chromosome, etc.). When students make models of DNA, they often ask 'Where is a gene?' 'Where is a chromosome?' Or teacher can ask for students to indicate difference between gene/ chromosome/ DNA to check their understanding. Students' models of DNA often give insight into whether they have understood pairing of bases (e.g. they may not have matched appropriate bases).

C: A copy of the genetic information inside a cell is made during the process of cell division	D: Different genes are 'switched on and off' in a cell	E: Genes can be manipulated.
Ask students about differences in number of daughter cells produced from mitosis and meiosis. Mix and match of terms. Give students two columns of mixed terms that they have to match. Provides insight into understanding, e.g. do students link 'black hair' in one column to genotype or phenotype in second column?	**Pictionary** – students draw and identify various "standard" representations of genetics. In pedigree analysis, when asked to predict the offspring with a certain trait of individuals in the pedigree, if students ask: 'But how do we know what the genotypes of the parents are?' This indicates they haven't understood the meaning ofgenotype.	

	IMPORTANT SCIENCE	
This CoRe is designed for students in Middle –Upper secondary school (i.e. Year 10).	**A:** **Genetic instructions are passed from parent to offspring**	**B:** **There is variation between individuals within a species**
What you intend the <u>students</u> to learn about this idea.	In sexually reproducing organisms both parents contribute equally to the genetic makeup of the offspring, and so offspring are not identical to parents. In asexually reproducing organisms, offspring is an exact genetic copy of the parent.	Within a species there are differences between individuals, both internally and externally. There are different sources of variation: (1) the re-arrangement of genetic information from both parents (during formation and fusion of sex cells); (2) external factors (such as chemical mutagens).
Why it is important for students to know this.	This is the basis of an understanding of heredity.	Need to recognise that there is diversity amongst different life forms as well as uniqueness within a species.
What else <u>you</u> know about this idea (that you do not intend students to know yet).	Fine details of mitosis and meiosis.	Fine details of processes leading to variation (e.g. crossing over).
Difficulties/ limitations connected with teaching this idea.	Teachers need to be sensitive to both known and unknown aspects of students' biological family situations.	Students need to have a concept of 'species' (and that there is more than one definition)
Knowledge about students' thinking which influences your teaching of this idea.	Many students would be unaware of asexual reproduction, and the processes of reproduction in organisms other than animals. Students tend to think that particular characteristics are inherited from mother and particular characteristics from father.	Students tend to be interested in why variation exists within a species.

IDEAS/CONCEPTS		
C: The total amount of variation within a species is relatively stable	**D:** An individual's characteristics are determined by interaction between genetic information and the individual's environment	**E:** Evolution is a process that results in heritable changes in a population spread over many generations
A new variation is a relatively rare occurrence that only occurs when the genetic information is disrupted or changed by a mutation. Mutations can only be passed on to offspring (or next generation) if they occur in sex cells.	Genetic and environmental factors act together to determine an individual's characteristics. Phenotype (i.e. observable characteristics) = genotype (i.e. genetic information) + environment.	A population is a group of individuals of the same species living in a particular place. The frequency of particular characteristics in a population can change as a result of a change in the environment. Over many generations, the consequences of such changes in characteristics can lead to changes in a species or the emergence of new species. This process is called evolution. Natural selection is a mechanism for evolution.
Important to know that mutation is a source of new variation.	It is not genetics or environment alone that determines an individual's makeup.	Need to know there is a relationship between heredity and change, over time.
Different types of mutations and their effects on protein formation.	Details of environmental triggers on protein production.	Details of evolution as a change in allele frequencies. That there are different forms of evolution (e.g. cultural, biological).
	This is a complex issue since there is no single answer about which characteristics and to what extent the interaction occurs between these aspects.	The scientific language used has very different meanings from those in everyday life (e.g. adaptation, fitness, selection).
Students tend to think that changes in a species arise as a result of a "need" to fit in with the environment and that mutations occur "on demand" in order for species' needs to be met. Also that an individual adapts rather than the species. The common language around 'adaptation' may exacerbate this problem. Students don't realise that mutations in somatic (body) cells aren't passed on to the next generation.		Need to take into account students' religious beliefs. Students often have the misconception that evolutionary changes and mutations are a response and adaptation to the environment Students often have the misconception that evolution and natural selection operates at the individual level, rather than on a population. Students generally haven't studied much about history of life on earth.

	A: Genetic instructions are passed from parent to offspring	B: There is variation between individuals within a species
Other factors that influence your teaching of this idea.	This is a personally interesting topic for many students. Need to spend time establishing this idea before progressing to other ideas.	Ethical and environmental issues. Need to spend time establishing this idea before progressing to other ideas.
Teaching procedures (and particular reasons for using these to engage with this idea).	Survey – Students conduct survey of family characteristics – helps students to observe differences within family and why a family member may have a characteristic that their parents don't have.	Comparison study – Students look at specimens of different organisms from the same species (e.g. dogs, clover) to identify similar and different features (maintaining awareness of developmental variation). Students investigate different selective breeding techniques to consider characteristics that have been selectively bred and possible reasons for this (e.g. cats, potatoes). Use of PTC paper (ability to taste PTC is a dominant trait) – students can test themselves and calculate probabilities of someone in class being able to taste it (and compare with general population where $p = 3/4$).
Specific ways of ascertaining students' understanding or confusion around this idea (include likely range of responses).		"Vegetable people" activity that requires students to build parent organisms according to given information and predict characteristics of several offspring – demonstrates understanding of phenotype and genotype.

C: The total amount of variation within a species is relatively stable	D: An individual's characteristics are determined by interaction between genetic information and the individual's environment	E: Evolution is a process that results in heritable changes in a population spread over many generations
		Evolution and natural selection don't make sense without a concept of 'deep time', which most people find difficult to conceive. The religious versus science debate portrayed in the media can have an impact.
	Popular culture – Use examples from popular culture (e.g. Harry Potter) to explore the inheritance patterns of particular alleles within a family/population. Involves some speculation about wizarding as dominant or recessive trait. Genetic barley: grow barley that has green or white (albino) phenotype in dark and in light. In the dark, offspring always albino, in light, offspring green and albino, so students work out that phenotype = genes + environment. Construct a pedigree – Give students original data about a genetic condition (e.g. Huntingdon's disease). Students enjoy constructing pedigree and trying to work out inheritance pattern. Use of software – e.g. 'Pea plant genetics' and 'Drosophila genetics' to generate data from a real experiment. Students collect data and work out the likelihood that certain phenotypes, etc are reproduced.	Use of software to model natural selection so students can see changes occur over many generations (e.g. in frogs) and is not instantaneous. Also helps them to see what happens when the environment changes and that *the variation already existed* when the change occurred. Ask students which variation is at a selective advantage and why. History of life on planet Earth – construct a scale time line on a 2m strip of paper. Include important geological events and biological events (e.g. when did first plants appear in fossil record?). Different student groups can be given the task of researching and constructing time line for different geological periods and then all can be stuck together.

INTRODUCTION TO PAP-ERS ON GENETICS

In this section of the chapter, the PaP-eRs on Genetics are presented. They are not organised in a specific order, nor are they intended to be read sequentially. Each PaP-eR should stand alone and be capable of illustrating how PCK is evident in the way the individual PaP-eR brings to life specific aspects of the CoRe.

9.1: A MENTAL MODEL FOR TEACHING GENETICS

In this PaP-eR, an experienced biology teacher discusses the mental model that she has developed for teaching genetics. This model underpins her approach of first introducing genetics terms and ideas to her senior high school students and then encouraging them to see the links between those terms and ideas. The PaP-eR takes the form of an excerpt from an interview with the biology teacher, Sue.

Sue: I've been teaching senior high school genetics for a few years and over that time I have come to organise my thinking about how the different genetics concepts are linked together using the analogy of a tree: the trunk is the topic of genetics, and the main branches are the key subtopics, and then the smaller branches off these are different concepts, and then the leaves on the tree and other little branches are different activities or ways that I can use to help the students to remember and understand the branches (concepts). Being able to think about the concepts and the relationships between them in this way is helpful because the topic of genetics is so large and complex; it is often hard for students (and teachers!) to see the connections between the various parts. So we need a way to recognise the different parts and then bring them together later to say, 'Well this bit fits with this bit,' so it becomes like leaves fitting into a pattern.

Interviewer: So are you saying that you give your students various activities and tell them these are like leaves that help to outline the shape of the tree? So then as you go, you are kind of filling in the shape of the tree with them, as it were?

Sue: Yes, and sometimes the wind can blow, so the leaves from one part of the tree or different branches are in close proximity which means there might be some sort of link between them, so the wind becomes part of the analogy in a particular context. For instance, if you are looking at the expression of a gene, that's connected with protein synthesis. Initially when you first start introducing the idea of genes as the units of inheritance, you wouldn't start talking about protein synthesis because it is quite different in terms of the level or depth you might go into when introducing a concept like that. But if you first introduce the gene as a unit of inheritance and then make a connection to DNA and the structure of DNA in terms of genes being made up of different sequences of nucleotides, then you can make the link to the statement, 'Well, these genes have the coding to tell us which proteins to make.' Then you can also go back to another branch and talk about alleles being alternative forms of these genes and how the leaves of the branches would be brought together in a different way in the context of looking at pedigrees and genotypes and phenotypes. So the idea is, it's not a tree that just stays still: the branches move. And so when some of the branches are brought together because of the wind blowing in a particular direction, you need to look at those terms or ideas that are now in close proximity, whereas if the wind blows in a different direction you look at a different set of ideas and terms that are now close to each other. And when you look at typical exam questions in genetics, you're not just looking at being able to recall the shape and structure of the tree, but at seeing the application to unfamiliar situations as the wind brings different parts of the tree together - and that's what the students need to be able to do. So, the way that I teach genetics, in junior classes too, is not just about recall, it's about trying to get the students to link key terms and concepts together – and to recognise that this new language of biology they are learning can be put together to construct helpful mental models.

Interviewer: How do you decide what contexts to use in your teaching to help students to make links across those different leaves and branches?

Sue: Well, a really good way is to use things that are in the recent media, so it may be newspaper articles or, as is more frequently the case, *New Scientist* articles. *New Scientist* has some quirky little stories – the novelty of the story, the fact that it's not in a text book and the fact that it's not old news is just so exciting – the things that are happening in genetics and genetic engineering grab the students' attention and imagination. So when using that sort of story, I first get them to have a look at that article and to highlight or pick out what are the key biological terms; sometimes I give them a list of genetic terms that they may or may not be familiar with, and they have to find them, like a word game. Then we look at how those terms are grouped together and try to make sense of some sentences and maybe find out more to try to understand what that article is about.

Interviewer: Some of those articles are quite difficult to read.

Sue: Yes, so you need to select carefully as some of them have less complex biology terms that makes the article more accessible, especially to the younger students. Learning to recognise the language and not feel scared of the big terms is important since genetics, and biology more generally, is all about feeling comfortable with the language. There are so many new terms and then after you have learned the terms and their meanings, it's important to learn how those terms can link together. And then once you've got that linking together, that's when the rest of the picture will fall into place, and that is where the tree analogy with the branches comes in. You've got the terms and their meanings and seeing how they may link together is how you then get the idea of that particular concept across. For example, if you are looking at an article on inheritance of haemophilia or cystic fibrosis or whatever genetic disease or disorder, then you think, how can I use this context to show how the language works? So it is not just learning words in isolation but trying to recognise and translate the language so that it becomes something meaningful for students.

Interviewer: When you are making the selection of articles, presumably you are thinking back to the tree and the trunk analogy. So are there particular ideas on the trunk and the branches that are framing what you are thinking in this situation, for instance, in terms of particular big ideas in genetics? I assume there are some ideas that you feel students definitely need to understand that would guide your decision-making?

Sue: Sure! In genetics, most of the articles will, in some way, link back to DNA. I use different articles for different key ideas but I will always try to find some link to DNA, even maybe via a question (for example, where DNA isn't mentioned in the article) to try and help students to make that link to DNA and the structure of DNA. For instance, when we're thinking about ideas related to pedigrees, phenotypes and genotypes, we need to look at the genes and the alleles that are made up of DNA with different nucleotide sequences which will determine the different proteins that are produced or not produced. If the topic is genetic engineering, I might use an activity involving cutting and pasting DNA, so students are finding out about detecting particular sequences of DNA to predict whether a particular disease or disorder is present, or to identify a particular individual. So I guess I use different articles to show different linking and different examples of contexts, but always bringing it all back to DNA in some way. All the time, I'm trying to be clear and explicit that all these ideas are part of the same big picture. Using this kind of mental model then becomes an important organiser for my thinking and for helping the students to organise their thinking also.

9.2: DEEP TIME

To understand the science ideas behind evolution, an appreciation of the vast time periods over which natural selection occurred is important. This PaP-eR consists of two separate sections: Part A presents students' perspectives of an assignment that involved developing a visual representation of the long time periods involved in the development of life on earth, while Part B presents the teacher's thinking behind the task.

PART A: THE ASSIGNMENT

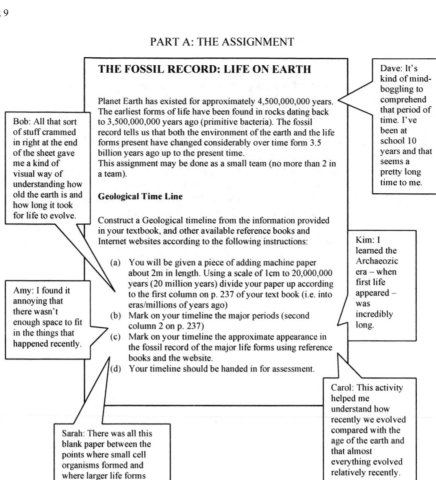

THE FOSSIL RECORD: LIFE ON EARTH

Planet Earth has existed for approximately 4,500,000,000 years. The earliest forms of life have been found in rocks dating back to 3,500,000,000 years ago (primitive bacteria). The fossil record tells us that both the environment of the earth and the life forms present have changed considerably over time form 3.5 billion years ago up to the present time.
This assignment may be done as a small team (no more than 2 in a team).

Geological Time Line

Construct a Geological timeline from the information provided in your textbook, and other available reference books and Internet websites according to the following instructions:

(a) You will be given a piece of adding machine paper about 2m in length. Using a scale of 1cm to 20,000,000 years (20 million years) divide your paper up according to the first column on p. 237 of your text book (i.e. into eras/millions of years ago)

(b) Mark on your timeline the major periods (second column 2 on p. 237)

(c) Mark on your timeline the approximate appearance in the fossil record of the major life forms using reference books and the website.

(d) Your timeline should be handed in for assessment.

Bob: All that sort of stuff crammed in right at the end of the sheet gave me a kind of visual way of understanding how old the earth is and how long it took for life to evolve.

Dave: It's kind of mind-boggling to comprehend that period of time. I've been at school 10 years and that seems a pretty long time to me.

Amy: I found it annoying that there wasn't enough space to fit in the things that happened recently.

Kim: I learned the Archaeozic era – when first life appeared – was incredibly long.

Sarah: There was all this blank paper between the points where small cell organisms formed and where larger life forms started to appear.

Carol: This activity helped me understand how recently we evolved compared with the age of the earth and that almost everything evolved relatively recently.

PART B: THE TEACHER'S THINKING

Evolution is a change in organisms over time. The way I teach evolution is to look at the evidence first – so I get the students to look at past life on Earth and they can see by studying the past time periods and the organisms present that there has been considerable change, and then we look at the mechanisms of change, which is natural selection. Students haven't learned much about the history of life on earth in the junior curriculum, and although they may have learned about dinosaurs, they haven't put it all together. I get students to construct a scaled geological time line on a two metre strip of paper. They have to include important geological events. Then they have to add significant biological events that they've researched.

And so they look at the fossil record and what it tells us (e.g. when did first plants appear?), and the students match that up with the time periods. We also look at some of the geographic evidence like continental drift, and then we look at genetic evidence. So we look at evolutionary relationships by looking at genetic relationships.

The first thing they say is, 'Oh gosh, everything happened just recently. Nothing much happened back then.' And they begin to appreciate the vast periods of time we're talking about. And of course, when they say it happened "recently", it's still a time period going back 500 million years. They're starting to get this concept of 'deep time' as being so long ago that it's like distance in space, so hard for us to conceptualise because it goes back so far. And of course an understanding of that is so important to understanding evolution because without those long periods of time, natural selection just doesn't make sense. A lot of students (and adults too) find it very difficult to conceive of the changes that we believe occurred over time because they can't conceive of the time periods: they say, 'Oh, I don't believe it because it couldn't happen in that time,' because they are putting it into the time framework of their experience. So I spend a lot of time trying to get across this very difficult concept of the lengthy periods of time involved in the development of life on Earth.

At the end of this, they are ready for the mechanism for this development. I tell them that people were familiar with a lot of this evidence but they didn't know why it happened, so then we look at natural selection as a process.

After spending about five weeks setting the scene, I find I only need to spend about one week on natural selection. This is because the ideas about natural selection develop quickly and readily once students have a good grasp of deep time.

9.3: TERMINOLOGY TALK

This two part PaP-eR concerns issues of terminology and language in understanding genetics. In Part A, a teacher reflects on her approach in helping students to understand the meanings of terms and the links between them. In Part B, students talk to their teacher about some of the difficulties they have in making sense of the ideas, and the range of teaching approaches that help to support their learning. This is a PaP-eR that also illustrates how some aspects of the CoRe play out differently in classroom practice (and may, at times, initially appear contradictory) yet are important in illustrating the need to respond to different aspects of content knowledge – especially in relation to issues around language.

PART A

I believe when you are looking at important ideas or concepts, first comes the language. Next is how the language links together and how you can construct sentences and paragraphs with your language. Then you can build on your learning of the concepts, but if you haven't got the language you can't understand the basic ideas. Indeed, I find the biggest stumbling block for students in learning genetics is the specialised language and their confusion with some of the terminology.

So one of the things that I keep revisiting when I teach genetics is the terminology: that's because to learn the concepts, you have to learn the language to be able to use the concepts. I use various coloured flash cards which I make myself using some of the key terms. The key terms are printed on a card that relates to a particular concept and so sometimes you may have the same term on a different coloured card because you are introducing it in a different context. For instance, the term 'gene' relates to cell division, protein synthesis and to genetic engineering, so when you bring out all the cards, students can see that this word is connected to all these different areas. And so this activity is something that can be used very effectively to help students make links across concepts.

Sometimes I might get the students to look up the definitions of the words on those cards, and write them on the back, or make separate definitions cards and then get them to play a game of matching up word cards with definition cards. In later lessons, I might get students in teams to organise the cards on the floor into a flow chart or mind map, and as they move the cards into the different positions in the mind map I ask them to explain to each other how they see that the words are linked. For example, if the gene card is next to the allele card, they might explain that an allele is an alternative form of a gene; but then someone else might link the allele card to a genotype card, or homozygous or heterozygous cards, and explain these different links. I divide the class into groups of four students, to talk about the terms and their meanings and their links. And it's interesting that just in five or ten minutes – not very long – I can move around and listen to their dialogue, and hear who has got it and who hasn't and the sorts of questions that they ask each other like, "Just explain that a bit more because I don't get it." There is a lot of peer coaching that happens; and you can hear the misconceptions and gently probe them as they are occurring in the groups so that no-one feels silly. Then when we resume as a whole class group I can explore some of the major misconceptions by asking, "What are some of the things that you talked about that were new to you or different from what you thought?" I try to frame the questions in a non-threatening way. This gives students the chance to share and explain their views, and helps them to feel comfortable to use the language and explore meanings of terms, as well as showing them that often several people can share the same misconception.

PART B

Ingrid: I found the vocab [vocabulary] is one of the harder things in understanding genetics. There are so many new words that are only used in genetics – you wouldn't use them anywhere else, and because they are all quite similar when you first hear them it is quite confusing, although when you get into the habit of using them it gets easier. Like when we first started learning genetics, I always got mitosis and meiosis confused, but after we did lots of different activities I understood the ideas better and it was a whole lot easier.

Ann: I found it really difficult to remember the terms and understand what they mean, also. It seemed like every lesson there was a whole lot of new words to learn and you were still struggling to remember the words you learnt last lesson. The cards we made were helpful because I could keep looking through them and thinking, do I know this term? What does it mean?

Linda: I liked that too, and I liked making the mind maps using the cards in my group because we could talk about how we understood the different words and how they linked up together. Sometimes I could see, 'Oh yes, it's all part of the same thing.' Like when we did that activity to find how many links we could make between DNA and natural selection. That was fun.

Ms P (teacher):   What other sorts of activities did you find helpful to learn the vocabulary?

Rob: I liked it when we got into small groups and discussed stuff. When Jonathan explained things to me, I found it easier to understand than when you (Ms P) explained stuff because sometimes you use much more complicated ways of explaining than he does.

Jim: Ha ha. Even Jonathan's explanations are too complex for me sometimes! I like it when I can do some activities by myself first, to get the hang of stuff before I get into a group. Like, using the cards and matching the terms with their definitions. That was good – as long as the definitions weren't too complicated.

Sally: I think that when we saw all that complicated vocab it was like, well, this must have complicated meanings, too. And it made us a bit worried that we wouldn't understand it even before we started.

Ms P (teacher):   I think one of the issues can be that it's not that the processes we're learning about are themselves so complicated. It's just that there are many new terms to learn to explain how these processes work, so you end up having a lot to think about and that's when the confusion starts.

Ingrid: Yeah, but also there are lots of steps in the processes, like transcription and translation, so even though each step isn't so very complicated, and perhaps overall the idea isn't that complicated, when you put all the steps together and all the language, that's when you start to say, 'Ahh ... I'm lost!'

Jan: And don't forget you can't even see the stuff because most of what we talk about is so small. The drawings and micrographs of the same structure also look different, so how do you know what these things actually look like? That makes it hard to learn too.

Ms P: That's true.

This conversation with her students helped to remind Ms P about some of the difficulties her students encountered as they grappled with the extensive and complex terminology of genetics. It was not surprising that her students experienced these difficulties – after all, even scientists have difficulty keeping up with the new terms and changes of terminology. Yet at the same time, Ms P's familiarity with genetics as an experienced Biology teacher sometimes led her to forget just how overwhelming it can be for students to encounter all this new terminology. It was important for her to talk with them regularly about which approaches were helpful for different students so that she could shape her lessons accordingly. She needed to be sensitive to their threshold levels for learning new terms and to be selective in the terminology and approaches to learning that she chose to present to them.

9.4: UNDERSTANDING HOW NATURAL SELECTION WORKS

In this PaP-eR, a teacher uses a newspaper article that supports a Lamarckian view of natural selection to probe and develop students' understanding of the mechanism for natural selection. The newspaper report concerns the spread of cane toads across Australia. Previously these toads were concentrated in and near the cane fields in the Australian state of Queensland. Cane toads are exotic to Australia, and have become a pest there since being introduced in the early part of the twentieth century.

Mr Pell tells his students about a report in the newspaper: Apparently cane toads are evolving longer legs as they are spreading south and across Australia because they need the longer legs to travel further distances. At least, that is what is reported in this article. What is your take on it?

The students seem intrigued. They ask lots of questions to establish what actually was reported in the newspaper article and what actually was observed, and suggest possible explanations.

Claire: The article says toads with longer legs can travel further. That would means toads with shorter legs are less genetically fit than those with longer legs and would die out. But **is** that the case? I don't know!

Tim: Maybe the explanation is the ones that the reporter found have travelled furthest just happen to have longer legs. But they may not necessarily be more genetically fit. (Pauses.)

Sarah: (interrupts) Wait, wait. Individuals can't evolve to suit their environment. Whole populations evolve and individual frogs don't just develop longer legs **because** they need to travel further. If they have longer legs, it's just because of a random mutation. And then having longer legs allows them to also travel further. And then they breed and their offspring have longer legs. But they are not growing longer legs **because** they need to travel further.

Ha: Has the reporter just taken the liberty of linking longer legs to distance travelled? If there is no link, then it could be just an example of continuous variation like for us humans – they could just have varying leg lengths like we do – it doesn't just mean their legs are longer because they travel further.

Sarah: Yes. The reporter has done the "changing to suit the environment" thing – that is, he's given a Lamarckian view: it's like concluding if a poison has been introduced to kill off rats,

'Oh, look! That rat survived! It must have developed a resistance because of the poison!' No, it doesn't happen that way, the rats already had the resistance. And with the toads, they already had the longer legs, and they could travel the longer distances.

The students listen to Sarah's remark without comment. While Sarah seems to have pinpointed the misconception in the newspaper article, Mr Pell suspects that the other students are not ready for closure on this issue, and that some are still unsure about how science views the mechanism for natural selection. He waits to see how the discussion progresses.

The students begin to speculate about why the cane toads are actually moving across Australia from their original habitat.

David: Maybe the reason they are moving away from their habitat is because of predators, not because of their longer legs?

Mr Pell: Unfortunately they don't have any predators in Australia. That is why they are such a pest. So why else might they move away from their original habitat?

Nigel: Too much competition for food.

Lucian: There are more of them so they need more space.

Mr Pell: How does having longer legs fit in to the explanation? The allele frequency changes in the group that is moving because the toads with longer legs have a selective advantage to move further, and the rest tend to die out in transit. (Some laughter at the latter comment!) Where do the longer legs come from?

Finally Tim resolves the issue.

Tim: Let's just say this. The toads are in the middle of Queensland, and it's getting crowded. Families of toads are now trying to go south to different places and get access to more food. Suppose all the toads have this instinct to get away from crowded areas but some of them can only go so far because their legs aren't as long. Now there is already variation in the population: some already have long legs and others have short legs, but the ones with long legs can travel further. Now some of the short legged ones might not be able to go so far and might die because they can't get access to enough food. Now I don't reckon it's sufficient time for there to be much change in allele frequency, even though I know they can have a lot of eggs and breed rapidly. I suppose there could be a slight change in allele frequencies of longer legs in populations that have spread further away from where they were first introduced. And if that's the case, the reporter would have been finding ones with long legs quite a way away from their original habitat, and obviously he has guessed, 'As the toads go further south, they'll get longer legs – that's evolving.' So he doesn't know what evolving means.

Mr Pell: Yes, and you can see how the general public doesn't understand evolutionary theory. So Sarah was right from the start when she said the newspaper reporter was presenting a Lamarckian view.

9.5: UNDERSTANDING THE ROLE OF CHANCE IN EVOLUTION

Misconceptions about the links between natural selection and evolution are common, and often related to a misunderstanding of the role of chance in evolution. In this PaP-eR, a teacher addresses this issue with a group of his Year 11 students, and later reflects on the difficulty of helping students develop an appropriate understanding.

A class of Year 11 students have been studying a unit on genetics. A small group remain after the class for an informal conversation about the unit with their teacher, Mr Roberts. As Mr Roberts suspected, they found macro-evolution was more difficult to understand than micro-evolution.

Sam: I find it hard to imagine how chance produced every bit of a living thing. Like how did an eye form? How come the mutation that produced it just happened to be one that made us able to see?

Mr Roberts: I suppose one of the misconceptions is that it just happens – because it doesn't just happen!

Sam: I thought it was by chance that a mutation happens?

Mr Roberts: The mutation occurs by chance, but the eye doesn't just appear. It has its own evolution through micro-steps.

Matt (chimes in):   Yeah, the eye that we've got today wasn't the result of someone waking up one day and saying, 'Oh, my God, what's this?!'

The group laugh.

Sam: But isn't it all life due to chance along the way?

Mr Roberts reminds the students about an activity they did with playing cards to simulate natural selection: "Remember that little exercise with the cards? We only did it for a few little minutes. You were working in pairs and you both had packs of cards. One of you in each pair just had to keep shuffling until you got the pack in order – that simulated pure chance, where the probability of getting them in the right order is just enormous. The other student in each pair also shuffled their pack but as soon as they got an ace at the top they took it out of the deck. Then they kept shuffling and as soon as they got a two they took it out of the deck. And so on. Suppose we did that activity right now. Think about what would happen to the second group compared to the first group: who'd end up with an ordered set of cards quicker?"

Matt: The group that's taking out cards and lowering the probability?

Mr Roberts: Exactly! And that's what natural selection is like – it's acting on structures that are already there as opposed to just randomly producing changes the whole time. So natural selection is not just the result of pure chance – the occurrence of a mutation is due to chance but natural selection is refining the process over time.

Sam is not yet convinced. She argues: But there is still a chance, like with the cards analogy, that you actually get the ace in the first place, and the accumulation of chance events like that is hard to imagine.

Rob: But the deep time involved, and the rate of mutation gives a huge numbers of events. And most of those are going to be dead ends …

Later on in the staffroom, Mr Roberts recounted the conversation to a colleague, adding: 'The more I teach evolution, the more I realise the difficulty students have in understanding the influence of chance in evolution. We tend to teach it from the simplistic point of view of natural selection: on the surface it can seem quite simple because we tend to talk about one phenotypic characteristic and the effect of something like camouflaging predators, and it is very easy to understand how that could happen. But it's much more complex than that, and I think modern evolutionists are now understanding that chance played a much greater role in small populations. The concept of genetic drift is so much more important for understanding major evolutionary change. I think a lot of people can accept micro-evolution – natural selection leading to adaptation – but it's that big jump between species that people find hard to understand. The wing of the bird is so well developed, where did it come from? And people also talk about the evolution of the eye – how could that have happened? So those major evolutionary jumps are what people find very difficult to understand. That's why as a teacher I often introduce articles like the one about cane toads (see PaP-eR 9.4: *Understanding how natural selection works*) because it helps to draw out misconceptions and gives students the opportunity to clarify their ideas about chance and natural selection.'

9.6: INTRODUCING DNA WITH SWEETS AND SONGS

Many Year 10 students have heard of DNA although they are not sure what it is. In this PaP-eR, a teacher explains how she begins her lessons on Genetics with her year 10 students by introducing them to a physical model of DNA using sweets. She also uses songs to help students learn the vocabulary of genetics and to understand the links between the ideas she wants them to remember.

The first thing I do in the year 10 Genetics Unit is introduce the term DNA and explain what the letters stand for. Then, to make the idea concrete and to encourage students' interest, I use a physical model that students construct using sweets so that they can see that there is a sugar phosphate backbone in DNA and a combination of four nitrogenous bases attached to that backbone. But while the sugar and phosphate molecules alternate in a constant manner, the sequence of the nitrogenous bases is different and it is in that sequence that the "language", the genetic message, is stored.

I think the students find it quite fascinating when they start to realise that this sequence is the basis of how we are all different and the ability of living things to be able to reproduce and pass on traits, etc. is linked to this sequence of nitrogenous bases being different. I use pink marshmallows for the sugar – nice and sweet – and liquorice blocks held together by toothpicks for the phosphates. Then, coming out of each of the pink marshmallows, another toothpick with one of four colours of jelly babies to represent a nitrogenous base; thyamine (green), adenosine (yellow), cytosine (orange) or guanine (red). Next we make another sugar phosphate molecule.

For students to learn about complementary base pairing, they have to follow a rule that for every green jelly baby, a yellow one has to be its partner, and for every orange jelly baby, there has to be a red partner. Then students can compare their sequences.

The idea that genetic mutations are due to changes in one of the bases is also easy to illustrate using this model. So already, by using the sweets activity, students are looking at the structure of DNA, the complementary base pairing nature of DNA and the different sequences that are possible. The good thing about the structure is that if they twirl it around a little bit they can see a double helix shape. They usually recognise the twisted ladder shape because they have seen lots of pictures of it as part of their everyday life, but they don't really know the specifics of the structure. Through this activity, students begin to connect their mental image with the chemical structure.

Beginning with that sort of novel activity where the students can physically create and see a model of DNA and feel it, enables them to experience what I consider to be the "essential core" of genetics.

Building on the activity

While most students have already heard of DNA, they may not know what it is. So while they are making their models and chatting with each other, I go around to small groups and ask them what they know about DNA. Their responses help me to frame what I do next, and to know which students have a firm grasp of the various ideas and concepts and those that do not. Then, later in a whole class discussion, I am able to draw in those different students at different times. For instance when I ask, 'So can you tell me again what you said about DNA?' I can build on the background knowledge that already exists in the class, and help some of the students to feel like experts; which shows that I value their ideas: 'I really liked what you said about DNA. Can you say that again for the class?' In this way, the ideas are framed in student language which is a helpful start to developing their understanding.

Typically what students already know about DNA comes from watching crime shows on TV; for example, that DNA has something to do with paternity cases and forensic cases. They've heard that some diseases can be genetically inherited, for example, haemophilia. Some have heard of the 'elephant man' or read articles in the newspaper about genetic diseases. Some have family members who have genetic diseases such as thalassemia or conditions such as red/green color blindness. Many have heard of genetic fingerprinting and know a bit about genetically modified food – although they don't really know how it works at a molecular level. For example, they may know that producing transgenic tomatoes involves cutting out a piece of the DNA and somehow changing or rearranging what is already there, or putting a fish gene into a tomato to make it less susceptible to frost. (Typically it is more the science fiction type of changes that that they seem to remember.)

My experience in through this activity is that students start to build up a shared language for talking about DNA which then gives me something to refer to as I introduce more complex ideas and develop more sophisticated explanations with them. Some of the terminology can be confusing, because often they just don't know it. The new language is definitely a stumbling block and they need "friendly" ways to be able to remember it.

Developing understanding

Something else that I do is to teach students a song I wrote to the tune of the nursery rhyme, *Twinkle, twinkle little star*:

DNA is in my genes

Tells me how to make proteins

Got my genes from mum and dad

Mixed them up and made me glad

DNA is in my genes

Tells me how to make proteins

The first two lines of the song help them link DNA and genes and, later on the song tells them the function of genes and DNA – 'how to make proteins'. I also wanted them to know where the genes come from – 'got my genes from mum and dad' and so they get the basis of genetic inheritance as a strong concept as well. 'Mix them up' helps them learn, without going into meiosis, about random assortment and fertilisation etc. and that you don't get all of your genes from one parent or the other. I added the line about 'made me glad' because I just wanted the song to be uplifting and happy. I use this song across all the different class levels, even with my year 12s (final year of high school). For senior students I add three more verses that go into the triplets and codons, including start and stop codons. I also introduce hand actions so that as the students are singing, they are making little symbols for codons - like ATT and TAC. In this way, I am hoping to increase their genetics vocabulary in a fun way, and to link the language with its meaning. But even if students can only remember that 'DNA is in my genes, Tells me how to make proteins, Got my genes from mum and dad, Mixed them up' then I'm glad because that is a lot of information and language that is being musically "glued in" to them. It's a bit of a joke, but it's surprising just how well they retain the ideas, and these ideas are the core of what I am trying to teach.

So the way that I think about how all the ideas fit together is a Genetics Tree (see PaP-eR 9.1: *A mental model for teaching genetics*). I use a pointer to show students when we sing the song, that we are following quite a few branches and making those connections between branches very quickly. I often do the song alongside the DNA model using the sweets activity and ask students to make their own verse about the structure of DNA as they construct their model.

I've found it helpful to give students at any level a list of words that rhyme with the ends of some of the key biological words so the song writing doesn't take too long and students are not worried about trying to find a rhyming word. It's interesting how singing tunes that they all know, this activity is not such a threat. Even the year 10 and 12 boys – the big football players who are not kids anymore – don't mind singing these songs because it helps them start to make sense of the terms and their meanings.

These two activities of song writing and model making are a useful way of giving students a reason to use the vocabulary of genetics in a fun context. Importantly, through doing the activities students are developing their understanding of the terms because each term has a specific meaning and links to other terms in particular ways depending on the context. The songs that they come up with then give me a good insight into the depth of their understanding and that is the crucial part of all of this because it helps to inform me about their learning and how I can build on it through my teaching.

9.7: SCIENCE IS DIFFERENT WHEN YOU HAVE TO TEACH IT

This PaP-eR has been constructed from a conversation with a teacher who was a scientist, in order her ideas about teaching have developed. As this PaP-eR illustrates, the need to understand teaching as demanding different ways of helping students understand content beyond the "facts" is a most important aspect of science teaching. This teacher knows that there is not one way of teaching a topic (in this case genetics) and that trying to think like a student is an important way of helping her to teach the content in engaging ways for her students as she begins to recognize some the difficulties, issues and questions they might have of the content. It is this purposeful linking of teaching and learning in light of deep knowledge of the content that influences what it means to develop pedagogical content knowledge (PCK). This PaP-eR illustrates that very point through the topic of genetics.

I find it interesting that my content understanding of genetics differs from when I was working as a scientist in that field. As a scientist doing experiments with chromosomes, I didn't have to remember exactly every stage of cell division, and I could refer to a poster of the different stages of mitosis if necessary. Since becoming a teacher I've re-learned the details so I can teach my students, but as a scientist I focussed on different things. For example, when I worked with chromosomes, the level of detail was completely different – I was looking at their shape, I was counting them and I was looking at proteins that attach to the chromosomes. In one sense, although that kind of work presupposes an understanding of mitosis, it can be done without remembering what pro-metaphase really means. As a scientist, in your everyday work you don't have to think about content knowledge of genetics and the connections between the various ideas in quite the same way you do as a teacher. That's because as a teacher you have to be able to deal with questions from students right there and then. So teaching calls on knowledge in a much more immediate way. It's a way of thinking that wasn't quite the same when it was all about just my own understanding as a scientist.

As a teacher, my job is to develop an understanding of the content and the process of learning in my students. To do that means I have to look at the content and students' learning. I have to pay attention, I have to observe the difficulties that my students have in understanding it. Engaging in the learning that way doesn't necessarily help me understand the content any better (although I can think of times in genetics teaching when it certainly has) but the point is that it helps me understand the way my students think and what makes that work better for them. That is certainly something that, as a teacher, even though I know about misconceptions and all of that, I don't really have a good understanding of what a particular student's picture of the world might be because I can't remember what it was like when I didn't know that stuff. The teacher's job though is to be able to draw it out and to be able to help them construct a deeper understanding – and not just so they can pass the test.

If I think about genetics as a topic, it's not just the teaching of it, but preparing myself to go into class and finding out what's going on in the world, or some of the research in the field, and trying to make sure I'm up to date so that I can make things interesting and relevant and current for the students. It's about helping them to understand all this stuff that is in the newspaper and not just accept what they read, but question it, you know about the ethics, the science, the purpose, stuff like that. So I feel like I probably keep up more with science news than I used to, well maybe in a different way because I'm asking questions of myself like: 'What would this mean to my students?; or, What makes sense here?; or, What is hard to understand?; and sometimes, Why does this matter?' So that process is about helping me to understand things from a different perspective and that is important so that I can have better conversations with my science teacher colleagues so that somehow through that process, I get closer to knowing how to play with these ideas in productive ways with the students.

Maybe what it really means is that I know now that each time I teach mitosis I have to re-learn some things, and each time I guess I've got this whole other bag of experience that comes with it so it's a richer mental image that I've got, but I know that the content alone isn't enough to be able to engage the students in learning it.

Teaching is partly about me and my understanding, but also about how others understand and how to help them develop that understanding; and that is different. What I mean is that I see now that when students ask me questions, they start a process of engaging me in a conversation about the content. Because of that I have to think about what they understand and don't understand and what I know (and perhaps don't know), and how to find ways to get them to understand the ideas as something more than just facts. Through that conversation, my understanding gets stronger and hopefully so does theirs and so it becomes obvious that the best way to learn something is to have a conversation and talk about it; ask a question.

Now that I hear myself say that, I suppose that is what is at the heart of the idea of PCK. You see, talking about ideas helps you understand them differently; understand them in a teaching and learning sort of way.

CHAPTER TEN

EXAMINING THE USE AND VALUE OF CoRe(s) AND PaP-eRs

This chapter is designed to offer different perspectives on the use and value of CoRes and PaP-eRs. The chapter opens with two vignettes of different users of CoRes and PaP-eRs. The first vignette is that of a student teacher who used the Circulatory System Resource Folio while completing her practicum (school teaching experience). Her perspective on CoRes and PaP-eRs illustrates how the use of the Circulatory System Resource Folio helped her to think differently about how to plan and organise her teaching, and create a more interconnected and meaningful approach to teaching the topic.

The second vignette is that of an experienced teacher who used the Electric Circuits Resource Folio as a source of ideas for her teaching of the topic with her students. Interestingly, beyond using PaP-eRs as a way of thinking about new activities in her teaching of the topic, she also came to see the conceptualization of CoRes and PaP-eRs as a new way of thinking about her practice. They offered a framework through which she began to think about and structure her teaching differently.

The vignettes offer one way of looking into the use of CoRes and PaP-eRs, and are a precursor to another way of viewing them through one part of a research project that was designed to study the applicability, value and usefulness of CoRes and PaP-eRs for teachers. That project comprises the major part of the chapter and is written by Adam Bertram whose doctoral research into CoRes and PaP-eRs comprised a two year longitudinal study in which he examined how his participating teachers came to understand a CoRe and PaP-eRs conceptualization of PCK. His account in this chapter is one part of his larger study (Bertram, 2010) that was initiated in response to his own interest in PCK; which was a major shaping force in his thinking about his science teaching and his students' learning.

Together, the vignettes and the research account offer insights into how CoRes and PaP-eRs might be used and understood and as a group together illustrate how CoRes and PaP-eRs can shape not only how science teachers might think about their knowledge of practice, but also how that thinking can influence their teaching in productive ways.

VIGNETTE 1: A STUDENT TEACHER'S RESPONSE TO THE PCK BOOK

Nicole is in her final year of a four year double degree in science and education (BSc/BEd). In her science degree, she is majoring in mathematics with a minor in physiology. Prior to her studies she worked for many years in the corporate world and was involved in training and designing of training programs for businesses. She plans to teach at the secondary level. As she explains below, Nicole has found ideas in the PCK book to be valuable in helping her to think about and plan her teaching.

How did you come to use the book?

I was doing a teaching practicum in the first semester this year, and taking a Year 10 sports science class. The teacher said, 'Well, they're up to the circulatory system, you can teach that,' but when I asked if there was a text book, she said, 'No.' Well my initial reaction was that I could hardly remember what I'd learned about the circulatory system in Year 10, so I thought I'd better find a text book to help me find out. And I remembered there was something about the circulatory system in the PCK book (which was as a required text in my Biology Methods unit). So when I flipped through and found the chapter on the circulatory system, it was like a godsend because it answered my question, 'What do I need to teach Year 10?' as it had a whole lot of information about what is required of a Year 10 class that is studying the circulatory system, and more.

I found the CoRe especially useful when I was planning my teaching. The first part of the CoRe told me what students needed to know, so I put that down under my learning outcomes for my lessons. This meant I had a clear idea of what I wanted the students to take away from each of the lessons I was teaching. And then I think probably the second most useful bit of the CoRe for me was the row about why students need to know these ideas because it is closely related to therow about what students need to know, which helped me work out how I would tackle teaching each of the big ideas. And of course the row with the teaching activities was really useful. I also found that the row about the knowledge that the teacher would have but the students wouldn't have to be helpful because it's often hard to know as a beginning teacher how much detail we need to make available to students. So by the time I had developed all my learning outcomes and was clear about what students needed to learn and why they needed to know it, along with a lot of suggested activities, I felt like I was well equipped to teach the right level of material in a way that students would get it!

I've always thought 'forewarned is forearmed', and I felt after reading the CoRe and PaP-eRs that I knew what to watch out for, even though I had no experience of teaching that topic. In fact I actually felt like I had taught all this before, and knew what students might have trouble with, what they might have misconceptions about, and what would be a great way to start teaching the topic. So I went into the classroom feeling not only like I knew the content really well, but that I'd had experience teaching it just because I'd read about other people's experience teaching it. So I think I got much more help from the PCK book than I would have from a text book because text books just focus on the knowledge that students need to have and it is left up to the teachers to work out how to make that knowledge available for students.

What was the most valuable aspect of the PCK book from your perspective?

I think one of the biggest things I got out of reading this book was the interconnectedness of ideas. As a student teacher you only get to do a short amount of teaching and possibly because of that I thought about science teaching in terms of chunks of information to be taught. Before reading the book, I hadn't really seen how interconnected everything is; now I feel like I've opened that door. I've got a better appreciation of the theory that if students can connect to something they already know, their knowledge is so much richer. If you are just teaching this bit of information and then moving on and teaching another bit, then you are really missing a lot of opportunities to build and connect the richness of their learning.

The year before, I taught a Year 8 class about the heart and the circulatory system and I didn't touch at all on how interconnected it is – my approach was, 'Here is the heart, this is what is looks like, let's cut one up, how fantastic!' whereas now I say, 'OK, what is over-riding all of this is how interconnected it all is.' So if we're talking about the circulatory system, I'll ask, 'What is it doing for your brain? And what is your brain doing for it? And what is the circulatory system doing for your lungs and what are your lungs doing for your circulatory system?'

What made you feel that your new teaching approach worked?

From the teaching perspective, I felt that what I was doing had a structure, and the students responded so well to the activities. I think they found it was really quite interesting and engaging to think about how things are interconnected in the body. When we talked about how the circulatory system is interconnected, the students were saying upfront, 'Well, it doesn't do anything for the lungs, the lungs bring in air' and so then we had a bit of a conversation about what the circulatory system is and how it goes to every single cell in the body and there are cells in the lungs, and they said, 'Oh! OK.' And if you give the students exercises where they have to decide what are connections between a whole list of things, they will initially say, 'Oh, they're not connected,' but then somebody always finds one, even connections that I haven't thought of. And I found having a whole class discussion about whether they felt it was a valid connection really gave me access to a style of learning that was richer than if I'd just said to them, 'Here's the system.'

Has the book changed about the way you think about teaching science?

Yes. Previously I was just looking for a whole lot of little ideas to teach whereas now I realize that when I start teaching a topic, I need to be looking at the big ideas, and links between them and what feeds into them. I realize that even if the students don't learn all the detail, they might just get the big ideas. So I now look for a structure, even when I teach mathematics, rather than just presenting a series of unrelated ideas.

I think I now look differently at the knowledge to be taught. Previously I would have opened a text book and asked myself, 'OK, we need to know these twenty things – how will I make this information available? – well, I'll tell them this bit and they can discover that bit.' Whereas now I probably organize the information a bit differently – in fact, it's probably organized differently in my brain. And I really think about why do students need to know this, do they need to know this, and look for rich practical and connecting activities. And I think about the possibilities for connections between what they have previously learned, or even something they are going to look at in the future, and whether I should maybe give them a bit of a preview and come back to it later on.

What did you mean when you said you organize things differently in your brain?

Well, I like structure and to have things organized. I like to know the big picture and if I haven't got the big picture then I can't organize what is going on underneath. And I think the book has allowed me to have access to structure, whereas before I might have had all the science information I needed to teach but struggled to organize it. It's a long time since I studied this stuff and even though I know it, it's not in the forefront of my brain. The book has helped my content understanding, but also helped me to think about how to make the content available to the students. If I had one of those CoRes available for every topic and every year level, then I would feel 120% prepared to teach because all the other stuff I can do. And I picture myself in a couple of years as a totally competent teacher, having stored lesson plans about topics that will contain the information in the CoRes – the big ideas and their interconnectedness, what students need to know and why, the activities, and so on.

In all honesty, this book is what I've been lacking in all the years of this course. I feel it just saved me hours of time.

VIGNETTE 2: AN EXPERIENCED TEACHER'S RESPONSE

Marion has 25 years teaching experience. She has taught physics for the past 10 years and has lots of experience teaching middle school science. She has a biochemistry degree with a physics sub major. She was introduced to CoRes and PaP-eRs at a workshop for physics teachers on teaching electric circuits. During this workshop, teachers read and discussed PaP-eR 8.4: 'Why one teacher avoids using $V=IR$', and considered the importance of models in teaching electric circuits. In her teaching, Marion likes to emphasise the human aspects of physics and the historical development of science ideas in order to help students better understand where science ideas come from and how they might be relevant to their lives and experiences.

How have you used the book in your teaching?

The book has been extremely useful. So far, I've only used the chapter on Electric Circuits. Probably the most helpful thing has been the Jelly Bean Role Play (see Electric Circuits CoRe and PaP-eR 8.1) as a means of starting off the topic of electric circuits, because I am able to continually refer back to it when I'm trying to help students' understanding. Once the students have the idea of the separate entities of charge and energy, and their analogues in the role play, I often respond to their questions by saying, 'Just remember the jelly beans' or 'What happened to the jelly beans?' or 'What happened when you moved around the circuit?', as this seems to help them understand the concepts more easily.

I also used the idea of comparing an electric field to a gravitational field (see Electric Circuits CoRe and PaP-eR 8.3) and found it helped students who ask, 'How do current electrons "know" what to do and where to go and how much energy to give up?' My response was, 'They don't need to know – they're in a field and they are just acting the way the field tells them to act', and of course not everyone understood this still, but the kids who were engaged and really interacted with the ideas did seem to grasp the concept.

A real eye opener for me was the activity of just asking to students to connect up a torch light globe, wires and a battery so the globe lights up (see Electric Circuits CoRe). One thing that hadn't occurred to me before reading it in the book is that students don't necessarily know how the globe conducts electricity, or that it's actually got two terminals, and that providing globe holders – which is the standard thing to do – gets in the way of students developing understanding about this. I found that rather than setting the equipment up carefully for them, it was more useful for student learning to say, 'Here's some stuff – have a play.' In fact, I was quite amazed that three or four students out of 14 thought putting one wire on the globe would make it light up. I hadn't picked this up before in my teaching so obviously I've been providing them with too much information, rather than letting them figure things out for themselves. I've also realized that it's better to ask questions like, 'How do you think things are going to work?' to encourage students to work things out themselves, rather than saying to them, 'That's not right' or giving them the answer. So now I don't do much actual "telling" in my teaching – my approach focuses on getting them to do some activities with me just filling in the gaps when I need to.

I certainly didn't at any time really dwell on Ohm's law – I took that right from the workshop [described in the introduction to this vignette] because I recognized that it is just so common in physics for a student to ask, 'What formula do I use?' and that this is a sign that they haven't got a clue what they are really doing. Instead, Ohm's law emerged as a result of some laboratory activities on parallel and series circuits, and potential difference and power in a circuit. During these activities they were asked to develop some relationships that included potential difference and current, and so they developed Ohm's law themselves. And I'm not saying that every student understood everything perfectly but I just found that those who were paying attention and interacting and working through things did have a better understanding and more confidence as well.

What made you think your students' understanding was better?

Things the students said in discussion, and their ability to predict what is going to happen when you do different things to a circuit. For example, when you short circuit a component with a switch, they could predict what happens when you close the switch, and quite a few were able to say, 'Well, that globe is going to go out' because we had talked so much about resistance and what that actually meant, and they understood the idea of current going in different tracks in a parallel circuit.

I don't recall any student thinking that charge got used up in a circuit – that was a big difference from before I used the approaches in the book. Like when I asked what the ammeter reading would be if I placed it at different points in a simple circuit, I didn't get anyone saying the charge is used up – and I have always had that response before. One thing that still did happen, and I know this is mentioned in the Electric Circuits CoRe, a few students said, 'The electrons are recharged' when I asked what happened in the battery. That terminology is so ingrained, and I'm not too sure what I should do about that, other than reiterate that while in everyday language 'recharge' means 'energise', in science 'recharge' means something different, a bit like the scientific difference between weight and mass.

Has your experience of using the ideas in the book changed the way you teach science?

Yes, there has been more interaction with the bigger ideas, and a greater focus on developing an understanding of the concepts and less attention to the details. I was more interested in the fact that the kids understood the concepts behind electric circuits. I think once they've got the big ideas, we can sort out the fine detail more easily as we go along – like the rules and the terms, and, for example the difference between joules and electrons.

Did you find the big ideas of the CoRe useful?

They were indeed. Sometimes in text books you can get bogged down and you tend to follow through a process and the progression of points just because of the resources around you rather than because you've thought about, 'What am I trying to get across here?'

But somehow the CoRe has made you think more deeply about the big ideas?

That's right, and the limitations. And it's made me think more broadly around teaching. Like having those question prompts down the left hand side of a CoRe, and answering them, has made me think differently about teaching a topic. 'What you intend the students to learn about this idea?' is something I've always thought about, of course, but having to think about, 'Why it is important for the students to know this?' is a question that has actually made me think more broadly beyond my initial response, 'Because they need to know it!'

I think the question prompts of the CoRe have just crystallized some things for me. 'What else do you know about this idea?' This sort of stuff comes out along the way when kids say, 'But miss, what about this?' So this row in the CoRe helps me to think about whether I need to develop my own knowledge so I can answer these students' questions. I find it much easier to explain things to kids when I have a much broader knowledge than they have so that I've got some resource bags to dig into. It might also just help me to question whether I really know why an event is happening, or whether I'm just regurgitating something I learned in school, and to think about pitching my response to students' questions at an appropriate level.

'Difficulties and limitations connected with teaching this idea' – I liked that idea of not just thinking about what is going to work well, but also about the limitations with the models I'm using. For example, often you start off talking about the water model in electricity and suddenly you come unstuck. Having the difficulties and limitations in the CoRe helps to remind me that we are talking about models, and when they break down we have to refine them or find new ones; and that I need to talk about that to the students. I think it is extremely important that kids aren't just served things up as though this is the way it is. Rather, I think it's important that they understand that this is the way we think it is and this is what works for us now, and it has changed a lot in the past, and will no doubt continue to change; and it's just brought me back to my idea of what science is, and how science has really progressed, and how we should present it to students.

I think I have probably thought about all of the questions in the CoRe before but not in a structured way that was obvious. Often all you do as a teacher is write down what you are going to teach, and the activities you are going to use, and nothing else. Sometimes you forget what the difficulties are with a particular idea or activity until you teach it again and you suddenly remember that you had this problem last time you taught it.

So the CoRe has provided you with a stronger framework for thinking about your teaching?

Yes, framework is a good word – and it is not just a framework because it's on paper, it's a framework also in my head that I can use in other areas as well.

RESEARCHING CoRes and PaP-eRs

Adam Bertram

As a senior Physics teacher and Science Co-ordinator I first became interested in PCK through my Masters research. Then when I enrolled in a doctoral program I pursued the topic further. As a construct, I thought PCK could be very helpful in developing science teachers' professional knowledge. I was therefore drawn to CoRes and PaP-eRs as a way of researching the field as a consequence of my earlier experiences as a teacher and beginning researcher. Because I was interested in the usefulness of CoRes and PaP-eRs to practicing science teachers I devised and undertook an extensive research study (my Ph.D.) designed to investigate them as a tool for understanding PCK. This chapter briefly reports on that study.

The research into the use of CoRes and PaP-eRs that I conducted over a two year period demonstrated that they provide a unique platform for beginning to untangle the complexities of teachers' understandings of content and pedagogy in the amalgam that is PCK. Emerging from that research has been clear and concrete examples of (participating) teachers' reasoning about their thinking and actions in the classroom that comprise aspects of their PCK; CoRes and PaP-eRs have helped that to be made explicit and visible. As a consequence, I can state that the research has illustrated well that the use of CoRes and PaP-eRs offers teachers the opportunity to develop a shared language of their expert practice. In so doing, they are an effective means of disseminating aspects of PCK to others. The inherent value in working with CoRes and PaP-eRs then is that they create new ways of developing teachers' professional knowledge and as such, contribute to the scholarship of science teaching.

EXPLORING SCIENCE TEACHERS' KNOWLEDGE OF PRACTICE

Over the course of two years, six practising teachers (three middle school science teachers, one senior science teacher and two generalist primary school teachers) participated in the research on which this section of the chapter is based (for full study, see Bertram, 2010). The participating teachers were involved in a pre-, mid- and post-test study into the use of an intervention into their existing practice based on their learning about, and use of, CoRes and PaP-eRs.

Two participants (Delta and Gordon) were generalist primary school teachers. When the study commenced, Delta had been teaching for three years while Gordon had only been teaching for six months. Three teachers (Julie, Rani and Samantha) were teaching middle school science to students in Years Seven through to Ten. Jerry was a senior physics teacher and was teaching students in Years Eleven and Twelve.

The study

The overarching primary research questions of the study were:

- how does an understanding of PCK, through CoRes and PaP-eRs, influence (participating) science teachers' thinking about theirprofessional practice?; and,

- how do CoRes and PaP-eRs impact how (the participating) science teachers engage with their own pedagogical content knowledge?

To investigate these research questions, a longitudinal, ethnographic study (involving extensive interviewing over two years) was conducted. Given that teachers' knowledge is often tacit and therefore difficult for them to convey to others (Gess-Newsome, 1999; Korthagen & Kessels, 1999), a framework was adopted for the study consisting of pre-, mid- and post-intervention stages in order to be most likely to have sufficient depth of data to answer the research questions.

In the pre-intervention stage, the first interview (Int. 1) asked participants to describe their current views on teaching and learning. Following this, in a separate interview (Int. 2), an introduction to PCK was provided and CoRes and PaP-eRs were fully explained. (At this point, participants were asked to make initial comment on their thoughts about the value and usefulness of these constructs.)

In the mid-intervention stage, participants created their own (and/or contributed to a small group) CoRe based on a science unit or topic that they would soon be teaching (and had previously taught). Following CoRe completion, participants were asked to comment on the process of making the CoRe and to offer their views on how that process influenced their thinking about teaching and learning, and their understanding of PCK (Int. 3).

In a following interview (Int. 4), participants were asked to describe a recent teaching episode (based on content from their CoRe), and to provide as much information as they could so that a PaP-eR could be developed from that interview. Once a PaP-eR had been developed participants were asked to comment on the process of making the PaP-eR and any influence that that process had on their thinking about teaching and learning, and their understanding of PCK (Int. 5).

In the post-intervention stage participants were interviewed to see whether CoRes and PaP-eRs (individually and as a combined instrument) had any impact on their long-term practice (Int. 6).

At the conclusion of the study, teachers were presented with their initial pre-intervention views on teaching and learning in the form of a summary document. They were then asked to reconsider these views and contrast them to their current (post-intervention) views on teaching and learning and to ascertain any changes that were apparent to them and to add anything new. This was set as an individual 'homework task' and was then followed up in an interview (Int. 7) designed to draw out in detail their understandings from the 'homework task'.

Finally, a concluding interview (Int. 8) was conducted to explore participants' final views on the entire study (CoRes, PaP-eRs and PCK and how they impacted or influenced their professional practice).

The open interview format adopted for the study allowed teachers to offer narrative accounts of rich data that provided great insights into their thinking.

FINDINGS

In the earlier chapters of this book, the authors proposed various ways that CoRes and PaP-eRs might address current issues surrounding PCK research in science education and the possible benefits that CoRes and PaP-eRs might have for science teachers' practice. The study has, to some degree, tested some of these ideas with the participants. The sections that follow are not an attempt to revisit and thoroughly summarise all of the detail of the full research study. Rather, they offer a summative description of those results that are most pertinent to the research questions and the contentions of the earlier chapters.

PCK is difficult for teachers to access - a framework and shared language is needed

In the opening chapters, Loughran and colleagues contend that PCK is a difficult and elusive aspect of science teachers' professional knowledge that is rarely explicitly accessed in their practice. In order for science teachers to meaningfully engage with and access the ideas of PCK they suggested that a special shared language is necessary to facilitate and provide an appropriate platform. Various researchers have also claimed that a shared language is fundamental to the specialised professional knowledge of teachers (Loughran, 2002a, 2003; Mitchell & Mitchell, 2005, 1997; Munby, et al., 2001; Zeichner & Noffke, 2001). Given that teachers have been known to share their knowledge and skills of practice through stories and anecdotes (Clandinin & Connelly, 2000; Conle, 2003; Fenstermacher, 1997; Northfield, 1997), Loughran and colleagues designed PaP-eRs to purposefully explore teachers' narrative accounts of their practice, and in so doing considered that they could offer insights into their PCK.

In an attempt to make PCK accessible and useable within the notion of creating and nurturing a shared language, Loughran and colleagues believed that CoRes and PaP-eRs together might achieve this end.

Through my research, participants were introduced to the construct of PCK (via sample CoRes and PaP-eRs from the first edition of this book). As a consequence, the study was able to explore participants' views on the process of making CoRes, PaP-eRs and, therefore, PCK. As the study progressed, participants' responses increasingly became shaped by a new language (influenced by the CoRes and PaP-eRs approach) through which they were able to effectively describe their PCK.

All participants in the study recognised that constructing their own CoRes encouraged structured reflection and helped them to be much more conscious of their students' learning. They began to describe CoRes as being centered on and preparing them for, teaching particular content in particular ways to their particular students. Explicitly (Julie, Rani, Jerry and Gordon) or implicitly (Samantha and Delta), participants illustrated that CoRes "forced" them to uncover and connect with their tacit knowledge of teaching and learning, for example:

> Well, it certainly helped me map out what the students' prior knowledge and expectations were ... It did make that explicit whereas before I sort of would have vaguely known about it and not actually talked about it, had I not been asked about it. (Jerry, Int. 3)

As such, CoRes (the prompts and the Big Ideas) offered a language for participants to begin to better articulate their knowledge of practice. Similarly, after seeing their PaP-eR in final form, all participants reported that their PaP-eR had prompted meaningful consideration of their practice – helping them to better cater to their particular students, as well as helping them recognise their own strengths and weaknesses.

> [W]hen you do a reflection like this, it helps you develop your content better and you ask yourself some good questions ... like, 'What should I cover in depth?', 'What will the students get out of this content?' or 'Would they explore it further?', 'Would they be interested in exploring the content further?' (Rani, Int. 5)

Loughran and colleagues contended that a shared language was critical to unveiling teachers' PCK. Through my research, it was clear that a shared language was essential for teachers to be able to talk, articulate and think about their practice in ways that conveyed meaning when considered in the relation to the notion of PCK. Both CoRes and PaP-eRs effectively facilitated the development of this language and appeared to be an effective instrument for teachers to frame and talk about their professional practice. Each of the following sections illustrates this notion of a language and a framework for conceptualizing practice as underpinning the specific research outcomes being demonstrated, i.e. in each section, a shared language and framework are sub-themes that help to support that specific issue being examined.

CoRes and PaP-eRs offer concrete examples of science teachers' PCK

PCK can be elusive and difficult to articulate (Baxter & Lederman, 1999; Gess-Newsome, 1999; Korthagen & Kessels, 1999). Loughran and colleagues suggested that CoRes and PaP-eRs offered a method of capturing and portraying science teachers' PCK through concrete and meaningful examples.

While a CoRe's prompts (on the left hand side of the CoRe) are designed to draw out explanations and detail in the way participantsthink about the content, many struggled to respond to particular prompts. At some prompts, some participants (Julie, Rani, Delta and Gordon) simply listed content or teaching procedures without offering any reasons as to why they were important to the particular content area. Some prompts were left blank or had very scant detail (Jerry and Delta). Prompts were designed to provoke teachers to consider the content to be taught through the lens of PCK and all participants found this to be challenging as they struggled with the difference between listing content as propositional knowledge and actually displaying deeper thinking about the content.

My study illustrated that participants required an opportunity to work with a CoRe to develop a familiarity with the process in order to manage the demands inherent in completing the task. Identifying 'Big Ideas' in particular was a challenge. Initially, they were not big science ideas (as per Loughran et al.'s description in Chapter 3); rather they were labels for the sub-sections of content to be taught. Interestingly, Gordon negotiated with his students what they would like to learn and developed his Big Ideas in view of that approach to the content (Rockets). Jerry's Big Ideas focussed on exploring propositional knowledge. Delta included a 'Bringing it all together' Big Idea which merged her other Big Ideas in such a way as to view them as one Big Idea in effect making the others sub-themes of the one Big Idea. Samantha and Rani's Big Ideas illustrated their thinking from a social (not just science) perspective.

Essentially, most participants struggled with the concept of Big Ideas, and they generally did not elaborate the reasons for their choices in particular detail in their responses.

PaP-eRs are designed to prompt teachers to talk about their teaching of a particular lesson in ways that might reveal their pedagogical reasoning about specific actions or teaching procedures. All of the participants were able to share and describe their reasoning particularly well about one teaching episode based on content from their CoRe. Rich aspects of their PCK could be captured and documented from their narrative accounts.

A strong example is that of Delta who was able to articulate her reasoning about: the content; pedagogical knowledge; knowledge of her specific students; knowledge of herself in terms of her limits of knowing the content; and finally, being able to view her own teaching through a PCK lens. For Delta, her PaP-eR revealed aspects of her teaching that were not previously explicitly known to her. She claimed that she 'definitely' learnt more about herself as a teacher, and that, as a consequence, she would focus more on her students' understanding.

> I'm probably questioning more [as a result of creating the PaP-eR], 'Why am I doing this activity? What is the point of it? What are the kids going to get out of it? What skills are they going to learn? How's it going to benefit them?' (Delta's PaP-eR)

PaP-eRs proved to be an effective instrument for capturing instances of participants' PCK and provided an avenue for participants to talk about and share (i.e. through a common language) their knowledge of practice. PaP-eRs added specific instances of PCK to the broader instances captured through the CoRe, and demonstrated the useful and symbiotic nature of both instruments as a means of capturing and portraying a more complete picture of teachers' PCK.

Participants' post-intervention views on PCK, CoRes and PaP-eRs illustrate that they viewed the resultant Resource Folio (combined collection of CoRe and PaP-eRs) to be thought-provoking and insightful into their professional practice. Four of the six participants (Julie, Samantha, Jerry and Delta) stated explicitly that they believed their experience of the study had provided them with a means of viewing their practice specifically through a PCK lens. All participants claimed that CoRes and PaP-eRs had provoked them to examine science content for teaching in deep and meaningful ways, to understand their students better and then to marry this to develop a pedagogical approach specifically designed to improve their students' learning. In terms of their future development, all participants reported that particular aspects of their professional practice had been improved as a result of completing and using CoRes and PaP-eRs. Indicative responses include:

> The study has helped me to actually become more aware of misconceptions, and I ... have really developed that a great deal since then. (Julie, Homework Task)

> It's broadened that ... spectrum so to speak, about the content that you can deliver. (Rani, Int. 8)

> The study has helped me reflect on the number and type of different learning activities I provide to accommodate different learners. (Samantha, Homework Task)

> The thing that I can take away from this is – trying to be sympathetic to my students' modern understanding of science. ... I now understand that you can use it as a way to not just explain but to understand the scientific process where you move from one idea that was the best idea at the time to another idea which is better. (Jerry, Int. 6)

> Yeah, it [the study] has [changed my long-term view of teaching and learning] in that I definitely reflect more. (Delta, Int. 8)

> [The study] influenced my view of teaching insofar as I think ... teachers need to actually think about what they've done and what they've done successfully or not, more often. (Gordon, Int. 8)

Contributing to professional practice

In reviewing the main findings of the effect of working with CoRes and PaP-eRs on participants in the study, four major themes emerged: reflection; shared language; professional knowledge; and, changes in practice. These are now discussed.

From participants' responses, it was apparent that the whole process of the study had increased their understanding of reflection on practice. They came to see CoRes and PaP-eRs as important tools which "forced" them to reflect. They began to embrace and understand reflection as crucial to understanding themselves as teachers but most importantly as the stimulus for improving their professional practice. All participants commented on the importance of reflection:

> [PCK is] 'very important' because it gives [teachers] a framework. It gives them the avenue to reflect and understand why they're teaching specific content to that specific group. So ... [it is] 'very important' for that. (Rani, Int. 8)

> I would think the PaP-eR is about an ongoing reflection and improvement to processes the teacher already has in place. (Jerry, Int. 6)

> I would never have done this much reflection, previously. ... [I] reflected on many more aspects than I would have previously. (Delta, Int. 8)

> Some people can't really reflect upon their teaching in the way that they go about it. They probably need that little push and they need that professional discussion which is what this is and it is my understanding that it is what the CoRes and the PaP-eRs are designed to do. (Gordon, Int. 6)

This reflective process (offered via CoRes and PaP-eRs) helped to break down the barriers of how participants perceived "normal" classes as a collection of "teaching" lessons or content topics. Essentially, it gave them a framework for discussing and thinking about their PCK in ways that they did not do beforehand. In this way, the participants developed a common language in which to frame, share and discuss PCK and to reveal aspects of their practice that were previously tacit. Notably, their responses in the study, particularly over time, clearly show changes in their ways of thinking about their professional knowledge. In fact, all participants claimed their current views on teaching and learning had been influenced, changed or developed as a consequence of the study.

> [The study] influenced my view of teaching insofar as I think ... teachers need to actually think about what they've done and what they've done successfully or not, more often. ... In terms of students, I suppose it's probably made me consider the enquiry-based learning aspects further and just different ways to make that interesting for students and to keep them involved in that process ... Looking at my [pre-intervention] views, I was quite intrigued to see the way that I had changed my perspective on science teaching ... I'd said that there were some elements [of science content] which I found quite difficult to teach ... because I didn't have the knowledge about those things. But ... I've realised that's something that I need to push myself on and really work to develop because I've seen the merits of it, particularly in science-based programs, in enquiry-based learning. (Gordon, Int. 8)

Impact of CoRes and PaP-eRs on the participants' views on teaching and learning

Essentially, all participants claimed that their pre-intervention views on teaching and learning had been influenced, changed or developed as a result of the study and two participants (Rani and Delta) claimed it affirmed their sense of feeling valued as teachers.

Of the impact of an awareness of PCK in regard to their practice (as brought about by CoRes and PaP-eRs), each participant described how it affected them personally. Julie claimed she had significantly improved how she understood her students' misconceptions and how the study had challenged what learning meant to her. For Rani, the CoRe had 'loosely contributed to her development' of PCK and as a teacher. For Samantha the study offered a framework for structured reflection from which she could view her teaching through a PCK lens. Jerry suggested that his general teaching philosophy had steered away from viewing teaching as just facilitating and that PCK had been a 'contributing factor in the ongoing shaping' (Jerry, Int. 7) of his practice. Delta felt that the construct of PCK had helped her to evaluate the varied approaches she had used to cater to her differing students' learning styles. Tacit knowledge had also been made explicit for many of the participants. Finally, Gordon claimed that as a result of understanding PCK, he had changed how he now assessed his students' understanding.

For five of the six participants (Julie, Samantha, Jerry, Delta and Gordon) PCK, through CoRes and PaP-eRs, offered a structured way for them to reflect in a meaningful and purposeful manner. Julie, Jerry and Gordon claimed that the study had caused them to rethink their general views on teaching and learning. For others (Rani, Jerry and Gordon) the study had great impact on the way they developed or their thinking about their students' learning.

Five of the six participants (Julie, Rani, Jerry, Delta and Gordon) directly (or indirectly, in the case of Rani) stated that they believed the study raised and enhanced their awareness of their own PCK. These same five participants also believed that the changes to their post-intervention views on teaching and learning may have been because of an awareness of their PCK developed via the study. These five participants all agreed that PCK (through CoRes and PaP-eRs) offered teachers an important and useful construct for shaping their professional knowledge. They expressed how the study made them consciously and purposefully reflect and evaluate their practice to produce more meaningful lessons for their students.

Limitations of CoRes and PaP-eRs

Throughout the study, limitations around the use of CoRes and PaP-eRs for regular practice were apparent. The most substantial of these, reported on many occasions by the participants, was the enormous investment of time required to produce a CoRe. Although all participants mentioned this as a limitation, Jerry explained the paradoxical nature of time invested in relation to outcomes achieved:

> I complained before about it [in the making of the CoRe] being expensive in terms of time, that's because it has to be. And if you've got a shortcut to it, you'll get a shortcut outcome as well. (Jerry, Int. 6)

Although all participants asserted that CoRes and PaP-eRs were useful, they also stated that because of the significant investment of time required in their production, they could not foresee using them on their own initiative. Delta and Gordon suggested that perhaps CoRes could be incorporated into the normal curriculum routines of the school or at least adopted as a common approach by their head of faculty. However, if CoRes were used regularly again and again for the same topic year after year, then the whole process could become trivialised.

Responding to the research questions

All participants claimed that CoRes and PaP-eRs had given them greater depth in examining how they understood the content, their students and marrying this knowledge together in ways which could improve student learning. In so doing, all participants believed that they had developed a deep and rich understanding of their own PCK and that this could ultimately improve their professional practice.

Also, some interesting themes emerged about the ways in which CoRes and PaP-eRs appeared to impact how these teachers framed their professional knowledge. Firstly, CoRes and PaP-eRs were demonstrated to have encouraged meaningful reflection on the participants' practice. This reflection then provided them with a base from which to begin to discuss and effectively communicate their ideas about teaching and learning. In this way, they had developed a shared language:

> I think [CoRes and PaP-eRs] are good.... We know that as a teaching tool, to get someone to enunciate their thinking ... to actually try and explain their thinking ... is good for their learning. You know, what was their rationale behind their thinking? ... [To] defend why they are teaching it,

why it is important for students to know and to talk about how they teach it, then … that has to be … useful and helpful. (Samantha, Int. 4)

Through this new common language, participants began to recognise and think meaningfully about aspects of their professional knowledge, including that which was previously tacit. In so doing, an awareness, recognition and understanding of their own pedagogical content knowledge was developed. Through coming to see their practice through a "PCK lens", improvements and changes in their practice were observable. These changes were evidenced by differences in, and new ways of thinking about, teaching and learning through a comparison of their pre- and post-intervention views.

Participants' views on teaching and learning had, to various degrees, been influenced by the development of their understanding of the concept of PCK through CoRes and PaP-eRs. In this regard, CoRes and PaP-eRs helped participating teachers think differently about their professional practice. Other evidence also indicated changes in their thinking. The CoRe prompts provoked participants to begin to think beyond their normal approach to practice and to reframe their views in line with a PCK perspective. PaP-eRs also helped them to think differently about their practice by drawing out the intricacies and complexities involved in the thinking.

Concrete portrayals of participating teachers' PCK were captured from both CoRes and PaP-eRs in the study. In this way, they proved to be valid instruments in helping participating teachers draw out their PCK. In order to capture these portrayals, participants needed to be able to articulate their responses in ways which described their individual and personal PCK. This effectively translates into meaning that the participants were able to meaningfully connect with their PCK which enabled them to discuss that knowledge in a clear and overt manner.

Overall, the study has illustrated the following generalised outcomes:

Professional practice

- helped teachers to rethink how they could improve their teaching;
- helped teachers to reflect on their practice;
- "forced" teachers to explicitly think about and connect with their intuitive and tacit knowledge about teaching and learning; and,
- offered benefits to inexperienced teachers as well as experienced teachers.

Student learning

- helped teachers to think specifically about the importance of knowing their students;
- helped teachers to think about how they recognised and evaluated student learning; and,
- helped teachers to be aware of, and think about how to, approach drawing out and responding to students' alternative conceptions/misconceptions.

Content

- helped teachers to recognise the range of teaching strategies they had expertise in and using these for the teaching of particular content;
- helped teachers to think specifically about the depth and breadth of content; and,
- helped teachers think about how to approach and plan for new or unfamiliar content.

SUMMARY

Since its introduction to the academic literature, PCK has offered a framework for beginning the in-depth exploration of the personal and often intrinsic aspects of science teaching. This study presents an exploration of the practical and real value of PCK for practising science teachers. At the heart of this research, the concept of PCK was developed through the two instruments of CoRes and PaP-eRs.

The study investigated if the idea of PCK helped participants teach more effectively; if it helped them better communicate their knowledge of practice; and if it helped them to reflect on and understand their own practice. The study found that CoRes and PaP-eRs portray and highlight PCK through capturing the particular approaches used by teachers in teaching particular content for particular reasons. CoRes and PaP-eRs have been demonstrated to be useful in helping teachers develop their knowledge of science teaching. Essentially, the study demonstrated that CoRes and PaP-eRs were effective in helping the six participating science teachers to develop an awareness and understanding of pedagogical content knowledge and, as a consequence, influenced and improved the ways they viewed their professional practice.

While PCK has been well recognised as an elusive construct, this study has illustrated that a CoRes and PaP-eRs approach is effective in capturing and portraying concrete examples of participating teachers' PCK. The use of CoRes and PaP-eRs prompted the participating teachers to meaningfully reflect on their practice. This led to the development and use of a language of practice which in turn positively influenced their ability to communicate their views of teaching and learning in meaningful ways. Hence the participants' understanding of PCK developed, and as a consequence, their professional knowledge of practice was essentially enhanced.

CHAPTER OVERVIEW

This chapter was designed to illustrate how CoRes and PaP-eRs (Resource Folios) have been used and understood by some teachers. The vignettes at the start of the chapter offered insights into the nature of CoRes and PaP-eRs as a different way of thinking about PCK as a framework for conceptualizing practice. Betram's study builds on the views highlighted in the vignettes and makes the point that there are a range of possibilities for the use and application of CoRes and PaP-eRs in planning and developing the science curriculum. The use of CoRes and PaP-eRs as a way of explicating PCK has benefits for the ways in which science teachers come to understand and interpret their practice and create a new focus for professional learning and the growth of science teachers' professional knowledge. As has been well illustrated in the academic literature, and reinforced through the views and research documented in this chapter, teachers typically adapt and adjust things to suit their context and their needs when adopting what they see as helpful ideas, processes and practices. The research that led to the development of CoRes and PaP-eRs was built on a concern to better understand, and to try and "concretize" PCK in a way that might be helpful for the profession. The research was not designed to create a curriculum planning tool, nor some new form of syllabus or lesson planning rubric. The research was designed to unpack and portray the PCK of science teachers.

It is a testament to the nature of expertise in teaching that teachers have come to interpret and use CoRes and PaP-eRs in ways not necessarily envisaged (or intended) by the researchers. That, in itself, is a good thing and is perhaps an indication of the creative and innovative thinking that underpins expert practice. It could well be argued that such thinking is, in fact, a key attribute to the ongoing development of teachers' pedagogical content knowledge.

CHAPTER ELEVEN

SCIENCE TEACHING AND SCIENCE TEACHER EDUCATION

There is an inherent difficulty in science teaching whereby complex and abstract concepts and ideas need to be taught in ways that make them accessible and understandable for learners. As a consequence, teachers' attempts at simplification may inadvertently reduce such subject matter to propositional forms that, sadly, foster reliance on rote learning as opposed to encouraging the development of rich and deep understandings. Paradoxically, many science teachers themselves come from that sub-set of students who successfully managed to learn science despite the difficulty and associated teaching and learning tensions within this very situation. Therefore, it is not hard to see how they may in fact actually find themselves unwittingly recreating the same situation again for their own students, all of whom are not likely to learn "just like they did".

In considering this situation, it is important to be reminded of the different contexts in which learning about science teaching and learning takes place. There are two obvious contexts - schools and pre-service teacher preparation programs - and the teachers, teacher educators and student-teachers that work within each are important players when it comes to thinking about how one might begin to respond to the teaching and learning challenges in science education. By paying attention to these contexts, the knowledge of practice actively created in each by these participants is able to be focussed upon and create new possibilities for capturing and portraying such knowledge so that it might be better shared within the profession and ultimately, impact the nature of science teaching and learning more generally.

Therefore, in the first instance, a clear and strong focus on science teaching in schools is important. However, a field sometimes overlooked is that of teacher education where the emerging science teachers begin their more formalised education of science teaching and learning. Within this field of pre-service teacher preparation, science teacher educators are clearly crucial as they not only shape the agenda of what the science teaching and learning curriculum might comprise, but also how it is enacted, thus impacting the learning experiences of science student teachers.

The notion of PCK (and all that it entails as outlined in the previous chapters) is then an aspect of practice that needs to permeate the work of all three groups (teachers, student-teachers and teacher educators) if the paradoxical situation outlined above is to be addressed in meaningful ways. If it were to be addressed, then not only would there be a greater likelihood that quality science teaching and learning would be an outcome, but it might also be that the knowledge, skills and ability of expert science teachers might be better understood and be more highly sought and valued. It might also create a real prospect of something to aim for in one's own professional learning (whether as a student, beginning or expert teacher/teacher educator of science).

We would argue that in teaching generally, but in science teaching in particular, paying careful attention to the notion of PCK is one way of better valuing teachers' professional knowledge of practice while simultaneously creating an expectation for such development as integral to professional learning.

Across the fields of teaching and teacher education, explicitly linking experiences of learning science with the practice of, and knowledge about, teaching science offers access to ways of developing science teachers' PCK and is something we believe needs to purposefully be encouraged.

UNPACKING SCIENCE TEACHING

In reflecting upon one's own experiences of teaching and learning in science, it can sometimes be difficult to look back and see the changes in practice (and the reasons for those changes) that led to the manner in which one teaches at the present point in time. This can be difficult to do because such changes tend to be gradual and incremental. As teachers develop and refine their knowledge and skills of teaching through reflection on experience over time, the growth in their own wisdom of practice may not be recognized as being specialized and sophisticated, but rather as idiosyncratic and intensely personal. Personal perceptions of the distinction between the perceived value of the wisdom of practice are exacerbated by the fact that teaching is generally an individual and isolated experience. Further to this, as so much knowledge of teaching is tacit, it can be extremely difficult for teachers to articulate such things as: the reasons for teaching particular content in a particular way; how the context shapes those aspects of the content that are highlighted, simplified or ignored; what specific concept attainment equates with understanding a given topic and why; what comprises a teacher's own understanding of the content; or, what influenced that learning.

Of course, being unable to articulate responses to queries such as these does not mean that answers are non-existent, rather that the nature of teaching does not overtly encourage such articulation or create a strong professional expectation for so doing. Yet, through such articulation the specialist knowledge, skills and ability of expert science teachers becomes more obvious and, we would argue, is encapsulated in the notion of PCK. Therefore, through paying careful attention to PCK and its development and use, it is possible to focus serious attention on expertise in, and quality of, science teaching so that it may be better understood within (and outside) the profession. To illustrate the point, it can be helpful to think about PCK as:

> ... a continuum of models of teacher knowledge. At one extreme, PCK does not exist and teacher knowledge can be most readily explained by the intersection of three constructs: subject matter, pedagogy and context. Teaching, then, is the act of integrating knowledge across these three domains. For convenience, I will call this the Integrative model. At the other extreme, PCK is the synthesis of all knowledge needed in order to be an effective teacher. In this case, PCK is the transformation of subject matter, pedagogical, and contextual knowledge into a unique form – the *only* form of knowledge that impacts teaching practice. I will call this the Transformative model.
>
> The distinctions between these two models are subtle – the integration of knowledge versus the transformation of knowledge. An analogy from chemistry may help make the distinction. When two materials are mixed together, they can form a mixture or a compound. In a mixture, the original elements remain chemically distinct, though their visual impact may imply a total integration. Regardless of the level of apparent combination, the parent ingredients in a mixture can be separated through relatively unsophisticated, physical means. In contrast, compounds are created by the addition or release of energy. Parent ingredients can no longer be easily separated and their initial properties can no longer be detected. A compound is a new substance, distinct from its original ingredients, with chemical and physical properties that distinguish it from all other materials.
>
> When looking at models of teacher knowledge, the Integrative model is similar to that described for a mixture. Elements of knowledge from subject matter, pedagogical and context domains are called upon and melded in classroom practice. Upon reflection, the parent domains can be found in the justifications for planned and interactive classroom decisions. The Transformative model implies that these initial knowledge bases are inextricably combined into a new form of knowledge, PCK, in which the parent domain may be discovered only through complicated analysis. The resulting amalgam is more interesting and more powerful than its constituent parts. (Gess-Newsome, 1999, pp. 10 - 11)

Clearly science teachers do not exist, forever fixed, in one place along the continuum between the Integrative and Transformative models. At different times and in different contexts, where one might reside along the continuum varies as the development of knowledge of practice ebbs and flows as a result of the myriad of teaching and learning experiences one creates and encounters. However, it seems reasonable to suggest that at any given time, the closer one is to the Transformative end of the continuum, the more the "compound" created (or still being created) will be in evidence. Yet, unpacking the "compound" to its constituent parts is not easy.

This analogy of the compound and the continuum may also offer additional reasons as to why science teachers find it so difficult to respond to probes and prompts like those briefly noted above. Yet this does not mean that things must always be that way. As our research has highlighted, with a concentration on some of these issues (prompts in the CoRe), and with the help of colleagues through shared reflection and dialogue, ways of seeing what the "compound" looks like become possible and is demonstrated through the Resource Folios (comprising the CoRe and PaP-eRs as illustrated in Chapters 4 – 9).

In striving to develop Resource Folios we found ourselves both researching and workshopping ideas of PCK with experienced science teachers. On the one hand, our research uncovered interesting issues about the nature of PCK, while on the other, it also brought to the surface a wealth of previously untapped knowledge of science teaching and learning for many of the participants with whom we were working (particularly illustrated through the vignettes and the research study that comprised chapter 10).

Through our research, it was obvious to us that science teachers appreciated the opportunity to pursue understandings of PCK as they began to recognize and respond to the various alternative approaches to enhancing students' understanding of particular science topics and concepts. As they unpacked their own and their colleagues' knowledge and practice of science teaching, the strength of their own professional learning was constantly being highlighted and demonstrated through their views of the nature of their expectations of teaching. Through this process of exploring science teachers' PCK, the complexity of such knowledge as well as the rich variation that contributed to a recognition of the skills and expertise so fundamental to good science teaching and learning continually emerged.

As noted earlier, it is difficult for individual science teachers to recognize how their understanding of specific content has changed from the time they first started teaching. Yet being able to explain how one's understanding of particular subject matter content has changed and developed offers insights into how one's professional knowledge and practice may have been refined over time. For example, how one came to understand why a particular concept was difficult for students to grasp can be a catalyst for teaching in ways that better helps students to learn how to overcome these difficulties. Such teaching is clearly very different; it is much more skilful and indeed more specialized and sophisticated than simply restating the facts as constituent parts of the given subject matter content.

By exploring with science teachers how their understanding of practice has changed and developed, the factors that influenced that development, and how teaching particular content has altered their understanding of the concepts, it also becomes possible to link that knowledge and the subsequent teaching approach in ways that make it much more explicit for themselves and others. In this way, discussing science teaching moves from the common sharing of activities and ideas into richer explanations of content related pedagogy. It also highlights the underpinning pedagogical reasoning because it is the link to these deeper understandings of both subject matter knowledge and pedagogy that contribute to PCK.

Therefore, it can be instructive to reconsider instances or episodes that have been particularly influential in shaping understandings of practice. For example, remembering what it was like to be a learner of science in order to unpack some of the vivid memories of situations that were difficult or confusing, or alternatively, instances that were powerful and engaging, can be most revealing and informing to one's understanding of science teaching. Revisiting such experiences can lead to new insights into how one's own knowledge has changed and developed and create real possibilities for better building the relationship between learning and teaching in science. Building this relationship is surely fundamental to enhancing students' learning of science, an objective at the heart of teaching for quality learning, and indicative of exemplary practice.

EXPLORING SCIENCE TEACHERS' PCK

Not everyone looking into the classroom of a reputed master science teacher will be equally impressed all the time, but we have long known that some teachers are simply more personable, professional, innovative, engaging and ultimately effective than others. Just ask their students who are the ultimate consumers with their years of hard-won experiential data. … Certainly, in an arena as varied as the school classroom in a domain as complex as science teaching there can be no one best practice. However, if we allow that there are small groups of procedures and orientations that are more effective than others … we can feel quite justified in calling such practices exemplary. (McComas, 2005, pp. xviii - xix)

As we acknowledged earlier, PCK is not necessarily a term commonly used by teachers to describe or explore understandings of their practice. However, as McComas (above) notes, there are many other ways in which quality in science teaching and learning is discussed and through which a knowledge of practice may be shared within the profession. In considering that which comprises professional learning, it is clearly helpful to draw attention to what might more generally be described as exemplary practice. In so doing, the value of PCK emerges as a powerful way of moving beyond generic descriptors of good science teaching and introduces a more sophisticated approach to unpacking expertise in science teaching. It also creates a way of moving beyond perceptions of exemplary practice as simply comprising familiarity with a range of teaching activities. Therefore, in suggesting that exemplary practice should purposefully involve unpacking and valuing PCK, it is fundamental that opportunities for science teachers to work together to uncover and explicate their PCK be encouraged.

One way of so doing is through workshopping the development of a CoRe and PaP-eRs approach as it can help teachers think about, and share with others, their knowledge about how to teach particular science subject matter. For example, in science faculty meetings, working through existing topics in the curriculum using a blank CoRe (see Figure 3.1) offers a very different way of thinking about the nature of the content to be taught than is common in many curriculum documents and syllabuses as the notion of Big Ideas and the prompts in the left hand column help to unpack exemplary practice in new and different ways; through the lens of PCK. Using a CoRe in this way helps to make clear how important PCK can be in addressing the tendency to oversimplify complex subject matter as opposed to teasing out the central concepts and the associated implications for teaching and learning.

We have seen that using a CoRe and PaP-eRs approach offers a way of reconsidering practice. This issue has been evident to us through comments expressed by science teachers when considering their understanding of their practice, the point being clearly articulated by one science teacher who said that: 'Knowing the content is extremely important but knowing how to teach the content to particular students is also extremely important. It is necessary for me to have a large repertoire of various ideas (or different ways of teaching the same idea) so that students learn/understand the content.' We see this type of response as illustrative of the fact the exemplary science teaching is enmeshed with the notion of PCK. Therefore, encouraging science teachers to find ways of making their PCK explicit matters if exemplary practice is to not only be affirmed, but also be more carefully analysed and understood; particularly across different subject area specializations.

We are not suggesting that documenting and portraying PCK for science teachers should in any way be misconstrued as creating a recipe for how to teach given subject matter, for as McComas (above) so aptly reminds us, different things will be seen by different observers in different ways even when looking at exemplary classroom science teaching. However, what we are suggesting is that it is possible that the portrayals created in PaP-eRs offer windows into what could happen in a science classroom and therefore can create a strong, vicarious experience from which others might learn about science teaching. For example, science teachers have commented that: '[PaP-eRs are] a great guide that also gives you scenarios of what could happen in the classroom with certain activities'; and, '[Science teachers could] use PaP-eRs to help [other] teachers and students think about new dimensions to concepts/big ideas.'

In essence, through better valuing exemplary science teaching, by documenting, exploring and analysing such practice, we believe that PCK (as conceptualized through a CoRe and PaP-eRs approach), offers science teachers new and more meaningful ways of learning about teaching particular subject matter content. We suggest that this needs to occur at not only an individual and personal level in respect to one's own practice, but also at a collective level by creating an expectation for sharing PCK within the profession itself. However, if such a response is to transpire, there is a crucial need for the same expectation and actions to occur in pre-service science teacher education programs - both in coursework at university and during school practicum experiences; all science teachers/educators have an important role in both developing the next generation of science teachers as well as extending their own, and their colleagues' professional learning.

PCK IN SCIENCE TEACHER EDUCATION

Because of the difference in teaching experience and content familiarity, there is little doubt that there must be a difference in the extent to which PCK might exist and be recognisable in the practice of student-teachers in comparison with their science teacher educators. However, by introducing the concept of PCK, examining, analysing and modelling it in teacher education practice (both in school practicum and in university coursework), it is more likely than not that science teaching will be seen by science student-teachers as specialized and sophisticated practice, rather than simply comprising a variety of teaching procedures to make students' learning of science "more fun".

Exploring science student-teachers' PCK

It seems reasonable to suggest that as student-teachers initially face a myriad of concerns and needs that influence what it means to learn about teaching, different aspects of their development will assume different priorities at different times. At first glance, PCK is an idea that, although perhaps appealing, may not stand out for the individual student-teacher as being immediately important; perhaps too theoretical or jargonisitic (despite our arguments to the contrary in Chapter 3). This may change though when sufficient teaching experience has been gained that allows some of the more immediate concerns in learning to teach to be addressed (e.g. becoming comfortable with the teaching role, managing students' classroom behaviour, developing confidence in one's own knowledge of subject matter, etc.).

When these shifts in needs and concerns occurs, a way into framing the development of professional practice around the notion of PCK may emerge and not only be helpful, but in fact establish a way of thinking about science teaching that encourages learning about teaching beyond gathering an armoury of tips and tricks. However, in spite of this, it may also be that science student-teachers will simultaneously be confronted by a contradiction: a contradiction bound up in the need to be comfortable with some of the tips and tricks of teaching in order to move beyond tips and tricks alone.

In these circumstances, a decision to move from a sense of certainty in practice to one of uncertainty will need to be made, a decision that requires a growing sense of confidence in oneself. Further to this, because in their learning about science teaching student-teachers feel a need to accumulate a range of teaching procedures, there is a natural tendency for them to initially focus on their teaching as opposed to their students' learning. Therefore, it is important for both science teacher educators and their science student-teachers to see this contradiction as a problem to be acted upon; however, if it is not seen as a problem, it will not be acted upon. So, opportunities for science student-teachers to experience the sense of dissatisfaction associated with having apparently "taught the content well" only to find that their students "did not learn it" matters if they are to move beyond being comfortable with tips and tricks alone, i.e. see and feel the problem in order to decide to do something about it (Nilsson's (2008) research amply demonstrates this very point).

When such situations arise, the personal learning about the difference between delivering information as opposed to creating meaningful pedagogical experiences may then create an impetus for recognizing problems that they can choose to confront in their own practice. Such realization may make clear the importance of reframing pedagogy *and* content and be a catalyst for valuing PCK as a frame for developing science teaching in more sophisticated ways.

There have been a number of studies into ways of organising and structuring pre-service teacher education programs so that PCK might be a valuable tool for learning about teaching and create the impetus for action outlined above (see for example, De Jong, Van Driel, & Verloop, 2005; Lederman & Gess-Newsome, 1999; Zembal, Starr, & Krajcik, 1999). At the heart of many of these programs is a concentration on the mediating role of the teacher as a facilitator of learning as opposed to being a transmitter of knowledge (Woolnough, 2009). This point is well illustrated by Tobin and McRobbie (1999) who point out that:

> When students endeavour to learn something new they need to re-construct relevant prior knowledge. Two challenges confront learners, how to decide what is and is not relevant and how to re-present what is known in ways that best lend themselves to making sense of what they need to learn. Through conversations in which co-participation occurs the teacher can have a role in assisting students to identify and re-present relevant prior knowledge. Such conversations would focus on the knowledge of students and the appropriateness of different re-presentations for learning given science subject matter. A teacher can establish a climate in which students are expected to test the viability of their knowledge. … An initial first step in establishing an environment conducive to learning is to enable students to make their knowledge and thinking processes visible to others. … The teacher, who knows the subject matter to be learned, will recognize that a logical breakdown from the perspective of one who knows, may not be perceived as logical by those reconciling the extent of the fit of given teacher re-presentations with their own re-constructions. (pp. 230–231)

For student-teachers, it would obviously be helpful in their learning about teaching if they were to see such practice modelled by their teacher educators and school advisors/supervising teachers. But it would be even more powerful if they were to experience such practice firstly from a learner's perspective and then also be afforded opportunities to experience how to develop such practice in their own teaching.

DeJong, van Driel and Verloop (2005), when considering the development of PCK in student-teachers, illustrated how experiencing meaningful science learning generates a need for further learning. Such experiences, we argue, create real possibilities for student-teachers to begin to grasp not only the complexity of PCK but also to gain confidence in the value of living through the discomfort of moving from the certainty of transmissive teaching to the (initial) uncertainties associated with learning about teaching for understanding by experimenting with such practice in their own teaching. Perhaps a difficulty in creating such experiences is in the nature of authority within a teaching and learning environment and so the nature of "power" within a teaching learning environment needs to be recognized and appropriately addressed:

> Power within a community needs to be distributed such that all students have equitable access to resources to enhance their learning. … At issue is whether a person is able to participate verbally in the practices of the community. For example, perhaps a teacher is using a form of discourse that is inaccessible to learners. If that is the case they might not raise questions because of a fear that they do not know enough to ask a question, or they might not co-participate because the teacher does not provide the opportunities for them to participate. In each instance the teacher engages in a form of monologue and the students do not interrupt the flow of that monologue. The power of the teacher is constituted in a form of discourse that cannot be appropriated by the students, leaving them with little recourse other than rote learning. … Within each classroom the conditions under which co-participation is possible and encouraged needs to be negotiated and enacted such that learning can be optimized for all students. (Tobin & McRobbie, 1999, pp. 232–233)

Student-teachers no doubt experience (or have experienced) the disempowerment that the use of language, power and the monologue can create for learners. Hopefully, they remember such experiences in ways that encourage them to challenge the likelihood of repeating the same for their students as they develop their science teaching. It is, therefore, not difficult to see that science teacher education would be all the better if the conditions for co-participation were commonly experienced and viewed as essential to the development of exemplary practice. However, to do so requires a commitment by teacher educators to do just that in their teaching about science teaching and learning in pre-service education programs.

Exploring science teacher educators' PCK

Many science teacher educators were themselves successful school science teachers. In the career change from school teacher to teacher educator, they would no doubt have encountered many of the experiences associated with the transition that has been well documented in the literature (for example: moving beyond basing their teaching on telling student teachers about how they taught science, just offering student-teachers an array of good teaching activities, and views of teaching as an innate ability to understand it as a sophisticated and specialized form of professional practice).

Within this transition is the realization that just being able to 'do good science teaching' is not in and of itself sufficient for teaching about teaching science. At some stage, the pedagogical reasoning underpinning exemplary practice emerges as a crucial element in teaching about science teaching because of the need to develop understandings of why certain teaching approaches work in some contexts and not in others, or why particular subject matter needs to be conceptualized and structured in different ways if students are to have more likelihood of learning for understanding.

Just as student-teachers need to be reminded of their experiences as science learners in order to shape their views of their expectations for their own pedagogical development, so too teacher educators need to be metacognitive (to think about their thinking, to question their own learning) in relation to their learning about teaching science teaching so that they can highlight and model the development of PCK in ways that accord with Tobin and McRobbie's (1999) views of co-participatory learning (above).

With this point in mind, the following vignette is offered in order to highlight how attention to such learning might not only be recognized but also acted upon in a science teacher educator's practice.

As a science teacher educator I was concerned to teach my student teachers in ways that did not reinforce the traditional "science is all about facts and figures" approach that they had all no doubt experienced - and probably successfully mastered, through their own schooling. I had lots of interesting teaching procedures that, when used with appropriate science content, could engage them in learning and for the most part, they (and I), found these activities to be quite entertaining and seemingly useful in their learning to teach science. ... One session that is vividly etched in my mind was the time I decided to use a role play that I hadn't used before. ... The role-play was designed to explore the way the Moon revolves around the Earth. ... I started off in the normal way by getting students' prior views, listing them on the board, pushing and probing their ideas and generally trying to create a sense of interest in the topic. ... The next phase was to set up the problem. This was not difficult either, it was something like: "The Moon rotates on its axis once during its revolution of the Earth, so how is it that we only ever see the same face?" I'm not sure that before encountering this role-play I was ever aware of this myself (at least not beyond some esoteric link to my childhood and Pink Floyd's Dark Side of the Moon), so at first I think it probably made me stop and think, but not for too long as the problem was directed at the class (not me as the teacher). Besides, I was already fully occupied in teaching as I expertly stumbled through a teaching procedure (that I usually did not like) in a content area (with which I was unfamiliar). ... we [went outside and] spread out under the Oak trees next to the Faculty [and] I quickly organized everybody into their positions. I knew it couldn't be too hard. All I needed was a small group (4 - 5 students) to make a circle by linking their arms while standing back to back – so that they would all be looking outwards – that group would be the Moon. Then the same formation was needed for the remainder of the students and they would be the Earth. So far, so good. ... "Now Moon, start a revolution around the Earth, but while you do it, you have to organise yourselves to do only one rotation on your own axis. So Janet, from where you are now, you need to be facing the Earth again when you get back to that spot. Put a mark on the ground so you know where that will be. O.K., off you go." I said with great confidence.

I stood back and watched the role-play unfold. As the Moon slowly rotated in its revolution of the Earth I tried to visualize how it could be that if it rotated only once on its axis that only one side of the Moon would be seen from the Earth. I couldn't do it though. I just could not manipulate that in my mind to understand how it could be possible. But as I stood there watching it, I could see it happening before me. The abstract became very concrete. ... Suddenly I got what it meant to be involved in a role-play. Suddenly I saw a number of important pedagogical insights. Suddenly content matter started to take new shape as a developing understanding slowly emerged. Suddenly, our class became alive with learning; and I was part of it. ... Questions, issues and ideas about astronomy were initiated and different role-plays were envisaged as the students discussed the fundamentals of this approach in relation to other topics (summer and winter; day and night, etc.).

After the class I mused over the episode again ... what I knew – or thought I knew – before the experience was dramatically different to what I knew after the experience. Being involved in the experience was different to directing it for others. Abstracting the learning from this experience to other situations was intellectually challenging and engaging. What I saw in my students' approach to learning about teaching was new and different. What I began to see in teaching about teaching was a revelation. What I previously knew, I now understood. (Loughran, 2006, pp. 23 - 26)

What this vignette attempts to highlight is the importance of teaching about science teaching in ways that places PCK at the centre of pedagogical development. The vignette draws attention to the science teacher educator's learning about the pedagogy of teaching about the Moon (i.e. how the use of role play shed new light on important aspects of the content that were difficult to grasp). What the vignette suggests then is that teacher educators themselves need to be conscious of their own PCK, how it is developed and refined and how it might be made clear in their own teaching with their student teachers. If teacher educators do not use their own teaching, their own classrooms and their students' learning as a site for inquiry, i.e. foster co-participation, then they are really creating a situation in which student teachers are expected to discover for themselves that which they do not know they need to discover; the meno paradox revisited.

Teacher educators are faced by a number of tensions that shape their practice (Berry, 2004a, 2004b) all of which, when recognized and appropriately managed, bring to the surface the problematic nature of teaching for themselves and their student-teachers. One such tension is that of *telling and growth*. As Berry describes this tension, she demonstrates that just as student-teachers struggle to come to grips with how to teach for understanding so too do teacher educators. The need to create spaces and opportunities for students to learn for themselves and therefore grow in understanding is constantly being buffeted by the urge to "tell them what they need to know". In making this tension clear in their own practice, teacher educators can simultaneously make it a point of learning for themselves and their student teachers. If it is experienced together, through the co-participation, then reconstructing one's own knowledge and understanding as well as the problematic nature of teaching can be highlighted, acknowledged and responded to in different ways. In so doing, teaching about science teaching in ways that challenges the stereo-typical view of science teaching as the delivery of facts may move from rhetoric to reality; surely a good outcome in any teacher education program.

We are not suggesting that any of this is easy; however, we are suggesting that if PCK is not an integral part of the language, practice and experience of science teacher educators (both in school and in university), then science teacher education is not likely to offer a meaningful way of challenging the status-quo.

CONCLUSION

In concluding this chapter and the book, we wish to draw attention to three important features of change that we see as fundamental to responding to the possibilities inherent in the notion of PCK.

First, PCK in the way in which we have conceptualized and portrayed it in this book, offers a way of considering what might be possible in science teaching; a powerful image of what practice might entail and something worthwhile to aim for in teachers' professional learning. But, within such a "vision of the possible", it needs to be remembered that there is not one end point or one path to be followed. That leads to the second point which is that PCK has, by its very nature, a variety of "ways in" as pedagogy and subject matter combine in different ways, in different contexts and through different experiences to create various complex "compounds" all with their own special features and properties; such is the amalgam that is PCK. Thirdly, that the development, articulation and portrayal of PCK needs to be presented and re-presented in ways that highlight how the individual and collective journeys that science teachers take as they learn from, and with, their students and colleagues is continually refined in their professional practice.

In reconsidering the ideas about PCK that have been central to this book we close with a reminder of the importance of not trying to over-simplify the complex nature of science teaching and learning so much that the richness of the variation in ability and skills associated with managing the dilemmas and tensions of practice are overshadowed or lost. In considering the development of PCK as part of the fundamental professional learning of teachers, there is a need to continually encourage and value the questioning, probing, pushing, framing and reframing of the problematic aspects of teaching in order to further develop understandings of practice.

Finally, teaching for understanding is hard work and we believe that PCK can be a bridge to the theoretical and the practical aspects of science teaching in ways that bring to the fore science teachers' expert knowledge, skills and ability, so that they might not only be better recognized and appreciated, but be more highly valued within, and beyond, the profession.

REFERENCES

Appleton, K. (2002). Science activities that work: Perceptions of primary school teachers. *Research in Science Education, 32*(3), 393–410.

Baird, J. R., & Mitchell, I. J. (Eds.). (1986). *Improving the quality of teaching and learning: An Australian case study - The PEEL project*. Melbourne: Monash University Printing Service.

Baird, J. R., & Northfield, J. R. (Eds.). (1992). *Learning from the PEEL experience*. Melbourne: Monash University Printing Service.

Baxter, J. A., & Lederman, N. G. (1999). Assessment and measurement of pedagogical content knowledge. In J. A. Baxter & N. G. Lederman (Eds.), *Examining Pedagogical Content Knowledge: The Construct and its Implications for Science Education* (pp. 147-161). Dordrecht, The Netherlands: Kluwer Academic Publishers.

Berry, A. (2004a). Confidence and uncertainty in teaching about teaching. *Australian Journal of Education, 48*(2), 149–165.

Berry, A. (2004b). Self-study in teaching about teaching. In J. Loughran, M. L. Hamilton, V. LaBoskey & T. Russell (Eds.), *International handbook of self-study of teaching and teacher education practices* (Vol. 2, pp. 1295 - 1332). Dordrecht: Kluwer.

Berry, A., Loughran, J., & van Driel, J. (2008a). Returning to the roots of pedagogical content knowledge. *International Journal of Science Education, 30*(10), 1271–1279.

Berry, A., Loughran, J., & van Driel, J. (2008b). Special Issue: Developments and challenges in researching science teachers' pedagogical content knowledge: An international perspective. . *International Journal of Science Education, 30*(10).

Berry, A., & Milroy, P. (2002). Changes that matter. In J. Loughran, I. Mitchell & J. Mitchell (Eds.), *Learning from teacher research* (pp. 196 - 221). New York: Teachers College Press.

Bertram, A. (2010). Enhancing science teachers' knowledge of practice by explicitly developing pedagogical content knowledge. Unpublished Ph.D. Monash University.

Bullough, R. V. J. (2001). Pedagogical content knowledge circa 1907 and 1987: A study in the history of an idea. *Journal of Teaching and Teacher Education, 17*, 655–666.

Calderhead, J. (1996). Teachers: Beliefs and knowledge. In D. C. Berliner & R. C. Calfee (Eds.), *Handbook of educational psychology* (pp. 709 - 725). New York: Macmillan.

Clandinin, D. J., & Connelly, F. M. (2000). *Narrative inquiry*. San Francisco: Jossey-Bass.

Clarke, C., & Peterson, P. (1986). Teachers' thought processes. In M. C. Wittrock (Ed.), *Handbook of reserach on teaching* (3rd ed., pp. 255 - 296). New York: MacMillan.

Clermont, C. P., Borko, H., & Krajcik, J. S. (1994). Comparative study of the pedagogical content knowledge of experienced and novice chemical demonstrators. *Journal of Research in Science Teaching, 31*(4), 419–441.

Conle, C. (2003). An anatomy of narrative curricula. *Educational Researcher, 32*(3), 3–15.

De Jong, O., Van Driel, J. H., & Verloop, N. (2005). Preservice teachers' pedagogical content knowledge of using particle models in teaching chemistry. *Journal of Research in Science Teaching, 42*(8), 947–964.

Dharsey, N., Rhemtula, M., & Rollnick, M. (2005, August). *A case study of two Access Chemistry lecturers' practice of pedagogical content knowledge on chemical equilibrium*. Paper presented at the European Science Education Research Association, Barcelona, Spain.

Driver, R., Asoko, H., Leach, J., Mortimer, E., & Scott, P. (1994). Constructing scientific knowledge in the classroom. *Educational Researcher, 23*(7), 5–12.

Driver, R., Guesne, E., & Tiberghien, A. (Eds.). (1985). *Children's ideas in science*. Milton Keynes: Open University Press.

Dusting, R. (2002). Teaching for understanding: The road to enlightenment. In J. Loughran, I. Mitchell & J. Mitchell (Eds.), *Learning from teacher research* (pp. 173 - 195). New York: Teachers College Press.

Fenstermacher, G. D. (1997). On Narrative. *Teaching and Teacher Education, 13*(1), 119–124.

Garritz, A., Porro, S., Rembado, F. M., & Trinidad, R. (2005, August). *Latin-American teachers' pedagogical content knowledge of the particulate nature of matter*. Paper presented at the European Science Education Research Association, Barcelona, Spain.

Geddis, A. N., Onslow, B., Beynon, C., & Oesch, J. (1993). Transforming content knowledge: learning to teach about isotopes. *Science Education, 77*(6), 575–591.

Gess-Newsome, J. (1999). Pedagogical content knowledge: An introduction and orientation. In J. Gess-Newsome & N. G. Lederman (Eds.), *Examining pedagogical content knowledge* (pp. 3 - 17). Dordrecht: Kluwer Academic Publishers.

Gess-Newsome, J., & Lederman, N. G. (Eds.). (1999). *Examining Pedagogical Content Knowledge*. Dordrecht, Netherlands: Kluwer Academic Publishers.

Gunstone, R. F. (1990). Children's Science: A decade of developments in constructivist views of science teaching and learning. *Australian Science Teachers' Journal, 36*(4), 9–19.

Hoban, G. F. (2002). *Teacher learning for educational change: A systems thinking approach*. Buckingham: Open University Press.

Hollon, R. E., Roth, K. J., & Anderson, C. W. (1991). Science teachers' conceptions of teaching and learning. In J. Brophy (Ed.), *Advances in Research on Teaching* (Vol. 2, pp. 145–185). New York: JAI Press, Inc.

Hume, A., & Berry, A. (2010). Constructing CoRes: A strategy for building PCK in pre-service science teacher education. *Research in Science Education, DOI 10.1007/s11165-010-9168-3 (online frst)*.

Husu, J. (1995, July). *Teachers' pedagogical mindset - a rhetorical framework to interpret and understand teachers' thinking*. Paper presented at the 7th Biennial Conference of the International Study Association on Teacher Thinking (ISATT), Ontario, Canada.

Korthagen, F. A. J., & Kessels, J. (1999). Linking theory and practice: Changing the pedagogy of teacher education. *Educational Researcher, 28*(4), 4–17.

Leach, J., & Scott, P. (1999, August). *Teaching and learning science: Linking individual and sociocultural perspectives. As part of the symposium; In memory of Rosalind Driver: Advances in research on science learning*. Paper presented at the Meeting of the European Association for Research in Learning and Instruction, Goteborg, Sweden.

Lederman, N. G., & Gess-Newsome, J. (1999). Reconceptualizing secondary science teacher education. In J. Gess-Newsome & N. G. Lederman (Eds.), *Examining pedagogical content knowledge* (pp. 199 - 214). Dordrecht: Kluwer Academic Publishers.

Loughran, J. J. (1999). Professional development for teachers: A growing concern. *Journal of In-Service Education, 25*(2), 261–272.

Loughran, J. J. (2002a). Effective reflective practice: In search of meaning in learning about teaching. *Journal of Teacher Education, 53*(1), 33–43.

REFERENCES

Loughran, J. J. (2002b). Understanding and articulating teacher knowledge. In C. Day & C. Surgue (Eds.), *Developing Teachers and Teaching Practice* (pp. 146–161). London: Routledge.

Loughran, J. J. (2003). Exploring the Nature of Teacher Research. In A. Clarke & G. Erickson (Eds.), *Teacher Research* (pp. 181–189). London: RoutledgeFalmer.

Loughran, J. J. (2006). *Developing a pedagogy of teacher education: Understanding teaching and learning about teaching.* London: Routledge.

Loughran, J. J. (2010). *What expert teachers do: Teachers' professional knowledge of classroom practice.* Sydney, London: Allen & Unwin, Routledge.

Loughran, J. J., Milroy, P., Berry, A., Gunstone, R. F., & Mulhall, P. (2001). Documenting science teachers' pedagogical content knowledge through PaP-eRs. *Research in Science Education, 31*(2), 289–307.

Loughran, J. J., Mulhall, P., & Berry, A. (2004). In search of pedagogical content knowledge in science: Developing ways of articulating and documenting professional practice. *Journal of Research in Science Teaching, 41*(4), 370–391.

Loughran, J. J., & Northfield, J. R. (1996). *Opening the classroom door: Teacher, researcher, learner.* London: Falmer Press.

Magnusson, S., & Krajcik, J. S. (1993). *Teacher Knowledge and Representation of Content in Instruction about Heat Energy and Temperature* (No. 387313 ERIC Document).

Marks, R. (1990). Pedagogical content knowledge: From a mathematical case to a modified conception. *Journal of Teacher Education, 41*(3), 3–11.

McComas, W. F. (2005). Foreword: Exemplary practice as exemplary research. In Steve Alsop, Larry Bencze & E. Pedretti (Eds.), *Analysing exemplary science teaching* (pp. xv - xx). Maidenhead, Berkshire, England: Open University Press.

Mitchell, I., & Mitchell, J. (2005). What do we mean by career long professional development and how do we get it? In D. Beijaard, P. Meijer, G. Morine-Dershimer & H. Tillema (Eds.), *New directions in teachers' working and learning environment.* Dordrecht: Springer.

Mitchell, I., & Mitchell, J. (Eds.). (1997). *Stories of reflective teaching: A book of PEEL cases.* Melbourne: PEEL publishing.

Mulhall, P., Berry, A., & Loughran, J. J. (2003). Frameworks for representing science teachers' pedagogical content knowledge. *Asia Pacific Forum on Science Teaching and Learning, 4*(2), 1–25.

Munby, H., Russell, T., & Martin, A. K. (2001). Teachers' knowledge and how it develops. In V. Richardson (Ed.), *Handbook of research on teaching* (4th ed., pp. 877–904). Washington D.C.: American Educational Research Association.

Ndlovu, T. B., Rhemtula, M., & Rollnick, M. (2005, August). *A case study of South African Township teachers' use of pedagogical content knowledge of the mole.* Paper presented at the European Science Education Research Association, Barcelona, Spain.

Nilsson, P. (2008). *Learning to teach and teaching to learn: Primary science student teachers' complex journey from learners to teachers.* Linköping university, Norrköping, Department of Social and Welfare Studies, Norrköping: The Swedish National Graduate School in Science and Technology Education, FontD.

Nilsson, P., & Loughran, J. (2010, March). *Understanding and assessing primary science student teachers' pedagogical content knowledge.* Paper presented at the National Association for Research in Science Teaching, Philadelphia.

Nilsson, P., & Loughran, J. (2011). Exploring the development of pre-service science elementary teachers' pedagogical content knowledge. *Journal of Science Teacher Education, On line first: DOI 10.1007/s10972-011-9239-y.*

Northfield, J. R. (1997, July). *It is interesting... but is it research?* Paper presented at the Australasian Science Education Research Association, Adelaide, Australia.

Novak, J. D. (1991). Clarifying with concept maps. *The Science Teacher, 58*(7), 45–49.

Novak, J. D., & Gowin, D. B. (1984). *Learning how to learn.* New York and Cambridge, U.K.: Cambridge University Press.

Novak, J. D., & Wandersee, J. (1991). Special issue on concept mapping. *Journal of Research in Science Teaching, 28*(10).

Osborne, R. J., & Freyburg, P. (Eds.). (1985). *Learning in science: The implications of children's science.* Auckland: Heinneman.

Parker, J., & Heywood, D. (2000). Exploring the relationship between subject knowledge and pedagogic content knowledge in primary teachers' learning about forces. *International Journal of Science Education, 22*(1), 89–111.

Pfundt, H., & Duit, R. (1994). *Bibliography-Students' alternative frameworks and science education.* Kiel, Germany: IPN.

Polanyi, M. (1962). *Personal knowledge: Towards a post-critical philosophy.* London: Routledge and Kegan Paul.

Polanyi, M. (1966). *The tacit dimension.* Garden City N.Y.: Doubleday.

Schön, D. A. (1983). *The reflective practitioner: How professionals think in action.* New York: Basic Books.

Shulman, L. S. (1986). Those who understand: Knowledge growth in teaching. *Educational Researcher, 15*(2), 4–14.

Shulman, L. S. (1987). Knowledge and teaching: Foundations of the new reform. *Harvard Educational Review, 57*(1), 1–22.

Sullivan, V. (1996). Strategy B1: Predict, Observe, Explain (POE). In Rosemary Dusting, Gillian Pinnis, Rola Rivers & V. Sullivan (Eds.), *Towards a thinking classroom: A study of PEEL teaching.* (pp. 32, 40–41). Melbourne: PEEL publishing.

Tobin, K., & McRobbie, C. J. (1999). Pedagogical content knowledge and co-participation in science classrooms. In J. Gess-Newsome & N. G. Lederman (Eds.), *Examining pedagogical content knowledge* (pp. 215–234). Dordrecht: Kluwer Academic Publishers.

Tobin, K., Tippins, D. J., & Gallard, A. J. (1994). Research on instructional strategies for science teaching. In D. L. Gabel (Ed.), *Handbook of research on science teaching and learning* (pp. 45–93). New York: Macmillan Publishing Company.

Van Driel, J. H., Verloop, N., & De Vos, W. (1998). Developing science teachers' pedagogical content knowledge. *Journal of Research in Science Teaching, 35*(6), 673–695.

Van Manen, M. (1999). The language of pedagogy and primacy of student experience. In J. Loughran (Ed.), *Researching teaching: Methodologies and practices for understanding pedagogy* (pp. 13–27). London: Falmer Press.

White, R. T., & Gunstone, R. F. (1992). *Probing Understanding.* London: Falmer Press.

Woolnough, J. (2009, September). *Developing preservice teachers' science PCK using Content Representations.* Paper presented at the European Science Education Research Association, Istanbul.

Zeichner, K. M., & Noffke, S. (2001). Practitioner research. In V. Richardson (Ed.), *Handbook of research on teaching* (4th ed., pp. 298–330). Washington D.C.: American Educational Research Association.

Zembal, C., Starr, M., & Krajcik, J. S. (1999). Constructing a framework for elementary science teaching using pedagogical content knowledge. In J. Gess-Newsome & N. G. Lederman (Eds.), *Examining pedagogical content knowledge* (pp. 237–256). Dordrecht: Kluwer Academic Publishers.

INDEX

A

adaptation, 197
addressing misconceptions, 123
albino, 199
alternative conceptions, 1, 7, 11, 13, 15
analogies, 28
analogy, 192, 200
application of ideas, 126
applying science ideas, 130
applying science ideas, 131
ascertaining understanding, 13

B

bacteria, 194
Baxter, J., 217
Berry, A., 229
Bertram, A., 211
bicycle chain analogy, 174–175
big ideas, 7, 11, 13, 17, 20
bleed, 94
blood, 944
blood vessels, 94
brainstorm, 91
breaking set, 5

C

cane toads, 204
capture and portray PCK, 16
cell division, 191
chalk and talk, 52
challenging understanding, 126
challenging Views, 123
changes in practice, 223
characteristics, 192
chemical Reactions, 47, 78
chromosome, 190
chromosomes, 192
circulatory system, 85, 212
Clandinin, J., 216
classification and interpretive discussion, 29
cloning, 191, 193
coded information, 190
codons, 208
common language, 217, 220
comparing models, 28
compound, 224
concept, 2, 7–8, 17, 87, 176, 220
concept substitution, 124
conceptual hooks, 7
conceptualization of PCK, 15, 20–21
conceptualizing practice, 10
confidence, 228
Conle, C., 16
constructivism, 13
constructivist approaches to teaching, 16
content knowledge, 5, 7–8, 10–13
contradiction, 226
conversation, 209
co-participatory learning, 228
CoRe, 13, 17–20, 211, 213

D

deep time, 201
defining the boundaries, 122
demonstration, 91
design a role play or model, 177
developing understanding, 122
diffusion laboratory exercises, 91
dilemma, 16
dirty tricks, 52, 54
DNA, 190, 206
doctoral program, 215
dominant, 192
Drosophila, 199
Dusting, R., 2

E

effective science teaching, 15
electric circuits, 159
electricity, 181
electrons, 181
environment, 192, 197
establishing a common form of communication, 122
ethical, 198
evaluating the appropriateness of a model, 176
evaluating the appropriateness of an analogy, 176
everyday life, 207
evolution, 202, 206, 228
exemplary practice, 9, 225, 227–228
expertise, 1
explain POEs scientifically, 126
eye color, 192

F

Fenstermacher, G., 216
force, 117
forensic science, 52
framework, 13, 220
fungi, 190

G

gene card, 203
gene technologies, 193
genes, 194, 207
genetics, 200
Genetics
    CoRe, 189
genotype, 193, 195, 197–198, 200–201, 203
geological, 199
Gess-Newsome, J., 215, 217
gravitational analogy, 172

H

heart dissection, 91
heredity, 190
historical research, 29
history, 199
Hume, A., 231

CPSIA information can be obtained at www.ICGtesting.com
Printed in the USA
LVOW091726231012

304096LV00002B/5/P